Postpartum Depression

TREATMENTS THAT WORK

TREATMENTS THAT WORK

Postpartum Depression

A Cognitive-Behavioral Approach to Recovery

THERAPIST GUIDE

ANNE STEWART
CHARLOTTE GRANGER
PETER LAWRENCE
HEATHER O'MAHEN
ALAN STEIN

OXFORD
UNIVERSITY PRESS

OXFORD
UNIVERSITY PRESS

Oxford University Press is a department of the University of Oxford.
It furthers the University's objective of excellence in research, scholarship,
and education by publishing worldwide. Oxford is a registered trade mark of
Oxford University Press in the UK and in certain other countries.

Published in the United States of America by Oxford University Press
198 Madison Avenue, New York, NY 10016, United States of America.

CIP data is on file at the Library of Congress.

ISBN 9780197759707

DOI: 10.1093/med-psych/9780197759707.001.0001

Printed by Marquis Book Printing, Canada

The manufacturer's authorized representative in the EU for product safety is
Oxford University Press España S.A. of Parque Empresarial San Fernando de Henares,
Avenida de Castilla, 2 – 28830 Madrid (www.oup.es/en or product.safety@oup.com).
OUP España S.A. also acts as importer into Spain of products made by the manufacturer.

FSC www.fsc.org MIX Paper | Supporting responsible forestry FSC® C103567

About ✓TREATMENTS *THAT WORK*™

Stunning developments in healthcare have taken place over the last several years, but many of our widely accepted interventions and strategies in mental health and behavioral medicine have been brought into question by research evidence as not only lacking benefit but, perhaps, inducing harm (Barlow, 2010). Other strategies have been proven effective using the best current standards of evidence, resulting in broad-based recommendations to make these practices more available to the public (McHugh & Barlow, 2010). Several recent developments are behind this revolution. First, we have arrived at a much deeper understanding of pathology, both psychological and physical, which has led to the development of new, more precisely targeted interventions. Second, our research methodologies have improved substantially, such that we have reduced threats to internal and external validity, making the outcomes more directly applicable to clinical situations. Third, governments around the world and healthcare systems and policymakers have decided that the quality of care should improve, that it should be evidence-based, and that it is in the public's interest to ensure that this happens (Barlow, 2004; Institute of Medicine, 2001, 2015; McHugh & Barlow, 2010).

Of course, the major stumbling block for clinicians everywhere is the accessibility of newly developed evidence-based psychological interventions. Workshops and books can go only so far in acquainting responsible and conscientious practitioners with the latest behavioral healthcare practices and their applicability to individual patients. This series, Treatments *ThatWork*™, is devoted to communicating these exciting new interventions to clinicians on the front lines of practice.

The manuals and workbooks in this series contain step-by-step detailed procedures for assessing and treating specific problems and diagnoses. But this series also goes beyond the books and manuals by providing ancillary materials that will approximate the supervisory process in assisting practitioners in the implementation of these procedures in their practice.

In our emerging healthcare system, the growing consensus is that evidence-based practice offers the most responsible course of action for the mental health professional. All behavioral healthcare clinicians deeply desire to provide the best possible care for their patients. In this series, our aim is to close the dissemination and information gap and make that possible.

Many parents suffer from depression after having a baby. This can be both debilitating and distressing for the affected parent and their families. Depression in the postpartum period often goes unrecognized, leaving parents struggling with its impact. Early identification and treatment of postpartum depression are essential in order to promote the best outcome possible for parents and their babies.

This book provides a step-by-step guide of an evidence-based treatment for postpartum depression and aims to be a resource for therapists treating the affected parent using this approach. The program is divided into four modules: (i) assessment and goal setting, (ii) behavioral activation, (iii) managing unhelpful thinking, and (iv) relapse prevention. There is an accompanying workbook for the affected parent undertaking this treatment including detailed worksheets and resources.

It is recommended that parents work through their own workbook with the therapist. The treatment is laid out in a clear format in this workbook, with resources and worksheets. Completing the worksheets and reading through the material can help parents consolidate the learning that occurs through the therapy.

David H. Barlow, Editor-in-Chief
Treatments *ThatWork*™
Boston, Massachusetts

References

Barlow, D. H. (2004). Psychological treatments. *American Psychologist, 59*, 869–878.

Barlow, D. H. (2010). Negative effects from psychological treatments: A perspective. *American Psychologist, 65*(2), 13–20.

Institute of Medicine. (2001). *Crossing the quality chasm: A new health system for the 21st century*. Washington, DC: National Academies Press.

Institute of Medicine. (2015). *Psychosocial interventions for mental and substance use disorders: A framework for establishing evidence-based standards*. Washington, DC: National Academies Press.

McHugh, R. K., & Barlow, D. H. (2010). Dissemination and implementation of evidence-based psychological interventions: A review of current efforts. *American Psychologist, 65*(2), 73–84.

Contents

Preface *xi*

Acknowledgments *xiii*

About the Authors *xv*

Chapter 1 Introductory Information for Therapists on Postpartum/Postnatal Depression *1*

Chapter 2 Development and Summary of the Oxford Postnatal Programme *21*

Module 1 Preparing: Finding Out What Is Going on for You

Chapter 3 Session 1: Understanding Your Depression *51*

Chapter 4 Session 2: Values and Goal Setting *81*

Module 2 Activating: Doing Things That Make You Feel Better

Chapter 5 Session 3: Looking After Yourself *101*

Chapter 6 Session 4: Routines and Social Support *119*

Chapter 7 Session 5: Nourishing and Depleting Activities *129*

Chapter 8 Session 6: Problem Solving *139*

Module 3 Thinking: Helping Your Mind to Help You

Chapter 9 Session 7: Understanding How We Can Get Stuck in Our Thoughts *151*

Chapter 10 Session 8: Finding Alternatives to Getting Stuck in Our Thoughts *161*

Chapter 11 Session 9: Understanding the Importance of Self-Compassion *171*

Chapter 12 Session 10: Putting Self-Compassion Into Action *183*

Module 4 Heading to the Future: Planning How to Stay Well

Chapter 13 Session 11: Preparing to Finish Therapy *197*

Chapter 14 Session 12: Finishing Therapy *211*

Additional Sessions

Chapter 15 Session 13: Understanding and Managing Intrusive Thoughts, Images, and Urges *221*

Chapter 16 Session 14: Understanding and Managing Traumatic Images or Memories *237*

Beyond This Treatment Program

Chapter 17 Booster Sessions and Moving On *255*

Chapter 18 Growth and Change Through Treatment and Beyond *261*

Appendix A Worksheets *271*

Appendix B Assessment Questionnaire *295*

References *301*

Preface

Many parents suffer from depression after having a baby. This can be both debilitating and distressing for the parents and their families. Depression in the postpartum period often goes unrecognized, leaving parents struggling with its impact. Early identification and treatment of postpartum depression are essential in order to promote the best outcome possible for parents and their babies.

This book provides a step-by-step guide of an evidence-based treatment for postpartum depression and aims to be a resource for therapists treating parents using this approach. The program is divided into four modules: (i) assessment and goal setting, (ii) behavioral activation, (iii) managing unhelpful thinking, and (iv) relapse prevention. There is an accompanying workbook for parents undertaking this treatment including detailed worksheets and resources.

It is recommended that parents work through their own workbook with the therapist. The treatment is laid out in a clear format in this workbook, with resources and worksheets. Completing the worksheets and reading through the material can help parents consolidate the learning that occurs through the therapy.

Many parents suffer from depression after having a baby. This can be both debilitating and distressing for the parents and their families. Depression in the postpartum period often goes unrecognized, leaving parents struggling without support. Early identification and treatment of postpartum depression are essential in order to promote the best outcome possible for parents and their babies.

This book provides a step-by-step guide of an evidence-based treatment for postpartum depression and aims to be a resource for therapists treating parents using this approach. The program is divided into four modules: (I) assessment and goal setting, (II) behavioral activation, (III) managing unhelpful thinking, and (IV) relapse prevention. There is an accompanying workbook for parents undertaking this treatment including detailed worksheets and resources.

It is recommended that parents work through their own workbook with their therapist. The treatment is laid out in a clear format in this workbook, with exercises and worksheets. Completing the worksheets and reading through the material can help parents consolidate the learning that occurs through the therapy.

Acknowledgments

We are very grateful to all the mothers and their babies in the original study who taught us so much about the challenges of coping with postpartum depression.

We are indebted to the Wellcome Trust, which provided funds to carry out the study.

We acknowledge many colleagues who contributed to the research, particularly Peter Cooper and Lynne Murray, whose expertise on postpartum depression and infant development was invaluable, and Clare Kempton and Louise Dalton, who conducted therapy with many of the mothers. Michelle Craske gave valuable advice and support throughout the research. Many people contributed to the research, particularly Elizabeth Rapa, Bev Davies, Elena Netsi, Jess Cardy, Tassie Rowbotham, and Valerie West. We are also grateful for the help of student volunteers who supported the project.

We are grateful to experts who contributed to the development of the ideas in the treatment program, notably Michelle Craske, Pasco Fearon, Marinus van IJzendoorn, and Marian Bakermans-Kranenburg. Liz Andrews from Netmums contributed to the development of behavioral activation in the postnatal period.

We are particularly grateful to Olivia (not her real name), a participant in the research, who has given us invaluable help and insights in writing both the Therapist Guide and the Parent Workbook. As well as contributing sections in the books, she has worked closely with the authors in developing and writing all the chapters, has read through both books in detail, and has helped with the accessibility of the language and concepts.

We are grateful to Anna Hemphill, health visitor, who gave us invaluable feedback in the early development of this manual. Louise Dalton read early drafts of the manual and gave us helpful comments. Verity Westgate gave us very helpful advice on particular issues for parents with neurodiversity.

In developing this program, we have drawn on models and ideas that have been developed by leading clinicians and researchers in the field. We are grateful in particular to the following, who are all referenced in the reference list:

- Ed Watkins for his model of understanding and managing rumination, which is referred to in Chapters 9 and 10 on rumination
- Christopher Martell, Sona Dimidjian, and Ruth Herman-Dunn for their model of behavioral activation for treatment of depression, which is referred to throughout the book but particularly in Module 2
- Zindel Segal, Mark Williams, and John Teasdale for their work on mindfulness and mental health, which we refer to in Chapter 7
- William Miller and Stephen Rollnick for their work on motivation, which we refer to in Chapter 3
- Paul Gilbert and Deborah Lee for their work on compassionate mind, which is referred to in Chapters 11 and 12
- The late Aaron Beck who pioneered the development and use of cognitive behavioral therapy for treating a range of mental health problems

We are very grateful to the team at Oxford University Press, particularly Sarah Harrington and Jade Dixon, for encouraging us to write the books and for steering us skillfully through the process, and to our editor, Kate Scheinman, who has provided expert advice, helped to transform our material into readable books, and been very patient with us throughout, as well as a pleasure to work with.

Finally, we would like to acknowledge our own families who have supported us in writing these manuals and accepted the long periods of time on the computer.

About the Authors

Dr. Anne Stewart

Anne Stewart qualified in medicine at the University of London, UK, and completed her psychiatric training in Oxford, UK. She studied CBT at Oxford Cognitive Therapy Centre and has practiced CBT for many years alongside her psychiatric role, including establishing teaching programs for CBT with young people. She was the clinical supervisor in the research trial investigating the psychological therapy described in this book.

She has worked as a Consultant Child & Adolescent Psychiatrist in Oxford for many years with extensive clinical experience in depression, anxiety, self-harm, and eating disorders (now retired from a substantive clinical role) and is an honorary senior clinical lecturer at the University of Oxford engaged in teaching and research.

Dr. Charlotte Granger

Dr. Charlotte Granger qualified as a clinical psychologist from the University of Oxford in 2008 and worked as a research clinical psychologist on the Oxford Postnatal Trial between 2010 and 2013, developing, manualizing, and delivering psychological therapies for mothers with postpartum depression.

In her current NHS role, she is the Consultant Clinical Psychologist for the Child and Adolescent Mental Health Service in Central Norfolk, working with individuals and families across the lifespan with specialisms in the areas of attachment, child and adolescent mental health, parental mental health, and foster care and adoption. Charlotte has recently completed a Post Graduate Diploma in Clinical Paediatric Neuropsychology at the University College London.

Dr. Pete Lawrence

Pete studied psychology at the University of Cambridge (2003), completed his doctorate in clinical psychology at the university of Oxford (2009), and earned his PhD (2020) at the University of Reading, supervised by Professors Lynne Murray and Cathy Creswell. He developed, manualized, and conducted psychological therapies for postpartum depression in Oxford and contributed to the randomized trial described in this book.

Pete took up a role as Lecturer in Clinical Psychology at the University of Southampton in 2014 and was promoted to Associate Professor in 2022. Pete is presently the Research Director for the Doctoral Programme in Clinical Psychology, and co-chair of the National Group of Trainers in Clinical Psychology Research group.

Prof. Heather O'Mahen

Heather completed her PhD in Clinical Psychology at the University of Georgia, and then undertook a postdoctoral fellowship in Perinatal Clinical Psychology at the Department of Psychiatry, University of Michigan. At Michigan, she adapted and trialed Cognitive Behavioral Therapy for perinatal depression in low-income and diverse populations.

Heather took up a Senior Lecturer role at the University of Exeter, England, becoming Professor of Perinatal and Clinical Psychology in 2020. She is also a National Clinical Advisor to NHS England's Perinatal Mental Health team. Since moving to England, she has conducted four additional trials of perinatal CBT, including two trials of treatment delivered via the internet. This work has been widely disseminated throughout the NHS, Sweden, and Japan. She has remained active in training and supervising perinatal mental health clinicians, including collaborations with Prof. Alan Stein.

Heather's transatlantic clinical and research experience in perinatal CBT for depression contributed to the content in this book.

Prof. Alan Stein

Alan Stein received his medical training in South Africa. He was awarded a Wellcome Trust Lectureship at Oxford University in 1988 and then held joint Senior Research Fellowships at the Universities of Oxford and Cambridge. In 1995, he became Professor of Child & Adolescent Mental Health at the Royal Free and University College Medical School and the Tavistock Centre. In 2001, he was appointed to the Chair in Child & Adolescent Psychiatry in Oxford, and in 2024, he moved to the Blavatnik School of Government. Throughout his career, he has also worked on projects in South Africa.

Alan was the principal investigator of the trial investigating psychological therapies on which these books were based.

CHAPTER 1

Introductory Information for Therapists on Postpartum/ Postnatal Depression

Aim of This Chapter

This chapter aims to provide information for therapists on postnatal/ postpartum depression, what impact it can have, and what treatments work. Depression following birth of a baby is referred to as *postnatal depression* in some countries and *postpartum depression* in others. We will mainly use the term *postpartum* in this book.

Outline

- Introduction 1
- Prevalence 3
- Introduction of six parents with postpartum depression 5
- Risk factors for postpartum depression 8
- Diagnosis of postpartum depression 9
- Postpartum psychosis 13
- Negative cycles in depression 14
- Outcome of postpartum depression 15
- Evidence for treatment of postpartum depression 17
- Key points 20

Introduction

Giving birth is a powerful emotional and physical experience. There is a hope and indeed an expectation that it will be positive and fulfilling. However, it can also be unpredictable, painful, and occasionally traumatic. When giving birth is experienced for the first time, it can be

Postpartum Depression. Anne Stewart et al., Oxford University Press.
DOI: 10.1093/med-psych/9780197759707.003.0001

particularly bewildering and unsettling. Following the birth, mothers have to cope with physical, social, and emotional changes that are hard to prepare for and a challenge to manage, as well as having to care for their baby. Many mothers battle with poor sleep, exhaustion, and low mood. Depression is common in the postpartum period and often goes unrecognized. However, there is an increasing focus on assessing mothers in the postpartum period for depression, and there is evidence that psychological treatment can improve outcomes for both the mother and the child. Fathers may be overlooked, but they can become depressed during the postpartum period too. Nath et al. (2016) found a prevalence of paternal depression of 3.6% at 9 months following the birth, indicating that addressing the mental health needs of fathers is also important. Parents report that they are most likely to engage with treatments that are specifically adapted for the postnatal period as they target the types of problems they are faced with, and this was the inspiration for this treatment program.

This book provides a step-by-step guide of an evidence-based treatment for postpartum depression and aims to be a resource for therapists treating people using this approach. There is an accompanying workbook for parents undertaking this treatment including detailed worksheets and resources. Worksheets appear in Appendix A at the end of this therapist guide and in Appendix A at the end of the parent workbook. Worksheets can also be accessed by searching for this book's title on the Oxford Academic platform, at academic.oup.com. Note that when more than one copy of a worksheet is required, you may photocopy the worksheets for the parent, ask the parent to make their own photocopies, or direct the parent to the book website to print their own.

We refer to *mothers* as well as *parents* in this treatment program but acknowledge that there are also people giving birth and becoming parents who do not identify as women. There are also many routes to parenthood, for example, through surrogacy and adoption, including with lesbian and gay parents. The research on which this program is based involved female individuals who had given birth, but it is likely that the ideas and strategies will benefit a range of people with different experiences of being a parent, including co-parents who become depressed.

Prevalence

Postnatal/postpartum depression is relatively common, affecting around 10%–15% of mothers within 12 months of birth (Zaidi et al., 2017) and considerably higher in the context of socioeconomic disadvantage (Segre et al., 2007). In lower- and middle-income countries rates can be up to double (Mitchell et al., 2023). Puerperal psychosis is much less common, affecting between 0.1% and 0.5% of mothers (Vanderkruik et al., 2017), but can have devastating consequences for mother and baby. Many women are fearful that if they are depressed, they are at risk for puerperal psychosis, which isn't the case. However, a history of bipolar disorder does increase the risk of postpartum psychosis (Jones & Smith, 2009). Suicide in the postpartum period is a leading cause of death and can occur in the context of untreated depression. Physical problems are also common in the postpartum period and can contribute to low mood.

The timing of postpartum depression is variable; some mothers become depressed within a few weeks of birth, but other mothers may not get depressed until at least 3 months after the birth. The definition of postpartum depression includes parents who become depressed within the first year after the birth of the child.

It is important to be alert to the possibility of postpartum depression. Some studies indicate that significant numbers of mothers who report symptoms of depression are not identified in primary care as having depression (Boath & Henshaw, 2001). This can happen due to potential barriers in recognizing depression in the postpartum period (Webb et al., 2023).

Mother-Related Barriers

Barriers in recognizing postpartum depression relating to the mother include:

- Knowledge of perinatal mental health problems. The perinatal period is a significant transition with many physical, relational, and lifestyle changes. It can be challenging for mothers to assess what emotions are "normal" in this context and what constitutes a problem. This can be compounded when symptoms present as anxiety or irritability rather than low mood.

- Mothers may feel stigma about perinatal depression, especially about being judged for being a "bad" mother, and fear having their child removed from their care. These concerns may result in women who have experiences with health discrimination being less likely to disclose their mental health problems. This is especially likely in Black/African, South Asian/Indian, Hispanic, and low-income populations (Jankovic et al., 2020; Rokicki et al., 2024).
- Mothers may not be aware of what treatment options are available or whether those options might be applicable to their situation. Those who have had mental health treatment in the past may have beliefs about what is or isn't useful, and this can shape their help-seeking behaviors.
- Treatment burden can be challenging for mothers. Mothers with many health appointments may be less likely to seek treatment for their mental health.
- Access to treatment can vary across different countries and settings. In some, treatment at point of access may be freely available or associated with small co-pays. In other contexts, mothers may face significant treatment costs, and these will disproportionately affect treatment access in women with greater economic deprivation. Treatment waitlists and provider unavailability can also negatively impact women's access to treatment.
- Mothers may face additional practical barriers to engaging with treatment, including lack of childcare; transportation burdens; in rural areas, distance from providers; and in the case of digital interventions, lack of internet or mobile access.
- Mothers often require the emotional and practical support of family or close others to attend and engage with treatment. Support can range from helping to care for children during treatment sessions, supporting transportation to and from treatment, and, for many, supporting the mother's decision to seek treatment. Those with poor support may face challenges in accessing treatment.
- Limited trust in healthcare providers can impede the mother's willingness to disclose her problem or to follow through with recommended referrals.

Clinician- and System-Related Barriers

Other barriers to recognizing postpartum depression include:

- Healthcare clinicians work with mothers who experience a wide range of emotions, many of whom may have mild, temporary symptoms. Providers may therefore struggle to distinguish when a mother is depressed. Actively asking about symptoms using standardized measures and having awareness of atypical presentations can help.
- Perinatal depression can appear at any point during pregnancy and the year following childbirth, and women may wait before disclosing their symptoms. Clinicians may not be aware of the timelines in which women may be at risk of depression.
- Clinicians are more likely to screen and comprehensively assess for depression when they are aware of available follow-on services. Lack of provision or awareness of these services can negatively affect clinician assessment and referral behaviors.
- Maternity and primary care providers frequently lack appointment time and may not have the capacity to fully assess a mother's mental health.
- Regular use of standardized assessments for depression can help to overcome risks of errors in clinician judgment about the severity of mental health need, but these are not always used.
- Primary care and family doctors may be more likely to suggest treatment options consistent with what they are familiar with, focusing on antidepressants versus psychological interventions.

Because of these barriers, it is important to regularly use validated measures to assess for postpartum depression and to follow up scores indicating potential depression in order to further assess the problem and efficiently refer for help when appropriate and desired by the mother.

Introduction of Six Parents with Postpartum Depression

All parents have their own unique characteristics, context, and background; and this treatment program can be flexibly used to suit the individual client. We use the stories of six diverse women throughout the book to illustrate how depression presents and how the strategies can be used with a wide range of women from varying backgrounds and contexts. These stories are put together using our experience of many women with postpartum depression, but none of them are identifiable. The six women are introduced here.

LUCY, AGE 18, CAUCASIAN BACKGROUND

This is Lucy's first child from a short relationship. Her male partner has subsequently left and doesn't want anything to do with their son Jackson. The birth was medically uncomplicated, and breastfeeding is going well. Lucy's parents live nearby, and although her relationship with them was stormy during her adolescence, they are now trying to be supportive and want to help. Lucy lacks confidence in parenting and is not sure how to respond to Jackson or how to interact with him. She feels resentful that she can't go out and see her friends as she used to. She was studying for a catering certificate but has had to take time off since having Jackson.

ZAINAB, AGE 28, PAKISTANI BACKGROUND

Zainab is married to Tauseef, a supportive husband, and Amir is her second child. The birth was a forceps delivery, which was upsetting for Zainab as she was expecting a normal delivery. She has a history of clinical depression in her teenage years, had postpartum depression with her first child, and feels very guilty that she has become depressed again. She is bottle feeding Amir as she struggled with breastfeeding with her first child, and this led to her feeling low. Zainab has friends but is keeping to herself and has become socially anxious and isolated. Her parents are supportive, but they live in Pakistan. Her older daughter Layla is age 4, and although she was very well-behaved previously, Layla has been upset by starting school and having a new baby in the house. She is missing the closeness with her mother and has started having temper tantrums. Zainab feels she is a bad mother and is letting everyone down.

KENISE, AGE 30, AFRICAN AMERICAN BACKGROUND

Kenise lives in a large city with her children and husband, Demar. She has a 6-year-old daughter, Maya, and has recently had twins, Jayden and Serena (now 6 months old). They were born prematurely and were in the neonatal intensive care unit (NICU) for a few weeks. Kenise has found it difficult to bond with them, particularly as she felt distant from them initially. They started bottle feeding in the NICU, and this has continued. Demar travels for work and is often away. Kenise is struggling with looking after the twins as well as Maya. She is sleep-deprived and exhausted. Her mother lives in another city, 4 hours' drive away, so she misses regular support from her. She does have some aunties, cousins, and friends living nearby. However, she is too tired to make contact and has been outside the house very little.

SARAH, AGE 38, CAUCASIAN BACKGROUND

Sarah and her husband, Richard, started trying for a baby a few years ago, but she had several miscarriages that put a strain on their relationship. They were on the verge of separating when Sarah became pregnant again, and they decided to stay in the relationship and bring up the baby together. Sarah went into labor 6 weeks prematurely and had a prolonged and traumatic birth, requiring an emergency caesarean section (C-section). Their daughter, Chloe, breathed normally at birth but required monitoring for a week in the NICU. Sarah lost a lot of blood and had to remain in the hospital for a week with Chloe. This difficult experience of pregnancy and birth led to high anxiety and lots of worries about Chloe, which has put further strain on the relationship. Sarah has struggled to regain her energy following the C-section, and when they came home, she found it difficult to cope with all the demands. Previously Sarah was a well-paid senior manager in retail, but now she feels very deskilled. Richard is trying to be supportive but doesn't know how to help her. Sarah has become increasingly depressed and exhausted, alongside experiencing recurrent images about the traumatic birth of her baby.

In addition, Sarah comes from a large extended family that has very strong views about women/mothers being "strong," so she finds herself judging herself against this family value. Instead of feeling strong, she just hears a voice in her head telling her she is failing.

MILA, AGE 32, EASTERN EUROPEAN BACKGROUND

Mila is in a long-term relationship with a female partner, Sophie. Marta is her first baby; she had an uneventful pregnancy and an uncomplicated birth. It took Mila by surprise when she became low in mood and tearful when Marta was 2 months old. She thought it was just the "baby blues" and she would get over it, but the low mood has continued; now she doesn't feel like going out of the house. She wants to do the best for Marta but is struggling to breastfeed and feels guilty about this. She finds the lack of sleep exhausting and is having difficulty looking after herself, often skipping meals. In addition, she has started having thoughts about wanting to harm the baby which just pop into her head and concern her. Sophie is supportive but has a busy job and comes home tired. Mila's immediate family are in Poland. Sophie's family live nearby, which can feel a bit difficult for Mila as they have strong opinions on how she should manage her daughter.

ISABELLA, AGE 26, LATINX BACKGROUND

Isabella's baby Margarita was born post-term by C-section and is now 3 months old. Isabella was assessed as an adult and found to be autistic, which she found a relief as it explained some of the difficulties that she has experienced in relating to others and coping with change. She has very few friends and feels as if her male partner, Jack, doesn't really understand her needs. Her mother, who lives 1-2 hours away, has come to help several times already. Isabella says she is glad for the support but finds that her mother can have strong opinions about parenting that differ from Isabella and Jack's approach, which can be a source of conflict. She has found breastfeeding a real struggle because she is very sensitive to physical sensations but has persevered, despite the challenges. She is socially isolated and finds it difficult to adjust to the new and often quickly changing routines of having a baby. Isabella was working in IT, where she met Jack. She felt she was good at her work: it was structured, and she could focus on specific tasks. She doesn't feel she is suited to managing an unpredictable little baby and misses the structure of her work.

We will meet these parents again throughout the book and follow the way they deal with challenges and recover from their depression.

Risk Factors for Postpartum Depression

There is a considerable body of research on risk factors for postpartum depression. The most common risk factors identified are a previous history of depression, high levels of life stress, lack of social support, marital/partner conflict/violence, current or past abuse, having socioeconomic disadvantage, co-occurring medical illness such as HIV, being a young mother (especially a teenager), having a family background of depression, and substance abuse (Elwood et al., 2019; Howard et al., 2014; Hutchens & Kearney, 2020; Silverman et al., 2017; Zaidi et al., 2017).

Other risk factors identified include being a first-time mother (Bradshaw et al., 2022), having a twin birth, having an interventionist delivery, and low self-esteem (Bradshaw et al., 2022; Ghaedrahmati et al., 2017; Silverman et al., 2017; Zaidi et al., 2017).

Although these factors increase the risk, women can also develop postpartum depression without having an increased risk.

Diagnosis of Postpartum Depression

It is common to have mixed feelings about pregnancy, birth, and parenthood. Postpartum depression needs to be differentiated from the "baby blues," which occurs frequently after childbirth and is associated with rapid changes in hormones: Mothers may experience mood swings, tearfulness, lack of concentration, and tiredness during this period. These symptoms normally disappear in the first few weeks, but 10%–15% of women will have persistent symptoms. Sometimes postpartum depression can have its onset beyond the first few weeks, even a few months after giving birth, or can begin in pregnancy and continue following the birth of the child.

Diagnosis of postpartum depression requires a comprehensive assessment with the mother, including her current mental and physical state; the nature of the birth; the timeline; current sources of support; any current stresses, conflict, and potential sources of domestic violence or coercive control; and any financial difficulties, as well as her individual and family background, including previous pregnancies, previous mental and physical health problems, and developmental history. This assessment may be conducted by a psychiatrist or other medical practitioner separate from the therapist conducting the treatment. The diagnostic features of depression will be outlined briefly before presenting a more detailed description of common symptoms in depression.

To make a diagnosis of depression (using the *Diagnostic and statistical manual of mental disorders*, 5th edition [DSM-5] classification [American Psychiatric Association, 2013]), the individual must be experiencing five or more of the following symptoms over a 2-week period, and at least one of the symptoms should be either depressed mood or loss of interest or pleasure (the DSM-5 needs to be consulted for the detailed criteria).

- Depressed mood most of the time
- Marked diminished pleasure or loss of interest in activities
- Significant weight loss or weight gain or a change in appetite (either increase or decrease)
- A slowing down of thought and a reduction of physical movement
- Fatigue or loss of energy most of the time
- Feelings of worthlessness or excessive or inappropriate guilt most of the time
- Decreased ability to think or concentrate most of the time.
- Recurrent thoughts of death, suicidal ideation

There are useful self-report questionnaires available which can guide assessment of depression in the postnatal period. Validated questionnaires include:

- Edinburgh Postnatal Depression Scale (EPDS) (Cox et al., 1987; Wisner et al., 2002). This can be obtained free of charge, with the scoring, from the internet (e.g., https://med.stanford.edu/content/dam/sm/neonatology/documents/edinburghscale.pdf med.stanford.edu/E
- Patient Health Questionnaire (Kroenke & Spitzer, 2002)
- Depression Anxiety Stress Scales (Lovibond & Lovibond, 1995)
- Beck Depression Inventory (BDI) (Beck et al., 1996)
- Ruminative Response Scale (RRS) (Erdur-Baker & Bugay, 2010)
- Adverse Childhood Experiences 10-item Questionnaire (Felitti et al., 1998). This can be obtained free of charge on the internet.

In the research trial for our treatment program, the EPDS was used at the start of treatment, at the review halfway through, at the end of therapy, at the first booster session, and when the child was 2 years of age.

See Chapter 3 (Session 1) in this therapist guide for details on how to assess the context and specific features of depression in the postpartum period.

Common Symptoms in Depression

The common symptoms that mothers present with will now be described in more detail:

- **Low mood and tearfulness**: Low mood that continues for longer than a few weeks and starts to impact the mother's well-being may be an indication that a depressive illness is developing.
- **Loss of pleasure and interest in usual activities**: The lack of ability to take pleasure in activities previously enjoyed or those that are expected to be enjoyable (e.g., interacting with a happy baby) is a cardinal symptom of postpartum depression and can be especially challenging for new parents who may feel bereft and hopeless about feeling cut off from expected joy with highly valued experiences at such a critical time in their lives. This may be especially difficult when this symptom affects their ability to enjoy and bond with their infant. Parents may struggle to engage with valued activities that no longer feel emotionally reinforcing (including parenting-related activities), and this avoidance can further maintain their depression and may lead to problems in the quality of the parent–infant relationship.
- **Sense of hopelessness**: Along with low mood, the mother may experience a feeling that the low mood is never going to end, and this can bring a sense of despair and hopelessness.
- **Negative thinking**: There is a tendency in depression to take a negative perspective to one's situation. People who are depressed tend to be more sensitive to criticism and rejection from people, even if it is not intended. They may also assume rejection from their baby. For example, if the baby is crying, the mother may assume that it is because the baby is not happy to be with them. Negative thoughts, for instance, "I am failing as a mother," "I will never feel normal again," and "My baby doesn't love me," can lower mood even further. In addition, the tension and

anxiety experienced by the mother can be transmitted to the baby, who then may be harder to settle.

- **Change in appetite or weight**: Changes in appetite and weight are common in postpartum depression, but it is important to determine the extent to which the changes are due to physical/practical postnatal factors and/or to depressive mood. For example, in the immediate postnatal period, significant weight loss is common, associated with changes in fluid retention and less body fat needed compared to during the pregnancy. At the same time, mothers who are breastfeeding may have an increase in appetite associated with the need for increased caloric intake to produce breast milk. These potential appetite and weight changes should be balanced against a generic loss or increase of appetite associated with reduced desire for food or using food to regulate emotion (e.g., "comfort eating") in the context of low mood and/or anhedonia.
- **Poor sleep or excessive sleep**: Sleep is likely to be disturbed with frequent nighttime infant awakenings and feedings. However, some mothers may also experience difficulty getting to sleep (both initially and after awakening with the infant) and/or with early morning awakening. These mothers typically report significantly less sleep than other mothers of infants. More rarely, some mothers report excessive sleep during both the night and daytime.
- **Lack of concentration and poor memory**: Poor concentration and impaired memory are both commonly reported in the postnatal period. When these start to affect day-to-day functioning, these symptoms may be part of a wider depression.
- **Fatigue/exhaustion**: Mothers with postnatal depression commonly report feeling exhausted most of the time, over and above what is normally expected in this period of life. They might also describe feeling overwhelmed with the tasks they have to do and have reduced energy to carry these out.
- **Irritability**: Irritability is a common symptom of depression and can be bewildering for those close to the person with depression. It may be closely linked to levels of sleep. Irritability can make it harder for the partner and family to interact with the mother, leading to an increased sense of isolation.

- **Lack of motivation**: Another troubling symptom in depression is lack of motivation. This can make it difficult for the parent to look after themself and their baby. Sometimes the parent may just want to curl up in bed and not do anything.
- **Anxiety**: It is common for new parents to feel anxious, particularly if this is their first experience of parenthood. Anxiety that is out of keeping with the situation may occur in the presence of low mood. The anxiety may relate to concerns about low mood and difficulty in coping with the baby, or it may be more generalized and include panic attacks. This anxiety can be very disabling and may lead to avoidance of situations that increase anxiety. Symptoms of anxiety are common in depression.
- **Suicidal thoughts/urges**: Parents experiencing postnatal depression will commonly report thoughts that life is not worth living or is too painful or difficult to endure. Parents may also report feeling trapped, disconnected, and hopeless. There is robust research evidence for the link between entrapment and suicidality (S. Li et al., 2018; O'Connor & Portzky, 2018). Key risk factors associated with suicidal ideation and behavior in the first postpartum year include a history of domestic violence, childhood abuse, and poor social support (Reid et al., 2022). Chapter 3 (Session 1) will include discussion on how to assess suicidal risk.

Postpartum Psychosis

Psychotic symptoms, for example, hearing voices or experiencing delusions such as paranoid delusions, may occur in the presence of depression, but they are uncommon. If psychotic symptoms are experienced, it is important to exclude postpartum psychosis, which is a rare condition affecting around 0.1% of mothers in the postpartum period. The main symptoms of postpartum psychosis are mania, delusions, severe depression, and psychosis. Specialist treatment is required, usually in an inpatient unit. Mothers suffering from postpartum psychosis are beyond the scope of this treatment program. Some mothers involved in this program may be fearful of developing postpartum psychosis, and it is important to clarify that this is a rare disorder.

If the parent is starting to experience poor sleep, low appetite, and feelings of exhaustion, a vicious cycle can develop, whereby poor sleep can lead to loss of interest in usual activities, which can lead to a reduction in usual activities and social isolation. This in turn can contribute to further lowering of mood and less inclination to get out and do things. Self-care can deteriorate, and this can contribute to further feelings of exhaustion, particularly if the mother is not eating well or has impaired sleep. See Figure 1.1 for an example of negative cycles in depression.

Let's look at Mila and see how her depression started:

Mila is feeling low 2 months after giving birth. She has stopped contacting her friends, is irritable with her partner Sophie, and is tired with low energy; it just feels like there is too much to do. Mila is struggling to breast-feed and feels like a failure as a parent. She often lies awake at night with

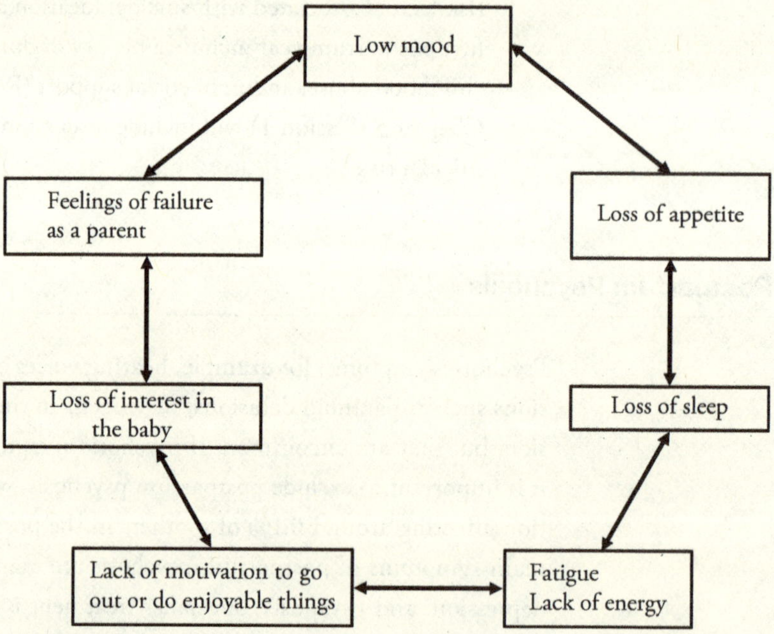

Figure 1.1

Negative Cycles in Depression.

negative thoughts going around her head about her ability as a mother. She is also ashamed about others seeing that she isn't coping as well as she'd like, and she lies awake worrying about how others might judge her. Consequently, Mila feels very tired the next day, struggles to look after Marta, and is neglecting herself. This is contributing to further low mood, and she is becoming increasingly socially isolated. This sets up a vicious cycle of low mood, lack of support, poor sleep, and exhaustion.

Mila is becoming depressed, and it is likely that her outcome and that of her baby will be influenced by how promptly she gets help. The next section reviews what we know about the outcome of postpartum depression.

Outcome of Postpartum Depression

It is important to promptly support and treat mothers with postpartum depression, not only because of the distress and functional impairment it causes for mothers but also because postpartum depression, especially if it becomes persistent, can increase the risk for problems developing in the parent–infant relationship: It also increases the risks for both short- and long-term negative cognitive, social, and emotional outcomes for the infant (Netsi et al., 2018).

Outcome in Mothers

A systematic review of 122 studies showed an association between postpartum depression and poorer maternal physical and psychological health (Slomian et al., 2019). A longitudinal study of parents and children in the United Kingdom (Avon Longitudinal Study of Parents and Children) showed that mothers with persistent and severe postpartum depression throughout the postnatal year showed elevated depression scores up to 11 years after childbirth (Netsi et al., 2018).

Impact on the Parent–Infant Relationship

A number of studies over the last 30 years have shown a significant association between maternal depression and reduced quality of the mother–infant interaction (e.g., Stein et al., 2014).

Impact on Infant Development

A considerable body of research has found that postpartum depression can adversely impact infant development., but this is certainly not inevitable. Cornish et al. (2005) found that chronic maternal depression lasting more than a year was associated with poorer infant cognitive and psychomotor development, with a similar effect for male and female infants. Brief episodes of depression did not significantly affect infant development. In their review Stein et al. (2014) found an association between postpartum depression and child emotional and behavioral difficulties, negative cognitive outcomes, and attachment problems. These effects were moderated by the severity and chronicity of maternal depression. Later studies have also found that children of women with persistent and/or severe postpartum depression are at an increased risk of behavioral problems in childhood and depression in the later teenage years (Netsi et al., 2018), as well as an increased risk of difficulties in the domains of sleep, cognitive, language, emotional, and behavioral development (Slomian et al., 2019).

It should be emphasized, however, that children of mothers with postpartum depression are not invariably negatively affected. Furthermore, some mothers manage to maintain high levels of sensitive parenting and interaction despite being significantly depressed. A number of studies have aimed to identify other factors that might contribute to the impact of postnatal depression on infants; these factors include parental disharmony and socio-economic adversity (Stein et al., 2014). McMahon et al. (2006) found that maternal attachment states of mind moderated the impact of postnatal depression on infant attachment. Milgrom et al. (2004) found that maternal responsiveness to the infant mediated the effects of postnatal depression on infant development.

Impact on the Wider Family

The impact of postnatal depression on the family has been studied. Boath et al. (1998) found that postnatal depression placed considerable burdens on partners and other family members, affecting social and leisure activities and placing considerable financial burden on the family. Postpartum depression also had an adverse impact on the marital relationship and on the partner's mental health. An example of this is seen in Sarah and her family.

Sarah's depression could be felt across the family. She struggled with feeling unsupported in caring for her baby. Her husband Richard could see she was feeling low and wanted to help but wasn't sure what to do with the baby. Sarah had worked out how to settle Chloe, but there were times when Sarah just felt she needed a break. She was anxious about letting Richard do things for Chloe because sometimes when they tried this the baby became upset, and then Richard ended up handing Chloe back to Sarah. She then felt like the situation was just more challenging than if she had done it all herself. Richard likewise felt helpless and upset and started to withdraw even more.

Sarah is becoming increasingly exhausted, and the family feel frustrated and powerless. Richard is also beginning to suffer from lack of sleep and is becoming irritable, which makes Sarah feel that she is not doing a good job as a wife or a parent.

Evidence for Treatment of Postpartum Depression

Having identified the presence of postpartum depression, it is important for parents to have access to evidenced-based treatments. A considerable number of studies have explored the efficacy of treatments for postpartum depression.

Medication

Antidepressants are in some cases prescribed by doctors for postpartum depression. Brown et al. (2021) conducted a systematic review and meta-analysis exploring the safety and efficacy of antidepressant drugs in comparison with any other treatment for postnatal depression. The results showed that there may be a benefit of SSRIs over placebo. However, there was insufficient evidence to assess the efficacy of SSRIs compared with other classes of antidepressants and of antidepressants compared with other interventions, including psychological interventions. A substantial proportion of women experienced adverse effects but there was no evidence of differences in the number of adverse effects between treatment groups in any of the studies. The authors concluded that there remains limited evidence regarding the safety and effectiveness of antidepressants in the management of postnatal depression.

However, a recent Norwegian study including over 60,000 women (Liu et al., 2023) suggests that treatment with SSRIs postnatally may have long-term benefits for women with postnatal depression and their offspring and is also associated with a reduction in risk for a number of adverse maternal and child outcomes associated with postnatal depression.

A recent article in the Journal of the American Medical Association points out that the "current American College of Obstetricians and Gynecologists (ACOG) practice guidelines recommend SSRIs as a first-line pharmacotherapy for perinatal depression and anxiety and that drug therapy should be individualized based on prior treatment response" (Schneider, 2025). In general, a cautious approach is recommended in the perinatal period, using the lowest effective dose, starting at a low dose and increasing gradually, with careful monitoring, including, in the case of breastfeeding, monitoring of the newborn for any adverse effects.

Psychological Treatment

There is a considerable body of research investigating psychological interventions for postpartum depression. The most widely studied interventions for postpartum depression are cognitive behavioral therapy (CBT)–based interventions and interpersonal psychotherapy. A meta-analysis of psychological interventions for postpartum depression in primary care found that compared with controls, psychological interventions resulted in lower depression scores at short-term and longer-term follow-up (Stephens et al., 2016). The interventions also led to improvements in adjustment to parenthood, marital relationship, social support, stress, and anxiety. There was no significant difference between the different psychological interventions reported in this review (7 CBT, 3 interpersonal therapy, 2 counseling, and 3 other nonspecific interventions). A systematic review and meta-analysis including 20 randomized controlled trials and 3623 participants found that CBT was associated with a better outcome than controls on both the EPDS and the BDI. Subgroup analysis suggested that in-house and telephone-based therapy led to an improvement in depression scores (Huang et al., 2018).

More recently, a systematic review of systematic reviews and meta-analyses reported that psychological interventions were effective at decreasing depressive symptoms in women with postpartum depression, with CBT being the most effective intervention (Branquinho et al., 2021), provided in different delivery formats (individual, group, face-to-face, or internet-based). Cuijpers et al. (2023) found an overall effect size for psychological treatment in perinatal depression to be 0.67.

A recent systematic review and meta-analysis by Pettman and colleagues (2023) found a moderate effect size of 0.53 overall, with additional significant effects for secondary features such as anxiety, stress, and perceived social support. This study also found that the type of CBT and the type of health professional and their training were significant moderators of the main effect (symptoms of depression), with higher effect sizes when the intervention was delivered by those with mental health training.

Regarding behavioral activation for postpartum depression, H. A. O'Mahen and colleagues (2013) found that an internet behavioral activation treatment for postnatal depression (Netmums) proved a promising treatment in reducing depression scores; but in this self-help-only program there was high attrition, and some women reported that without support it was a challenge to keep up with the program. A subsequent qualitative analysis with participants selected from this study suggested that support would reduce the impact of barriers and improve adherence (O'Mahen et al., 2015). The internet program was modified to take a modular approach, and guided support was added. The adapted program showed very low attrition and had a large effect size on depression, work, and social impairment at posttreatment and a large effect size on depression at 6 months. There were small effect sizes for postpartum bonding and perceived social support (O'Mahen et al., 2014).

The Oxford Postnatal Programme, on which this treatment program is based, was developed as part of a research trial (The Oxford Postnatal Treatment study (Stein et al., 2018)), which investigated the efficacy of psychological therapy in postpartum depression. The study found a significant improvement in the level of depression experienced by mothers immediately following the program, which was maintained at 12 month follow-up when the infants were 2 years of age. The treatment trial tested whether a specific focus on improving the mother–child interaction led to better child outcomes. Our findings indicated that the critical factor in improving child outcome was successful treatment of depression and that the specific focus on mother–child interaction did not make a significant difference. The research will be described in detail in the next chapter.

Key Points

- Postpartum depression is relatively common.
- Some women are more vulnerable to developing postpartum depression.
- Diagnosis and formulation require a comprehensive assessment.
- The outcome is good for mothers whose depression is treated effectively.
- If postpartum depression is persistent or not treated, there is a risk of negative outcomes for mothers and their babies.
- There is evidence for the effectiveness of psychological intervention in postpartum depression.

CHAPTER 2 Development and Summary of the Oxford Postnatal Programme

Aim of This Chapter

This chapter describes the background of the Oxford Postnatal Programme (OPP), how it was developed, and what is involved in it.

Outline

- Evidence base for this treatment program 21
- Models on which the treatment is based 25
- Key principles of the OPP 28
- Who is this treatment for? 31
- Duration of this treatment program 32
- Summary of the treatment modules 33
- Flexible use of the treatment program 35
- Engagement and the stance of the therapist 36
- Practical aspects of treatment 39
- What each session will involve 43
- Use of the parent workbook alongside this therapist guide 45
- Specific issues to be aware of in postpartum depression 46
- Key points 48

Evidence Base for This Treatment Program

The OPP was developed as part of a research trial (The Oxford Postnatal Treatment study) that investigated the efficacy of therapies in postnatal (postpartum) depression (Stein et al., 2018). All mothers in the trial

Postpartum Depression. Anne Stewart et al., Oxford University Press. © Oxford University Press (2026).
DOI: 10.1093/med-psych/9780197759707.003.0002

(N = 144) received a psychological therapy adapted for the postnatal period and designed to alleviate their postnatal depression. Drawing on the existing evidence base on effective treatments for postpartum depression, cognitive behavioral therapy (CBT) was the treatment of choice, using a largely behavioral activation (BA) approach. Behavioral activation is a key component of CBT but this has been expanded by Martell and colleagues (Martell et al., 2010) to be a stand-alone treatment which informs this programme. The standard program consisted of 12 sessions with two booster sessions, 2 weeks apart, at 4–5 months following the end of treatment. In the treatment trial, the average length of therapy was 10 sessions. A high proportion of the women completed the treatment: 66 out of 72 mothers (91.7%) received nine sessions or more in the index group, and 64 out of 72 (88.9%) received nine sessions or more in the control group.

This CBT therapy was delivered concurrently with one of two other psychological therapies. The index therapy for this study was video feedback therapy (VFT), which uses video feedback of maternal interaction with their infant to help enhance maternal sensitivity and support positive development of the mother–infant relationship. The active comparison group for the study was progressive muscle relaxation (PMR), which is a guided relaxation training program focusing on helping the mother identify muscular tension and release it. Thus the index group received CBT plus VFT and the control group received CBT plus PMR. Mothers were randomized to either of these treatments (72 in each group). The aim was to see if the mother–infant therapy (VFT) had a beneficial impact on child outcomes at 2 years compared to PMR (Stein et al., 2018).

Mothers aged 18 and over who were between 4.5 and 9.0 months postpartum and who were depressed were recruited from within Oxfordshire, United Kingdom, and the surrounding area via general practitioners, health visitors (specialist nurses who have additional training in community public health nursing and work in the community, primarily with preschool children and their families), and other psychological services and from posters and leaflets displayed in primary care facilities and children's centers. An assessment was made using a standardized clinical interview, known as the Structured Clinical Interview for DSM diagnosis (SCID). Women who had been depressed for at least 3 months were included in the treatment trial, following written, informed consent. The severity of the depression ranged from moderately-severe (58%) to severe (42%); 26.4% also had a generalized anxiety disorder, and 5.6% had post-traumatic stress disorder (PTSD). Their infants were between 5 and 9 months at the start of therapy (mean age was 6.8 months). The program described in this therapist guide has been broadened to be relevant to a wider range of people than were involved in the original study. As well as baseline assessments before therapy started, assessments were made at the end of therapy when the child was between 12 and 13 months of age and again when the child was 24 months old. At each time point depression in the mothers was assessed by both structured interview (SCID) and the Edinburgh Postnatal Depression Scale. The mother–child interaction was also assessed through structured observation in the family home using standard rating scales.

The primary outcomes included the child's cognitive and language development (using the Bayley Scale of Child Development), attachment, and child behavior. These were assessed when the child was 24 months of age. A range of other measures were taken, for example, mind-mindedness (the ability in the mother to view their child as having a mind of their own and be sensitive to what their child might be feeling, thinking, or wanting) (Pawlby et al., 2010).

Therapy was delivered in the parent's home. Some mothers arranged childcare, and in other sessions undergraduate placement students helped to look after the baby. However, many of the sessions were done successfully with the baby present. As the therapies were delivered concurrently, sessions lasted 90 minutes in total: 45 minutes CBT and 45 minutes VFT or PMR (whichever treatment the mother had been allocated to). A manual was developed to guide the therapists in delivering the program and ensure consistency. This therapist guide and the corresponding parent workbook describe in detail the treatment program for the mothers' depression. Details of the VFT and PMR are described in the research article (Stein et al., 2018).

The study found that the index psychological treatment (VFT) was not significantly different from the active comparison group (PMR) with respect to child outcomes. However, there was a marked improvement in *both* groups in the level of depression experienced by mothers immediately following the program, and these improvements were maintained at 1-year follow-up (when the baby was 2 years old), with rates of remission from depression reaching 85%. Child outcomes relating to cognitive development, language, and behavioral problems were no different from published community norms. These findings indicate that the critical factor in children's outcomes is the successful treatment of depression in their mothers.

Here are some comments from Olivia (not her real name), who was one of the mothers who took part in the study and agreed to share her perspective on it.

OLIVIA

I enrolled as a participant in the OPP study when my baby was 8 months old. I had been experiencing serious postnatal depression since giving birth and at the point I entered the study felt as if I was getting worse, not better. Through the study I had 12 sessions of the CBT described in this book over a 6-month period, plus two booster sessions (2 weeks apart) 5 to 6 months later, shortly after my baby turned 18 months.

I can say with certainty that the OPP was incredibly helpful to me. It helped me understand why I had become ill and that it wasn't my fault. It taught me that small changes in our daily routine could make a big difference and that it wasn't selfish to make plans that prioritized self-care and that helped me stay well. I was very afraid early in my illness of being alone in my house with my baby, without things to do, and the techniques I learned through the study helped me to get used to the idea that I could stay safe (and get some rest) in my own house—that being at home wasn't something I needed to find frightening. The most important and hardest thing I learned during my therapy was to be compassionate toward myself, that I hadn't failed at motherhood by becoming ill. Through my sessions I learned to take pride in the way I cared for my baby in very difficult circumstances, and I also discovered that it was OK to accept help from my family and friends when I was struggling.

That doesn't mean it wasn't hard at times to engage with the program because it was! This is because sometimes the material covered in the sessions was really upsetting but also because when I was ill, I wasn't very good at prioritizing my own health and recovery, and I found it hard to make the time to complete the home practice while caring for a small baby. However, once I had completed the program, I came to see how important it had been to keep going, including through the difficult bits. I also saw clearly that the change the program brought to my life wasn't just a result of the sessions but came about as much because of the work I did between sessions—either by completing worksheets like those in this book or by putting into practice some of the things we discussed in the sessions. At one point I did almost give up, but I was able to talk to my therapist about why I wanted to do so and talk through the decision with her. I am so glad now that, between us, we found a way for me to keep going.

There's one more thing I'll say at this stage, and that's that if someone had handed me a book when I was at my lowest point and told me to "read myself better," I would probably have thrown that book across the room. A book would have felt like a completely inadequate response to the crisis I was in. That's why THIS book has been designed to be used as a workbook for therapy, rather than as a substitute for it. The clinicians who developed this program haven't produced this book so that you can be left alone to get on with it but as a tool to allow the therapy model they pioneered to be available to as many people as need it. So, although it might be difficult, I really encourage you not to throw this book across the room but to work through it with your therapist and to stick with it. It will really help, I promise.

Models on Which the Treatment Is Based

The CBT that we used in the OPP has a strong focus on BA. It is adapted to account for the specific context of the postpartum period. This is a period of immense change for the parent and the family. The parent is likely to be sleep-deprived and will have fluctuating hormone levels that affect their mood. They may have worries about their competence as a parent—whether they will be able to feed their baby, whether they can meet their baby's needs, or whether they are becoming bonded to their baby, as well as worries about whether their baby is normal, is thriving physically, or is attaching to them. They may also have troublesome thoughts about wanting to harm the baby. The treatment is adapted to take into account these worries and helps the parent to focus on their own needs as well as those of their baby.

This treatment approach draws on the existing evidence base for effective treatments for severe and chronic depression. CBT and BA will now be described briefly.

Cognitive Behavioral Approach

CBT is based on the principle that the way we think about ourselves, others, and the world impacts how we feel and behave (Beck, 1979. Likewise, our mood and actions impact our thinking. A vicious cycle can occur that maintains problems such as low mood or anxiety. In postpartum depression, parents may experience a range of negative thoughts such as "I am useless as a parent," "I am never going to feel myself again," "It's all my fault that my baby cries a lot," or "I might as well give up." These negative thoughts can be paralyzing and lead to the parent adopting unhelpful behaviors such as isolating themself from friends or reducing their usual activities. See Box 2.1 for a summary of key principles of CBT.

Box 2.1 Key Principles of CBT

- The way we view ourselves, others, and the world impacts how we feel and what we do.
- CBT is based on principles that are intended to be personalized to the client in a formulation or case conceptualization and aims to identify the vicious cycles that keep problems going.
- Modifying thinking patterns and changing behavior can help to break the vicious cycles that maintain problems such as depression.
- CBT emphasizes collaboration and encourages the client to become their own therapist.
- CBT takes account of the client's past but is focused on making changes in the here and now.
- CBT is goal-focused and problem-oriented.
- CBT teaches clients to identify, evaluate, and respond to unhelpful thoughts, assumptions, and beliefs.
- CBT uses a variety of strategies to encourage helpful thinking patterns and behaviors including carrying out behavioral experiments.

BA

BA was developed by Martell and colleagues (Martell et al., 2010) and has been shown to be an effective treatment for depression (Ekers et al., 2014; Richards et al., 2016). It has been adapted for use with women with postpartum depression, both in person and online (O'Mahen et al., 2014). BA works on the principle that changing what we do can change the way we feel. It is highly collaborative, helping people to be their own therapist to work out solutions to the challenges they face. The main principles are summarized in Box 2.2.

Box 2.2 Key Principles of BA

- The therapist acts as a coach to help the parent find their own solutions.
- Changes in life can lead to depression and some coping strategies (such as staying at home), which may help in the short term but can keep people stuck.
- Helping people to change what they do is key to helping them change how they feel.
- Change happens from "the outside in rather than the inside out."
- Activities are scheduled that follow a plan rather than how the parent feels in the moment.
- It is helpful to change in small steps.
- A problem-solving approach can help to overcome challenges.
- Identifying and addressing the barriers to activation helps people to progress.
- It's best to do something rather than keep talking about it.

There are some additional components in the OPP that are particularly relevant for people suffering from postpartum depression:

- **Rumination**: In postpartum depression, it is common for parents to ruminate on their negative aspects, such as repeatedly going over in their mind ways in which they are failing as a parent or not relating to their baby as they should. In this treatment there is an active focus on helping the parent to find ways of overcoming the rumination.
- **Compassionate mind**: Many parents in the postpartum period find it hard to care for themselves or be compassionate toward themselves. A key component of the therapy focuses on developing the ability to be self-compassionate.

- **Intrusive imagery**: Some parents develop intrusive imagery in relation to their baby, which causes considerable anxiety. They may have intrusive imagery of harming their baby, which is concerning to themselves and those around them. There are strategies within this treatment to manage this imagery and reduce anxiety.
- **Traumatic memories**: Some parents experience difficult births, which may lead to symptoms of PTSD, depending on the nature of the trauma and the parent's vulnerability. The experience may also trigger memories of trauma that occurred earlier in their lives. In OPP, the parent is helped to develop strategies for managing traumatic memories and any troublesome symptoms so that they can move on and connect to their baby in the present moment rather than being preoccupied with what has happened in the past.

Key Principles of the OPP

Based on the above, there are eight key principles that are incorporated into this treatment, as follows:

- **What we do and think influences how we feel**: The way the treatment is carried out is very much influenced by the individual formulation, particularly the maintenance cycles, so it is important to work out with the parent how their thoughts, feelings, behavior, and physical state interact.
- **Doing things differently can help to lift our mood**: Following the principles of BA, the parent is encouraged to change their behaviors to be more in line with doing activities that they value and that help them to feel less depressed. Behaviors that have a net positive impact on mood are called *antidepressant activities*, and parents are taught to identify these activities and do more of them to feel better. A key point in BA is that people may have found themselves stuck in patterns where they are engaged in behaviors that in the short term seem to have an antidepressant effect but in the long term may be unhelpful. For example, a new parent may not be making much contact with friends or getting

out to an activity with their baby because it may feel too overwhelming. In the short term they may feel relieved by not doing these activities, but in the long term this might lead to feeling alone and guilty. You will discuss this with the parent. It is common for people to think "I cannot do any of that until I feel better," but the treatment is about "acting from the outside in" rather than from "the inside out." In other words, it is about identifying what is important to the parent and starting to take small steps to act differently with behaviors that are important to them, even when they may not feel like it at the start. To get the most out of these activities it can be useful to help people set up activities that they can become immersed in and engaged with.

- **Taking small steps one at a time can bring about big changes**: It is recognized that energy levels are low, that there are multiple demands on a parent's time and attention in the postpartum period, and that even texting a friend can be an enormous challenge. We encourage the parent to make small changes one step at a time at a pace that they can manage. It can be helpful to schedule these activities, rather than leaving it up to the chance that the parent might "feel up to it." When even small changes are difficult, we encourage the parent to problem-solve in order to work out how a change might be possible.
- **Dealing with unhelpful thinking patterns can break the vicious cycle of depression**: It is common in the postpartum period to develop a habit of ruminating about difficulties. Negative thoughts can go round and round the head, never getting anywhere and leading to behaviors that may be unhelpful. In the OPP the parent is taught how to manage these thoughts so that they do not interfere with function.
- **Planning routines can help us take control**: After giving birth it is easy to feel that everything has become chaotic and out of control. It can be a bewildering experience, particularly if this is the parent's first child and they have no prior knowledge of how to be a parent. During the treatment they will be encouraged to develop routines that benefit both them and their baby and increase their confidence as a parent. If they find it difficult to develop routines, they will be helped to problem-solve in order to find ways through the difficulties.

- **It is important to look after oneself first and be kind to oneself**: Throughout treatment, we emphasize to the parents that caring for themselves is a crucial aspect of learning to care for their baby as well as feeling better in themselves. Many parents are dismissive and critical of their parenting, and they benefit from specific guidance on self-care and how to be compassionate toward themselves.
- **We can become our own therapist**: A key principle in the OPP is teaching the parent to become their own therapist using Socratic dialogue and encouraging them to develop their own ideas for change and plan antidepressant activities. This will involve learning to problem-solve effectively so that parents can troubleshoot and find solutions. It's all a learning process, and even if things don't go as planned, just having tried is important. Being able to work out why things didn't work or what stopped the parent from trying is all part of the process of taking charge of themself. This is a skill for life.
- **Keeping on going with helpful strategies can help us stay well**: An important part of the OPP is maintaining wellness after the program has finished. The parent is encouraged to develop strategies to look after themself and maintain their progress so that they can continue to stay well after the program has finished.

See Box 2.3 for a summary of these principles. These eight principles are designed to help the parent get back on track and lead a life that feels meaningful and reinforcing. When discussing different strategies and skills throughout the program, it is important to relate these to the key principles and overall aim. This then provides a rationale for the strategies that are being suggested.

A critical principle is being kind to oneself. Taking a compassionate stance toward oneself is a core component of this program and will be referred to throughout the treatment program. Toward the end of the program there are two sessions specifically devoted to developing self-compassion.

Box 2.3 Key Principles of the OPP

- **What we do and think influences how we feel**: Remember, we can lift our mood by doing things differently.
- **Becoming more active can lift mood**: Getting out, taking some exercise, meeting up with friends can all help us to feel better.
- **Taking small steps, one at a time, is important**: It can be overwhelming trying to do too much all at once, so just take it one step at a time, and progress will be made that way.
- **Dealing with unhelpful thinking can break the vicious cycle of depression**: It is easy to get caught up in unhelpful thoughts that go round and round and make us feel worse. However, we can take control and manage these ways of thinking.
- **Planning routines can help us to take control**: When things seem out of control, setting a schedule for ourselves can be a way of taking charge and feeling back in control again.
- **It is important to look after ourselves first**: Unless we care for ourselves, it is hard to look after other people.
- **Becoming your own therapist is key**: Going through this program teaches life skills that you can put into practice long after you have finished therapy.
- **Continuing with helpful strategies can help us stay well**: It's important to keep going with the things that you have found helpful in keeping you well. These are skills for life.

Who Is This Treatment for?

This therapist guide is for professionals treating parents with postpartum depression ranging from mild to more serious. The research participants were all female, so in this therapist guide, the term *mothers* is used as well as *parents*. However, as noted in Chapter 1, the program may be helpful for a range of people with different experiences of being a parent (although we don't have evidence for this from our trial).

The term *therapist* is used throughout the program; but it is used as a general term, and the expectation is that a range of professional groups would be able to work effectively with this treatment, including clinical psychologists, CBT therapists, mental health nurses, community nurses for parents and young children (described as *health visitors* in the United Kingdom), mental health social workers, and psychiatrists. Ideally, the therapist should have recognized professional qualifications such as in mental health nursing, social work, psychology, or psychiatry, alongside training in the basic principles and delivery of CBT and regular clinical supervision. Clinical supervision is important for therapists at all levels, but it is particularly recommended for less experienced professionals using this therapist guide. This guide includes a comprehensive description of the model on which the treatment program is based and step-by-step guidelines for how to deliver it. A professional background with experience in developing a therapeutic relationship and working collaboratively is essential.

There is an accompanying workbook for parents with postpartum depression (*Postpartum Depression: Workbook*) that can be used alongside this therapist guide, which enables easy access to worksheets and resources for the client. Worksheets appear in Appendix A at the end of this therapist guide and in Appendix A at the end of the parent workbook. Worksheets can also be accessed by searching for this book's title on the Oxford Academic platform, at academic.oup.com. Note that when more than one copy of a worksheet is required, you may photocopy the worksheets for the parent, ask the parent to make their own photocopies, or direct the parent to the book website to print their own.

Duration of This Treatment Program

The treatment presented in this therapist guide and the corresponding parent workbook consists of a number of components designed for flexible use within four separate modules. There are also additional components (described in Chapters 15 and 16) that may be used when there are specific complexities such as coping with intrusive imagery or traumatic memories. The standard session number for each module is as follows: two assessment sessions, four activation sessions, four thinking sessions, and two future planning sessions. A review of therapy is held during the sixth session or approximately halfway through the program.

The early sessions of therapy are best done at least weekly to make it easier to engage with the parent and encourage early change. As the therapy progresses, the sessions can be spaced out to give the parent a chance to try things out on their own for a longer period. The final two sessions can take place at least 2 weeks apart. In the research trial, the participants also had two booster sessions (2 weeks apart) around 4–5 months after the final session of therapy. Many parents find this helpful as it gives the opportunity for an extended period on their own with two further sessions for consolidating and troubleshooting.

Summary of the Treatment Modules

The treatment is divided into four modules, although the boundaries between the modules are not rigid, and it may be necessary to return to earlier modules to do more in-depth work or to skip some elements of the modules if they are not relevant. Broadly, the modules cover assessment, behavioral work, cognitive work, and relapse prevention. They form the acronym **PATH**, which symbolizes the journey of recovery.

Module 1 Preparing: Finding Out What Is Going on for You

The first module (which is covered in Chapters 3 and 4) includes assessment of the parent's background, current difficulties, and mental state. It includes an assessment of the presence of depression and an assessment of risk, which includes risk to the baby and/or risk to the parent. You will encourage the parent to think about their values in life as a parent, within their family, and themselves as an individual and consider what needs to change for them to feel better about themself and get on with their life. Generally, this module takes between one and three sessions.

Module 2 Activating: Doing Things That Make You Feel Better

This module (which covers Chapters 5 to 8) looks at the links between mood and behavior and aims to encourage behaviors that are in line with the parent's values and improve mood.

The first session in this module (Chapter 5/Session 3) focuses on foundational self-care skills such as eating, sleeping, and exercising. This introduces the idea of setting small achievable goals and building a daily and weekly routine, which are then the focus of Chapter 6/Session 4. The idea of prioritizing self-care activities regularly is further extended in Chapter 7/Session 5, through focusing on recognizing nourishing and depleting activities. Chapter 8/Session 6 then introduces a structured problem-solving technique to directly counteract avoidance and encourage activation. At the end of this module, it is helpful to do a review with the parent on how things are going, what has improved, what the current challenges are, and what further work is needed.

Module 3 Thinking: Helping Your Mind to Help You

This module (which covers Chapters 9 to 12) tackles the negative thinking that can help to maintain the depression. There will be discussion about the impact of focusing on negative thoughts and ways in which the links between negative thoughts, feelings, and behavior can be broken. You will encourage the parent to think about themself in a warm and compassionate way, rather than in a critical or judgmental way. Some parents may require additional work on intrusive thinking or traumatic memories, which is covered in Chapters 15 and 16.

Module 4 Heading to the Future: Planning How to Stay Well

In the final module (which covers Chapters 13 and 14) the parent will review the progress they have made during treatment and be helped to identify goals for the future and plan ways of keeping well, including how to cope with difficulties and challenges. This module usually takes a couple of sessions to complete.

In addition to these standard four modules, there are two optional sessions that can be used with some parents as needed. These sessions aim to help the parent develop additional skills in dealing with intrusive thinking and traumatic memories where this is relevant. They can be used flexibly at any point throughout the program following Module 1.

Flexible Use of the Treatment Program

The first three modules can be worked through flexibly depending on the needs of the parent. Not all the skills described in this program will be relevant to all parents. The exact combination of skills and exercises will vary according to the individual. These two vignettes illustrate the diverse ways in which the program can be used.

LUCY

Lucy is a young single mother who had become increasingly low in mood following the birth of her baby, Jackson. She was referred for therapy and engaged well, working on routines that helped with her sleep and then scheduling in opportunities to get out a bit and have more contact with friends. The focus on behavioral activation really helped to lift her mood and increase her confidence as a mother. However, she still tended to get stuck in her thoughts about how she was a bad mother. She worked on this in the two sessions on rumination and was discharged from treatment after 12 sessions, having worked through the standard program.

SARAH

Sarah experienced a traumatic birth requiring an emergency C-section, following which she stayed in the hospital for a week and her daughter, Chloe, required a week in the neonatal intensive care unit.

Although initially Sarah appeared to cope, her mood became progressively low; and she began to spend long periods of time during the day ruminating on her memories of the birth. At night, she couldn't get the images of the birth out of her head, making it hard to sleep, and leaving her feeling drained the next day. She was referred urgently for treatment and engaged with the therapy. However, although her mood began to lift as she engaged with the therapy, she continued to be troubled by traumatic images of the birth. After completing sessions on problem-solving and addressing unhelpful thinking, she required additional sessions on imagery rescripting and rumination with more intensive work on her cognitions, particularly her view of herself as a bad mother. Overall, she had 14 sessions.

Engagement and the Stance of the Therapist

A crucial predictor of successful outcomes in therapy is a strong therapeutic relationship between therapist and client. Taking time at the beginning of treatment to ensure that this relationship is built has considerable benefits, particularly when the therapist and parent need to have difficult conversations or discuss challenging ideas. When thinking about engaging parents with young babies, it is important to consider the following fundamental skills:

- warmth
- acceptance
- collaboration
- minimizing blame
- paying attention to individual needs
- maintaining appropriate boundaries
- focusing on the process rather than the outcome

Warmth

Parents who are experiencing low mood are likely to be feeling overwhelmed, judged, self-critical, and anxious. Holding a deeply intentional stance of warm positive regard for the parent in therapy is crucial to building a strong therapeutic relationship. It is helpful for you, the therapist, to be mindful and observant of this dynamic in therapy and use supervision to monitor the development of this stance in the therapeutic relationship.

Acceptance

Practicing active listening is key in helping the parent feel understood and accepted. Active listening involves proactively communicating to the parent that you are hearing and accepting what is important to them. It is essential to allow the parent time to talk through whatever feelings emerge through the conversation, not moving too quickly into problem-solving or "fixing" what seems stuck, and naming and staying with difficult negative feelings such as overwhelming sadness or frustration. There are goals for each session, but it is also important to remember engagement is about attuning to what the parent needs in the moment.

Collaborative Work

In all sessions, it is helpful to encourage the parent to take an active role and share responsibility. It is important to convey that all results are useful, to focus on understanding what makes change difficult, and to work collaboratively to help the parent develop more effective action plans. This involves being responsive to the parent's behavior and then modifying agendas and interventions as appropriate.

Minimizing Blame

Parents with postpartum depression are very quick to blame themselves or feel a failure, so the therapist needs to work actively throughout the therapy to counter this feeling of blame. This will include taking a positive approach to times when a parent fails to do the agreed home activity. You can thank the parent for letting you know that the home activity was not completed and then indicate that it is helpful to understand the challenges and work on them together. A key goal is learning, so if things don't go according to plan, there is something to learn from that.

Individualization

Although this is a manualized intervention, it is based on core principles with flexibility to adapt the components to the individual needs of the parent in order to focus on the specific issues that have led to the parent developing low mood. Depression can lead to cognitive difficulties such as slowed thinking, as can the cumulative impact of sleep deprivation. As you begin therapy, observing and asking questions about how the parent learns, and reflecting on this in later sessions, can be useful. Consider with the parent what works for them, which may include reinforcing key concepts frequently, encouraging writing of notes in the parent workbook, and revisiting previous learning as and when necessary. Each parent will be different, so it is helpful to be curious about them as individuals, understanding what their unique issues are, how they respond to situations, what support they have, etc. The program will then vary according to these individual differences. The program can be adapted as needed for those parents with neurodiversity (as it was for Isabella).

Boundaries

Every therapeutic session or visit is an opportunity to demonstrate and model to the parent the importance of healthy boundaries and self-care. At the beginning of every session, make sure the parent is comfortable and knows what to expect for the session. Initiate and support thinking and implementing regular session self-care routines such as getting a warm drink or a snack. Think together proactively about how their baby's routine will be managed during the session: Does the parent need their phone on if their baby is being looked after elsewhere? Do they need to make up a bottle or have a comfortable cushion ready for the next feeding? Encourage recognition of the importance of making time for oneself through these practical preparations.

Focus of Work

It is important to keep a focus on the process of what is going on rather than the outcome and things that have been achieved. This will mean checking out how the parent is managing to put into practice the skills, whether they are deriving any positives from this, or whether they need more time to practice the skills (see later in the chapter for more discussion on this).

The therapist worked hard to engage Zainab in their second session. It had been agreed previously that Zainab should be seen at home (please see the next section on practical aspects of treatment for discussion on location of treatment).

The therapist arrived at Zainab's house for their second session to find that Zainab had forgotten the appointment due to an unsettled night with her son Amir teething and a challenging morning getting Layla ready for school. Zainab felt even worse for forgetting and expressed worries that it would be difficult to stick to regular therapy sessions in the middle of everything else she had to do. The therapist empathized with how hard it was all feeling, without trying to problem-solve or take Zainab's worries away. She encouraged Zainab to put Amir on the baby mat with toys and to make herself a cup of tea and breakfast. Once settled, Zainab talked to the therapist for some time about how overwhelming and miserable life seemed and that she felt she couldn't bear the daily grind of seemingly endless tasks.

The therapist listened actively, summarizing and reflecting on how Zainab was feeling. Zainab began to feel calmer, and the therapist began to move on to material for the therapy session, focusing on how low mood can develop and the Mood Monitoring Record (Worksheet 6). At the end of the session, the therapist reinforced the effort it had taken Zainab to complete the session, the slow small steps to progress, the importance of self-care, and that there were no judgments in the therapeutic space. Zainab felt more positive after the session, having had the opportunity to talk and be heard without judgment and having managed to complete her therapy session despite how difficult the morning had felt.

With Isabella the issues were different, due to her background of neurodiversity.

In the first couple of sessions, Isabella seemed uncomfortable and somewhat distant. The therapist was aware that Isabella was autistic so ensured that the sessions were predictable—at the same time and place each week—and that a quiet room with minimal distractions was used so that Isabella felt more comfortable and understood. When discussing abstract issues, such as the mother's values, the therapist aimed to be as concrete as possible, using examples from Isabella's life. The therapist encouraged her to give honest feedback about the sessions, and Isabella learned to trust the therapist enough to do this. This enabled them to find the best way to work together.

Practical Aspects of Treatment

Location

In the research program, all participants were seen at home, which resulted in benefits by increasing the accessibility of treatment, ensuring attendance, and potentially providing support with their baby if necessary. This may not always be possible, but it is helpful at the start of treatment to work out with the parent what would work best within the boundaries of what is possible. Some parents might prefer to get out of the house to attend a clinic appointment. Others may find this difficult and prefer a home visit or to video chat or to speak on the phone. Research has found that mode of delivery does not affect outcome (Branquinho et al., 2021; Pettman et al., 2023).

If the therapy is being conducted at home or online, it will need to be organized in advance where the parent will be doing the therapy and how to manage interruptions or potential involvement of other family members. Also, if the therapy is being conducted online, note that some parents may prefer to initially meet in person at least once. Others, particularly those who struggle with stigma, may prefer to start with online approaches but may be more open to an in-person visit(s) later in treatment. We acknowledge that in some circumstances in-person sessions may not be possible, and research suggests that the working alliance is not harmed by an online-only approach (Preschl et al., 2011).

Frequency and Length of Treatment

This treatment was originally developed to be delivered once a week for 10–12 sessions. However, it can be helpful to offer the treatment more intensively, particularly at the start of therapy. For example, the parent may be seen twice a week, in some circumstances, particularly if the depression is severe and debilitating. The additional session may be in person or via telephone/video link, whatever works best. Research has found that more intensive treatment is related to improved outcome (Cuijpers et al. 2023). However, some parents like the routine of weekly appointments, which may be fitted more easily into the busy postpartum schedule. Toward the end of therapy, the sessions may be spaced out to enable the therapy to finish more gradually. We also recommend booster sessions (discussed in detail in Chapters 14 and 17), but not every parent will want to have these. The important thing is to be flexible according to the parent's needs.

Toward the end of therapy, you will need to assess whether the parent is ready to finish therapy. This will depend on to what extent they have achieved their goals for therapy and how they are functioning generally. Things may not be entirely back to normal at the end of therapy but hopefully things will be good enough for the parent to continue working on their issues with support from family, friends, and/or their primary healthcare provider.

Participant Record-Keeping

When suffering from postpartum depression, it can be hard to keep track of what has been discussed in each session. Although the parent will have the parent workbook, there may be additional ideas discussed in the session that may be helpful for the parent to reflect on between sessions. To facilitate recall, it helps to keep a record of the session. At the start of therapy, you may have a discussion with the parent regarding how best to keep a record. You can encourage the parent to keep notes in their workbook, and the following are some additional options:

- The parent or therapist can record the whole session (audio or video) for the parent to listen to later (this may be overoptimistic for many parents, but some make the time and find it helpful).
- The parent or therapist can record the end of the session where summary points and home practice are discussed.
- For some parents, a summary email sent by the therapist following the session can be a helpful reminder of what has been discussed.
- Alternatively, it can work well to take 5 minutes at the end of the session to look at the summary points of the session together and encourage the parent to write down any other pertinent points that were covered in the session and any specific homework tasks.

These options can be brainstormed with the parents. Options may vary to the extent that parents find recordings acceptable, and they will have their own ideas about what works best for them. The important thing is that the parents have choice and control as to how they keep track of the content of the session.

Confidentiality and Consent

It is crucial at the outset of treatment, when discussing consent to treatment (which may be written informed consent, depending on your practice) to be clear that the sessions are principally confidential but that there are some limits to confidentiality where there is a serious risk of harm to self or others. This is particularly important for parents who may be experiencing negative intrusive thoughts about their baby or about themselves, which they are either embarrassed about sharing or anxious about what might happen if they share these thoughts. Generally, information can be kept confidential unless there is a concern that either the parent or the baby is at risk, in which case the therapist may need to share information with other professionals. This needs to be made clear to the parent in a sensitive way, reassuring them that, if possible, you would share with them your concerns first.

It may also be agreed that you will send a summary of treatment progress to the parent's family doctor, primary care physician, or other professionals as relevant.

Supervision

It is expected that any therapist undertaking therapy with parents with postpartum depression will receive supervision on a regular basis. The parent needs to be aware that their case will be discussed (anonymously) with other professionals to enhance the effectiveness of the program.

Involvement of Partner/Family

Some parents find it helpful to involve their partner or other family member in at least some of the sessions to discuss how their partner/family member can support them. This can also be an opportunity to let the partner or other loved one know about the depression and its impact and to work out together practical things they can do to help. Family members can often feel overwhelmed by the depression, so having practical things to do can help. It can be particularly helpful to involve loved ones in the last module when preparations are being made for ending therapy.

On the other hand, some parents prefer to be seen entirely on their own. Indeed, in the study, a few participants were reluctant to even share with their family that they were having treatment. It is important to take your lead from the parent and respect their confidentiality and privacy. Even if you do involve other family members, it is still crucial to give the parent as much autonomy and agency as possible. It is important to be sensitive to the possible fear of having their baby taken away as well as the shame of opening up about depression. It can be helpful to think of the partner (or other family member) as an "ally" rather than as a "carer."

What Each Session Will Involve

Sessions will generally last 45 minutes, but this will depend on the needs of the parent. The therapist should incorporate the elements below in all sessions (modified from Martell et al., 2010).

Maintain Session Structure

As is usual in CBT and BA, each session will start with collaboratively setting an agenda. The agenda will include:

- reviewing mood (using a 1–10 scale at the outset of each session), including engaging in a safety check
- reviewing how things are going since the last session, including how the parent is getting on with their new skills
- reviewing the outcome of between-session home practice
- discussing specific material related to the session/content for the week
- agreeing on home practice for the coming week(s)
- collaboratively summarizing the session
- evaluating the session and asking for feedback

Be Action-Oriented

All sessions should maintain a focus on activation and on countering any avoidance associated with low mood. This will include structuring and scheduling routine activities that follow a plan based on values (not a mood) and setting small goals that are manageable and meaningful. The emphasis is on engaging in activities that are naturally reinforcing and that involve attending to experience and taking a problem-solving empirical approach (i.e., working out a possible solution, trying it out, and reviewing the outcome).

Work Toward Identified Goals in Line With the Parent's Values

Through exploring goals and values and maintaining a strong focus on these in sessions, you can develop an understanding of the kind of life the parent would like to have. This helps shape individualized goals, moving towards these goals over the course of treatment.

Reinforce Examples of Helpful Behavior

As the therapist, it is helpful to keep alert to examples a parent gives of when they behaved in a way that improved their mood and to make sure to respond to these examples in a way that increases the likelihood that the parent will continue to engage in such positive change. You can look with the parent at how this change might impact on their individualized formulation/conceptualization.

Agree on Home Practice

At the end of each session, you will work out with the parent an activity, strategy, or self-monitoring assignment (including monitoring mood) to do between sessions using the worksheets. Worksheets appear in Appendix A at the end of this therapist guide and in Appendix A at the end of the parent workbook. Worksheets can also be accessed by searching for this book's title on the Oxford Academic platform, at academic.oup.com. Note that when more than one copy of a worksheet is required, you may photocopy the worksheets for the parent, ask the parent to make their own photocopies, or direct the parent to the book website to print their own. The aim of home practice is to come up with activities that are consistent with the parent's goals. Worksheet 9: Weekly Goal Planner and Worksheet 10: Weekly Goal Record help to keep the parent focused. Practicing these activities between sessions and keeping track of progress are likely to have a huge impact on the outcome of therapy, so this is an essential discussion to have with the parent at the outset of treatment.

Flexibility is important too, with some parents using a variety of ways to record progress, including on paper, post-it notes, smartphones, pictures, recordings, etc. If home practice proves difficult, you can discuss what the barriers are and brainstorm ways to achieve it.

Review How Things Are Going

Each session will involve a review of progress to date so that changes can be consolidated and the therapy can be modified to maximize the possibility of change. Although you need to be mindful of meeting goals, it is important to discuss progress with the parent in terms of process rather than outcome. Encouraging curiosity and learning is as important as meeting specified goals. For example:

- Is the parent engaging with valued activities?
- Is the parent learning from what they did during the week?
- What positives have there been from the way the parent did things differently this week?
- How does the parent feel they are getting on with the skill they discussed last session?
- Do they need more time to practice these skills before taking on new ones?

Halfway through the program (at around Session 5 or 6), there will be a more formal review of progress, looking at what has changed so far and what are the remaining things that need to be tackled. It can be helpful at this point to repeat a standardized outcome scale (discussed in Chapter 1) to get a measure of the level of depression, alongside specific questions regarding any depressive symptoms. As the order of sessions is flexible in this program, you will need to decide the appropriate stage at which to do this review.

Use of the Parent Workbook Alongside This Therapist Guide

It is advisable for the parent to have their own copy of the workbook that accompanies this therapist guide. The workbook includes resources, worksheets, and explanations that complement the therapy sessions and assist in the parent's progress. Using the worksheets, including self-monitoring, is an important way of keeping track of what is being done.

Specific Issues to Be Aware of in Postpartum Depression

Becoming a parent is a huge transition. If this is the first baby, the parent is suddenly responsible for a helpless baby without having any prior skills and experience; but even a subsequent child can provide new challenges for parents. They may have experienced a difficult pregnancy or a traumatic birth and may be feeling exhausted and debilitated. In addition, for mothers, hormones are in flux, making them vulnerable to low mood. It is a time when parents lose the stability and consistency of their usual life and are faced with unpredictability and uncertainty. If they are fortunate to have a supportive partner, this can be invaluable; but some parents may be struggling on their own or with conflict in their close relationships. It is not surprising, therefore, that low mood and depression occur at this time of life (Bradshaw et al., 2022). Although the prevalence of suicide is in fact lower than expected in the first year after childbirth (Orsolini et al., 2016), suicide is a leading cause of maternal death in the postnatal period, with 20% of postpartum maternal deaths caused by suicide (Lindahl et al., 2005). It is therefore important to screen for suicidal thoughts and urges.

Postpartum depression can affect how mothers feel about their baby in various ways:

- Some parents feel that postpartum depression has not influenced their relationship with their baby. Indeed, some parents report that having to care for their baby helped them get through the depression.
- Some parents find that they don't experience pleasure when with their baby.
- They may find it hard to love or feel bonded with their baby.
- They may feel angry toward their baby or blame the infant for their depression.
- Some parents may struggle to "read" their baby's signals and cues and feel they are not able to respond appropriately to their baby or that they "just don't get" their baby.
- They may also have intrusive thoughts of wanting to harm their baby. These thoughts are common and usually do not indicate a risk of harm to the baby, but as a therapist, you need to be alert to the possibility of risk. This issue is dealt with in detail in Chapter 15/Session 13.

Parents may have a mix of feelings toward their baby, or their feelings may change according to the fluctuation of their mood.

Some parents can feel very ashamed or embarrassed that they are suffering from depression when they should be enjoying having a new baby. It is important to listen empathically to what they are saying and endeavor to understand their situation and concerns. Engaging the client is the first step in any therapy and is particularly important when working with parents with postpartum depression who may already be feeling vulnerable and helpless.

Once therapy has started there will still be times when motivation flags and the parent may feel like giving up. In particular, the distress of engaging with therapy might feel like it is outweighing any potential benefit in the future. Accepting distress is inevitable during the program, and sitting with distress may be an important part of getting better. It is important to remind the parent of the reasons for doing the program that they identified at the start and to work out ways to make it easier to carry on, which might mean ensuring that they get some additional support, for example, from friends or their partner. Keep an open dialogue with the parent about how they feel about the therapy and what would make it easier to continue. If the parent is struggling with keeping going, it may be helpful to return to earlier components of the therapy. Encouraging small steps can bring a sense of momentum back and instill hope. Here is what happened to Sarah.

Sarah was keen to get started on the program but after a couple of sessions felt like giving up as she didn't feel any better and it was such hard work doing the home practice. She was close to her family, and her cousin reminded her that she wasn't going to get better straight away and that it is hard work getting through a depression. Sarah asked her cousin (who lived nearby) to join one of the sessions so that she could understand more about the treatment program and help her when she felt stuck around practicing at home.

Having a new baby requires building a new relationship with another being, which can be both pleasurable and exhausting or even sometimes irritating. The interaction with the baby can impact on mood, and conversely the parent's mood will impact on how they interact with their baby—for example, the rumination that often occurs in depression might impact on the parent's attention to their baby's cues. This treatment program addresses the interaction with the baby when the relationship with the baby is impacting on the parent's mood, as well as highlighting that doing activities with the baby in an absorbed and attentive way can have a positive impact on the parent's mood.

Key Points

- The Oxford Postnatal Programme was developed as part of research on effective treatments in postpartum depression.
- The research evaluation showed it was successful in remitting postpartum depression.
- It is based on cognitive behavioral therapy and behavioral activation and is a collaborative form of therapy.
- The treatment program can be used flexibly to suit the individual parent.
- Each session follows a consistent structure designed to encourage the parent to take responsibility.
- Home practice is an important part of treatment.
- Parents with postpartum depression can easily feel overwhelmed, so it is crucial to keep the treatment as simple and straightforward as possible.

MODULE 1

Preparing

Finding Out What Is Going on for You

The focus of Module 1 is on assessment of the parent's symptoms and concerns, drawing up a formulation/conceptualization, and setting goals. This module will set the foundation for the rest of the therapy, so it is important to take time to engage the parent and make a thorough assessment of the issues so that you understand how best to help them in the therapy.

The first chapter in this module (Chapter 3/Session 1) focuses on a detailed assessment of the parent's concerns, coping strategies, risks, and protective factors; and this session will involve doing a collaborative formulation/case conceptualization to make sense of the concerns and what might be keeping them going. A safety plan may be drawn up, if needed, which can be referred to throughout the therapy.

The second chapter in this module (Chapter 4/Session 2) considers what the parent's values are and uses this discussion to agree with the parent specific achievable goals.

CHAPTER 3 Session 1: Understanding Your Depression

Aim of This Session

The aim of this session is to engage the parent, describe the treatment, discuss expectations for therapy, assess current concerns and strengths, identify any risks, develop a formulation/conceptualization, set initial goals, and create a safety plan if needed.

As there is a lot to cover in this first session, you may need to allocate up to an hour and a half.

Outline

- Introduction and engagement 52
- Setting an agenda 53
- Description of the treatment 54
- Practicalities of treatment 54
- Brief background and any adverse childhood experiences 54
- Previous experience of therapy and expectations 55
- Motivation 56
- Assessment of context, current symptoms and concerns 56
- Coping strategies and strengths 63
- Social support 65
- Risks 66
- Formulation/conceptualization 69
- Future life and goals 72
- Managing risk 74

Postpartum Depression. Anne Stewart et al., Oxford University Press. © Oxford University Press (2026).
DOI: 10.1093/med-psych/9780197759707.003.0003

- Troubleshooting 78
- Home practice 78
- Summary of the session and feedback 79
- Key points 79

When to Conduct This Session

At the start of treatment for all parents

Materials Needed

- Assessment Questionnaire
- Worksheet 1: Preparation for Assessment
- Worksheet 2: Motivational Balance
- Worksheet 3: Coping Strategies
- Worksheet 4: How Changes in Life Can Lead to Low Mood
- Worksheet 5: Safety Plan
- Worksheet 6: Mood Monitoring Record

Worksheets appear in Appendix A at the end of this therapist guide and in Appendix A at the end of the parent workbook. Worksheets can also be accessed by searching for this book's title on the Oxford Academic platform, at academic.oup.com. Note that when more than one copy of a worksheet is required, you may photocopy the worksheets for the parent, ask the parent to make their own photocopies, or direct the parent to the book website to print their own.

Also note that the Assessment Questionnaire appears in Appendix B at the end of this therapist guide. The Assessment Questionnaire can also be accessed by searching for this book's title on the Oxford Academic platform, at academic.oup.com.

Introduction and Engagement

This is the first meeting with the parent, and it is important to be aware that they may well be anxious at the thought of meeting you. You will need to work actively to engage them and particularly to make sure that your questions/comments are not perceived as judgmental or critical. Parents with depression are very sensitive to the fact that they might be thought of as bad parents and will easily interpret statements in this light. It's also important to be aware that hopelessness, fears, and feelings of failure can be strong experiences in depression. So, when engaging with the parent, it's important to take this into account.

Developing a therapeutic relationship is crucial for the therapy. The qualities of warmth and acceptance as described in the previous chapter are essential, along with the ability to listen actively, paying attention to the specific issues of the parent you are working with and modeling being able to set helpful boundaries.

You will want to introduce yourself, explaining your professional role and how you will be working with the parent, and invite them to introduce themself, telling you about their current social/family context, how old their baby is, and what support they have. You may acknowledge that they have been given a diagnosis of depression and referred to you for treatment. This is a good opportunity to check their understanding of depression by briefly describing the nature of postpartum depression and answering any questions. You can also refer them to Chapter 1 of the parent workbook, which has detailed information about postpartum depression.

If they haven't already filled out a depression scale, you may give the parent a scale such as the Edinburgh Postnatal Depression Scale (this can be freely downloaded from the internet).

Setting an Agenda

Having done introductions and discussed the nature of postpartum depression, you can explain to the parent that at the start of each session you will set an agenda together that will include standard items such as review of progress and home practice as well as setting new home practice and getting feedback on the session. There will be specific agenda items that relate to the content of the program; in addition, it is important to give space to the parent to come up with any things they want to discuss.

Description of the Treatment

At this point, it is helpful to describe the key aspects of treatment and how it is going to work, as summarized in Chapter 2 of both the therapist guide and the parent workbook. This will include highlighting the principles of treatment and the different topics covered. You may refer to Chapter 2 of the parent workbook that explains what is involved in therapy. The parent is very likely to have questions about the treatment, and it is important to allow time to discuss what the therapy will involve.

Practicalities of Treatment

You may then discuss the practical aspects of therapy, as discussed in detail in Chapter 2. This will include agreeing where and when the therapy will take place, how to keep a record of sessions, issues relating to confidentiality and consent, and whether the parent would like any family members to be involved.

From now on you can use the Assessment Questionnaire, which appears in Appendix B at the end of this therapist guide, to structure your assessment. The Assessment Questionnaire can also be accessed by searching for this book's title on the Oxford Academic platform, at academic.oup.com. The parent will have an abbreviated version of this form (Worksheet 1: Preparation for Assessment, in Appendix A at the end of the parent workbook) to help them reflect on key issues prior to the assessment.

Brief Background and Any Adverse Childhood Experiences

As part of getting to know the parent and what they are bringing to therapy it is useful to find out whether they have had previous mental health problems and whether they have experienced any adverse experiences earlier in their life. The Adverse Childhood Experiences Questionnaire (Felitti et al., 1998)—available freely online—can be useful for checking out the range of events/circumstances the parent may have experienced. If their score is 4 or more, you can explore with the parent how much these experiences are still impacting them and whether they feel happy proceeding with the Oxford Postnatal Programme (OPP) or feel they need therapy to address these experiences.

Parents who have experienced adverse events earlier in their life may be more vulnerable to low mood and have less ability to manage their emotions, so this will need to be taken into account as you proceed through the therapy.

Previous Experience of Therapy and Expectations

It is helpful to discuss early in treatment whether the parent has had previous experience with therapy and what their expectations are for this therapy.

Useful Questions for This Part of the Session

Questions to ask the parent at this point in the session include:

I want to begin by talking about whether you have had any experience with therapy before and what you might expect from our sessions together.

- *Have you ever had sessions with a counselor or therapist in the past?*
- *Can you tell me how you found that?*
- *Are there things you remember being helpful or unhelpful?*
- *Can you tell me a bit more about any specific issues you have had in therapy that you found challenging?*
- *It sounds like it might be helpful for me to know how difficult that was for you, and it would be good to let me know if you feel we are going down the same path. Do you think you could do that? Is there anything that would make it easier for you to let me know?*
- *How do you feel things have been since you were referred for this therapy (OPP)?*
- *Has anything happened to you and the family?*
- *Have you had any contact with other health professionals?*

Motivation

Many new parents will struggle to fit in weekly sessions when their baby requires considerable time and energy, and they are likely to be sleep-deprived. It can be helpful to encourage the parent to reflect on what they are likely to get out of engaging with the program and what the downside will be. It is useful to think about the pros and cons of doing the treatment program both in the short term and in the longer term and help the parent work out the decisional balance. You can encourage the parent to fill out Worksheet 2: Motivational Balance.

In the study, a high proportion of the women completed the program. Sixty-six out of 72 mothers (91.7%) received nine sessions or more in the index group (cognitive behavioral therapy [CBT] plus video feedback), and 64 out of 72 (88.9%) received nine sessions or more in the active comparison group (CBT plus progressive muscle relaxation).

Let's see what Lucy thought about therapy.

Lucy was of two minds about starting therapy. She is a single mother and has to do everything at home. She was not sure whether she would have time to do the weekly sessions. However, she discussed it with her best friend who helped her think about how she would benefit from the therapy, and the friend encouraged Lucy to give it a go. At her first session, Lucy's therapist helped her look at the pros and cons of this treatment and decide what to do. She decided that she should give it a go. (See Figure 3.1.)

Assessment of Context, Current Symptoms and Concerns

Although you may have information available concerning the parent's history and current situation, it is important to conduct your own assessment. Depending on preexisting familiarity with the parent's situation and the complexity of the issues, this component may be completed in either one or two sessions and be divided at any point.

The format should roughly be followed as structured below; however, issues may be discussed in a different order, taking into account the importance of engaging the parent and establishing a therapeutic relationship.

Pros of doing this therapy	Cons of doing this therapy
There is a good chance that I will get over my depression	It's difficult to find a time each week to do the therapy
My baby will benefit from having a mother who is not depressed	It's hard work, and I'm really tired
If I put in time now, it will help me manage my time more effectively	Not sure if it is really going to work anyway
I will learn to problem-solve	I should be able to do this myself without help
I will find out how to sleep better	I don't deserve to have help
I may be able to work out how to get back to the things I used to enjoy doing	I don't think anyone can help me

Figure 3.1

Lucy's Completed Worksheet 2: Motivational Balance.

Current Context

If you are not already aware of the parent's current context, it is important to clarify the broad details of the pregnancy and birth; age, gender, and health of their baby; physical health of the parent and current family; and social and financial circumstances before moving on to discussing the depression and its impact.

Current Concerns and Mood

The first step is to clarify the parent's current concerns, the extent of their low mood, and how these impact both the parent and their baby.

Useful questions for this part of the session include:

- *Can you tell me what is concerning you about your current mood and when it concerns you the most?*
- *Have you had any days when you've felt* very low *(use the parent's own language)?*
- *What has that been like for you?*
- *Are there ups and downs across the day? Do you notice your mood changing over the day?*
- *How has that been for you while looking after your baby?*
- *How have you found yourself reacting?*
- *What do you do to look after yourself on a day like that?*
- *What makes a difference to how you feel?*

Self-Care (Parent's Sleep, Appetite, and Energy)

This is followed by a discussion on self-care.

Tell me about what it is like for you to do the practical and important things to keep going, such as eating, sleeping, and getting exercise.

Sleep

- *What has your sleep been like over the past week?*
- *What impact does that have on you?*

- *How is your mood on waking in the morning?*
- *How is your mood when settling yourself to sleep?*
- *How do you cope with difficulties in sleeping?*
- *Do you get any help with your baby overnight?*

Appetite

- *What has your appetite been like?*
- *When do you find yourself thinking about eating?*
- *Do you notice feeling hungry? What makes you notice/remember to eat?*
- *If you're not interested in eating, how is it for you feeding your baby/family or getting a meal ready?*
- *What bothers you most about your eating/appetite?*

Energy

- *How has your energy been?*
- *How does that affect your day?*
- *What difference does it make to your day with your baby if it's a day when you feel you have more energy? Or less energy?*
- *Do you have a time in your week to exercise or get out?*
- *Is that different from before your baby arrived?*

Pregnancy, Delivery, Early Months, Other Sources of Help, Medication

Once you have clarified the parent's current symptoms, it is important to find out more about the pregnancy, the context of the birth, and the time since the birth.

Tell me about your experience of being pregnant and the delivery of your baby.

Getting pregnant

- *What was it like for you when you found out you were pregnant?*
- *How did others react around you?*

- *What was important to you about having a child?*
- *Were you healthy through your pregnancy? Was it a stressful time?*
- *Were you well supported by your partner/family/workplace?*

Labor and first few weeks

- *How did the delivery go?*
- *Was it what you had hoped for/planned for?*
- *Did you feel well cared for?*
- *What was it like first seeing/holding your baby?*
- *When were you home again? And how were those early days?*
- *What was breastfeeding like for you?*
- *How were you yourself in the early weeks? Did this change as the weeks went by?*

Support from baby's co-parent

- *How did your baby's co-parent find taking on this role?*
- *Has it been a big adjustment for you both?*

Other sources of support

You can check out whether the parent is receiving any other professional support such as from an adult mental health service, local healthcare provider, primary care physician, general practitioner, or nurse practitioner. If the parent's mental health deteriorates, it may be helpful (with the parent's permission) to contact relevant people who are supporting the parent, in order to ensure a supportive, cohesive approach across different agencies/professionals.

Use of medication

Some parents may be receiving antidepressant medication alongside the psychological treatment, so it is important to check this out ensuring that it is taken as prescribed.

Activity Over a Typical Day and Week

Having ascertained the current situation and context, you can move on to finding out more about the parent's day-to-day functioning.

Tell me about your typical day and what you usually do throughout the week.

Changes during the day

- *What is it like for you in the morning and then as the day wears on?*
- *What is the most challenging part of your day?*
- *What usually goes well for you?*
- *What is a good part of the day?*
- *Do you notice anything that lifts your mood or brightens your day?*

Time for self

- *What bothers you most about looking after your baby and managing routine housework?*
- *What did you used to enjoy spending time doing?*
- *Is there any time in the day for yourself?*
- *Do you feel you have time to look after yourself?*
- *Are there things you would like to be doing for yourself?*

Return to work

- *How long will you be on parental leave?*
- *Will you still have your job to return to?*
- *Is the work and money side of things a worry for you?*

Managing Strong Feelings – Overthinking, Overactivity, and Avoidance

You can now focus on the parent's attitude to their current difficulties and how they manage.

Now I'd like to talk about whether you think repetitively about your current difficulties or try to stay busy to avoid doing this and how this affects your mood.

Presence of rumination

- *Do you find yourself worrying about things or thinking about things over and over, to the point where it can be hard to concentrate on other activities?*
- *What are you thinking about when this happens?*
- *Are these thoughts about what's happening now in the present, or is it about things past or in the future?*
- *Some parents describe "giving themselves a hard time" or "being strict" with themselves. Do you find you are critical of yourself at all?*

Triggers for rumination and consequences

- *How does this thinking get started? Do these thoughts just pop into your mind when you don't want them to?*
- *Once you have started thinking or worrying about something, can it be hard to stop? Does the thinking go round and round?*
- *When do you realize you are dwelling on this issue again?*
- *Is there anything that helps these thoughts to stop? Do you do anything to change what you are thinking about?*
- *How does this leave you feeling? Does it affect your mood? Does it stay with you?*

Some parents have told us that they experience feelings of shame (for example, wanting to run away, hide, feeling like a failure) or guilt about their parenting (for example, feeling like you would have liked to do things differently, having a guilty conscience).

- *Have you noticed any feelings of shame or guilt?*
- *Do you criticize yourself when you feel you have made a mistake?*

Overactivity

- *Parents often talk about being busy nonstop yet getting nothing done—is it like that for you?*
- *How much does that bother you?*
- *Are there activities that you would like to be doing in your week but have found difficult to do because of feeling sad or anxious about them?*

Avoidance

- *Are there any things that you are avoiding doing due to anxiety or worry?*
- *What would you like to be doing that you are not doing?*

Coping Strategies and Strengths

At this point in the assessment, it is important to inquire about coping strategies that are already being used and what the parent perceives as their strengths. This can lead to a broader discussion of the range of possible coping strategies, including distraction, slow breathing, muscular relaxation, physical exercise, having a relaxing bath, focusing on an enjoyable activity such as a favorite TV program, expressing oneself through writing or drawing, keeping connected with friends, etc. Check out what the parent already does and how helpful these strategies are. Look at Worksheet 3: Coping Strategies together, and discuss the range of coping strategies, working out with the parent what they might be able to try. It is helpful at an early stage of this program for the parent to become familiar with strategies that work for them. There may be points during the therapy when these strategies become very helpful, particularly if they are going through periods of extreme distress or low mood or if they have suicidal thoughts.

Coping strategies that the parent finds helpful can be included in the safety plan, to be discussed toward the end of this session.

Let's think about what helps you to cope with feeling low at the moment.

Existing Coping Strategies

Here are some possible questions:

- *What does it mean for you to be coping?*
- *Did you previously see yourself as a person who can cope with anything?*
- *What kinds of things signal that you are not coping?*
- *What does that then mean for you?*
- *How do you find yourself coping with the pressures you are under at the moment?*
- *Has that changed from how you would have handled things in the past (when under pressure)?*
- *Have you found any ways you used to cope still useful to you now, or are they not working so well for you now?*
- *What do you think your strengths are?*

Substance Use

A lot of people faced with overwhelming situations might find themselves drinking more than usual or using other drugs. Some feel it helps them cope better with stress.

- *Is this a way of coping you use yourself?*
- *Has it been different since your baby arrived?*

You may need to ask further questions, if necessary, on the nature, extent, and frequency of substance use; impact on self (mood/energy/sleep/memory/suicidal ideation and intent); and impact on others, especially caring for their baby. If you have any concerns, you may need to discuss with the parent's healthcare provider.

Social Support

It is now important to inquire about the presence or absence of social support.

Tell me about the people in your life currently who provide you with support.

Different Aspects of Support

You can now ask for more detail about specific support in the following areas.

Feeling supported

- *Who do you turn to when you need emotional or practical help?*
- *Who offers you a shoulder to cry on, or who can you confide in?*
- *Who can you talk to about how you're feeling?*
- *Who is there for you in a crisis?*
- *When would you call on them? Can you get hold of them when you need to?*
- *Who can come in and help with your baby?*
- *Who can support you with housework, making a meal, helping to get to appointments?*

Avoiding help-seeking

- *Is there anything that holds you back from sharing your feelings?*
- *How is it for you to ask for help? For some people this is difficult; others find they can ask for help. What is it like for you?*

Support network

- *Do you get to see your friends/keep in touch with friends? Are they parents too?*
- *How does your family (parents, family of origin) support you?*
- *How does your partner support you?*

- *Are you part of a parent and baby group? Do you have a network of friends?*
- *Is there a local community center or other center with baby activities that you like to go to?*
- *Do you use any of the online forums like Babycenter, Postpartum Support International, Parents.com, Reddit.r/New Parents, Baking Little Babes (on Facebook), netMums, and Mumsnet?*

Crisis support

- *Who would you go to if there is a crisis or if you need help urgently?*

Risks

There are several potential risks when working with parents with postpartum depression, including risks of injury or neglect to the baby or others, risks of self-neglect or self-harm in the parent, and risk of domestic violence (the latter has been found to increase during the postpartum period). All these need to be inquired about.

The clinical management of increased risk of harm (whether it is suicidal ideation with intent, self-harm, or harm to others, including their baby) should always be prioritized over any other part of any module in the OPP. The safety of the parent and their baby is a priority. In order to provide effective care for parents with severe and/or chronic depression it is necessary to monitor and address safety issues throughout assessment and treatment.

It is important to establish who is taking clinical responsibility for the parent's care. This may be the family doctor/primary care physician or other local healthcare professional such as a pediatrician. If there is a concern about the welfare of the parent and/or baby, then it will be important to liaise with this person.

Risk issues should also be discussed on a regular basis with your clinical supervisor. There may be situations when you feel that the parent cannot be safely left on their own or with their baby/children. If this is the case, you need to be able to urgently contact a senior member of your service or your clinical supervisor to discuss the next steps, which may be speaking with the family, arranging additional support, arranging more intensive treatment, contacting crisis support, or considering alternative care for their baby/children.

Risk Assessment

Risk can be assessed using the following structure and questions:

When people feel low, it is common for there to be thoughts of wanting it all to stop or for people to think about ending their own lives. Now I'd like to ask you about whether you have had these types of thoughts.

Presence of self-harm or suicidal ideation

- *Have you had thoughts of harming yourself?*
- *When do you have those thoughts?*
- *What were you doing at that moment?*
- *Have these thoughts become plans? Have you thought about how you would do it?*
- *Do you have access to the means to do it? Would you know where to get what you need to do that?*
- *Have there been times like this in the past when you've had these thoughts and/or acted on them? What happened then?*

Protective factors

- *What has held you back from taking steps to harm yourself?*
- *What would it mean for you if your baby/partner/family had to go on without you?*
- *For some people, their faith is an important reason for not taking such a step. Is faith also important to you? Does it help to keep you from acting on these thoughts?*
- *For some, it is a strong belief in life but not necessarily in a religious sense. Does that fit better for you?*

Previous incidents of self-harm or suicidal attempts

- *Have you ever tried to hurt yourself even if you didn't mean to die?*
- *Did you need any treatment in the hospital, or did you look after yourself?*
- *What has that experience meant for you? Did it make you think about self-harm/your life differently?*
- *Does it bother you if people can see the scars/signs of your distress and know how bad it must have been?*
- *What has helped you stay safe recently?*

Having identified the presence of risk to self, it will be important to create a safety plan using the information you have obtained on risks, coping strategies, and social supports. This is described later in this chapter.

Mila has been diagnosed with depression. She has low mood most of the time and feels really lacking in energy. She can't sleep at night and has stopped eating regularly. It is really hard for her to concentrate even on her favorite TV shows. Mila is aware that she is not going out very much and is keeping to herself at home. She is determined not to let the depression affect her care of her daughter, Marta, but there are times when she just feels too exhausted to feed the baby. Mila becomes tearful in therapy and tells her therapist that she has been having thoughts of wanting to end it all but has not made any specific plans or acted on these thoughts.

Mila works out with her therapist that the main problem is feeling exhausted and not getting any enjoyment from life. Mila feels guilty about this because she feels she should be enjoying having a baby more.

Mila's main strength is that she is able to talk about her difficulties with her partner, Sophie. This makes it easier for Mila to get support.

Before the session ends it will be important to create a safety plan with Mila—this is discussed later in the chapter.

Presence of Thoughts/Urges to Harm Others

As well as risk to self, it is important to inquire about any thoughts of harming others, including their baby. It is common in the postpartum period to have intrusive thoughts of harming one's baby; these need to be distinguished from intention or desire to harm the baby or others. This issue is discussed in more detail in Chapter 15. If you have any concerns about serious risk to others, these need to be followed up in the appropriate way, for example, discussing with primary care professionals and the family so that the right help can be provided.

Formulation/Conceptualization

Having developed a thorough understanding of the parent through the assessment and taken time to build the foundation for a strong therapeutic relationship, the next step is to help the parent understand how their depression has developed. This is done through introducing a simple cyclical formulation which will be developed and individualized over the course of the therapy. The aim of this formulation/conceptualization is to help the parent develop a non-judgmental, compassionate view of how their depression developed and to illustrate how the therapy will help to treat their low mood. You may find it works best to use another term for the formulation/conceptualization such as *diagram to understand your depression*. If you do use the term *formulation* or *conceptualization*, you will need to describe what it means exactly.

Maintenance of Low Mood

Use the formulation/conceptualization worksheet (Worksheet 4: How Changes in Life Can Lead to Low Mood). Begin with the circle that is titled "life events" and explain that the experience of conception, pregnancy, and the birth of a child is a major life event for everyone, which can test existing coping styles, lead to challenging and difficult experiences, and be a reminder of previous challenging experiences.

- Move to the circle titled "mood drops," and explain that these can lead to low mood developing, particularly when lack of sleep, exhaustion, and isolation can all result from looking after a small baby.
- Move to the circle titled "less rewarding life," and explain that these changes can lead to life constantly feeling less fulfilling, with reduced sleep, low energy, and little time for friends, hobbies, or self-care. Indicating the arrows, explain that this can develop into a vicious cycle, where low mood leads to lack of motivation to do rewarding activities, which then further deepens the low mood.

Make sure the parent has time to ask any questions about the diagram, including encouraging them to challenge it if there are parts they don't feel fit with their experience. It is better to raise and resolve these concerns at the start of the therapy than to begin it with these concerns not fully explored. You can now begin to fill in the diagram with the parent, using their own individual circumstances.

Let's see what discussion Kenise and her therapist had about the negative cycles in depression.

Kenise and her therapist looked together at Worksheet 4: How Changes in Life Can Lead to Low Mood. Kenise found this useful and, in the life events circle, wrote down how the twins being born prematurely and spending time in the neonatal intensive care unit was very stressful and meant she had very little sleep even before they came home. Once Jayden and Serena were home, she was very anxious about their physical health and spent a lot of time monitoring this, which meant that she needed help from her neighbor to walk with her older daughter Maya to school and take her to her swimming lesson.

Kenise missed this time with Maya, which made her feel worse; but she felt too exhausted and anxious to do anything different. Her own physical health was poor after a difficult birth, but she felt too overwhelmed and tired to do the postpartum exercises, leaving her feeling physically weak with frequent aches. She realized she spends a lot of time in the house and is often tearful and sad, blaming herself for not doing things better. Kenise wrote feelings of sadness, exhaustion, physical weakness, aching, and tearfulness, poor sleeping and staying at home in the low mood circle. She wrote not walking her daughter to school, not taking her daughter to her swimming lessons, not seeing friends, and not exercising in the less rewarding life circle.

Figure 3.2 shows Kenise's completed worksheet.

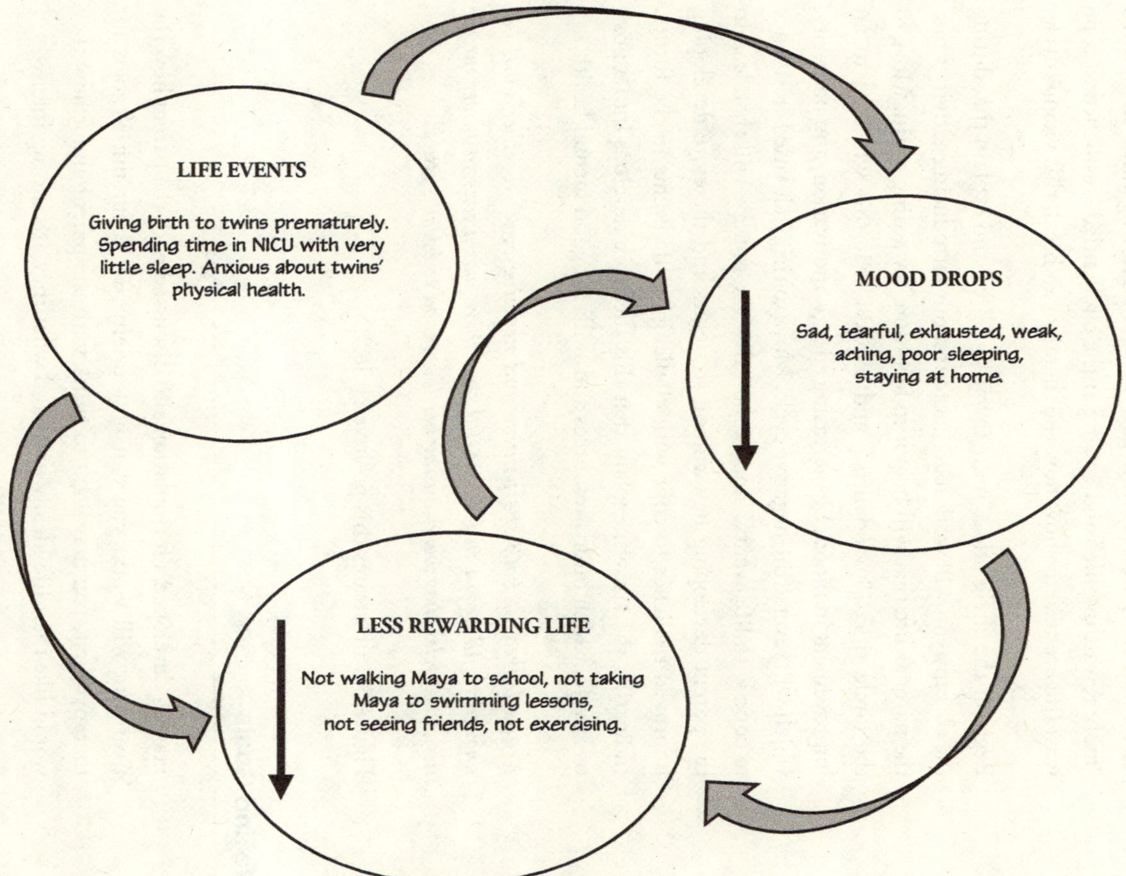

Figure 3.2

Kenise's Completed Worksheet 4: How Changes in Life Can Lead to Low Mood.

Note. NICU = neonatal intensive care unit

Developing a Positive Cycle

You can now think with the parent about how the cycle could be different, using Figure 3.3. Use this figure to show how this program (OPP) can help with the cycles of low mood. The explanation for this is reversed compared to the negative cycle, beginning at the circle titled "more rewarding life" and ending at the circle titled "resilience to cope with life events," to show how the therapy can break this vicious cycle.

Begin at the circle titled "more rewarding life," and explain that during the therapy you will work together to test out introducing activities into the parent's life that will help it to feel more rewarding again. Move to the circle titled "mood lifts," and explain that this will lead to an improvement in mood, by increasing energy, motivation, and positivity, which will reverse the negative cycle. Move to the circle titled "resilience to cope with life events," and explain that the therapy will then lead to the parent developing new coping strategies and therefore developing improved resilience to cope with challenging life events in the future. Indicating the arrows, explain that this therefore develops into a positive cycle, which builds resources and skills for good mental health.

Kenise looked at both the positive and negative cycles together with her therapist and began to feel hopeful that there was a way to interrupt the negative cycles that were causing her low mood to become stuck.

Figure 3.3 illustrates this positive cycle.

Future Life and Goals

Having developed a formulation and discussed with the parent how the treatment will work, you can now briefly ask about initial goals for therapy. First, you may want to think with the parent about how they would like their life ideally to be and what they are aiming for.

Having broadly ascertained how the parent would like their life to be, you may start to discuss the idea of developing goals that are achievable. There will be a further discussion of goals in the next session after identifying in detail the parent's values. You can refer to Worksheet 8: Setting Goals for Therapy. This is an essential step in behavioral activation/CBT.

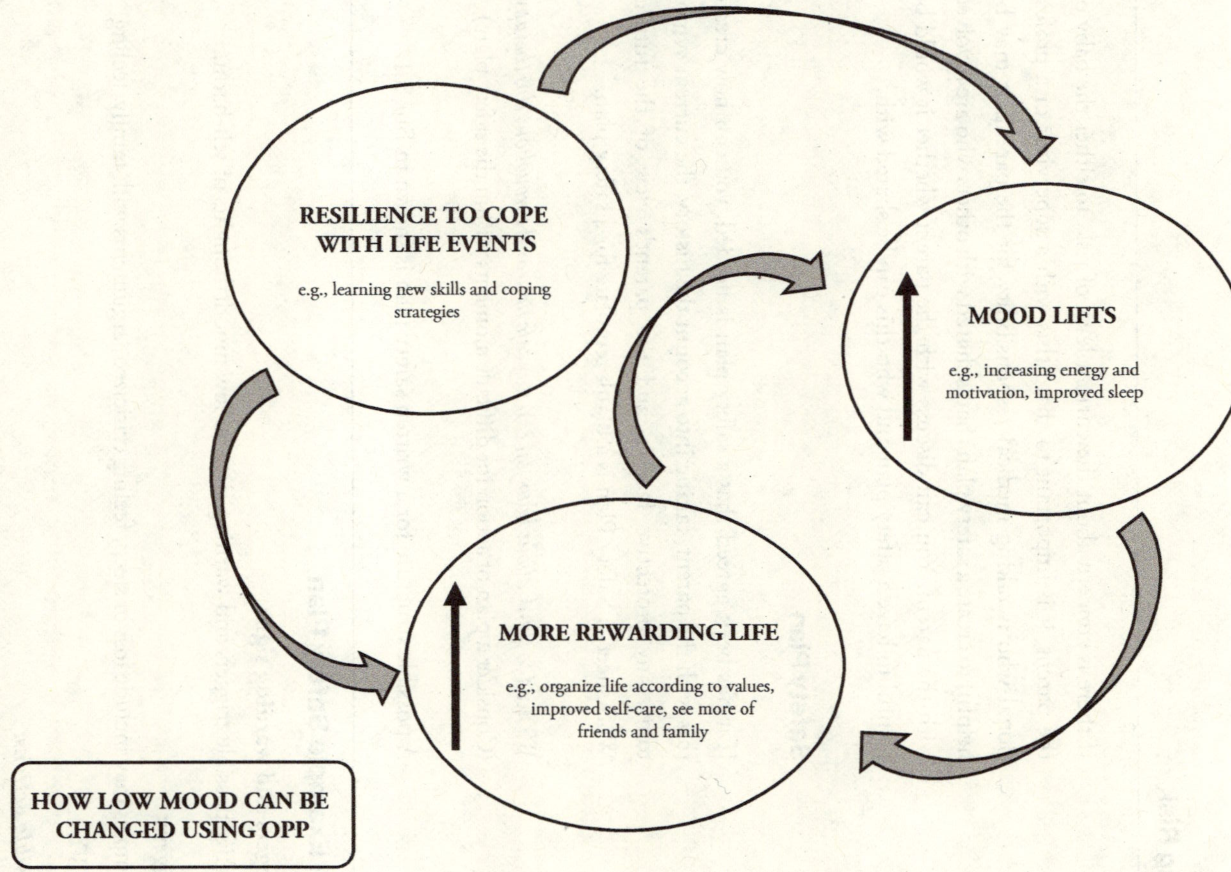

Figure 3.3
Building a Positive Cycle.

It helps measure progress and supports the parent to notice that each small change will add up over time. You can write the provisional goals into the Assessment Questionnaire and let the parent know that there will be a more detailed discussion of goals in the next session.

Managing Risk

If there is concern about the current level of risk, to either the baby or the parent, it is important to share this with a supervisor or a professional who is taking medical responsibility for the parent. It may be helpful to create a safety plan that is shared with others who are involved with the parent. You can discuss with the parent whether it would be helpful to have a safety plan and who this can be shared with.

Safety Plan

If it has been agreed that a safety plan is needed, you can now create this with the parent, taking into account the history, the current symptoms, any protective factors, and the parent's view of the future. Worksheet 5: Safety Plan is a blank template for a safety plan.

We need to think about how you can stay safe now and throughout this therapy. (Consider a plan of action for difficult moments within the safety plan.)

A possible structure for a written safety plan is shown in Box 3.1.

Box 3.1 Example Safety Plan

1. **Triggers and warning signs**
   Identify possible triggers and warning signs to low mood/thoughts of self-harm.

   Triggers:
   Examples may include loss of sleep, feeling criticized, arguments with family, feeling hungry.

   Possible actions:
   The parent should be encouraged to eat regularly and ensure they get sufficient sleep. They can also list some possible responses to negative thoughts about themselves arising from things that other people have said about them.

Warning signs:

The parent can identify the signs that might indicate there is a risk of self-harm. Examples include the parent keeping themself isolated, having images of self-harm, seeking out self-harm images, thinking through plans of how they might end their life, or stockpiling medication.

Possible actions:

Encourage the parent to distract themself from unhelpful thoughts/images by, for example, watching TV or a film or calling a friend.

2. **Coping strategies**

   The parent can be encouraged to write down some coping strategies in response to different situations. You can use ideas that have come up in the earlier discussion about coping strategies and refer to examples on Worksheet 3: Coping Strategies.

3. **Helpful social settings**

   Identify social settings that may distract from thoughts of self-harm or suicidal ideation, such as going out for a walk, going shopping, or sitting in a coffee shop with the baby.

   Identify who to talk to if the parent needs help, such as their partner, friends, parents, or wider family.

4. **Professional support**

   Make a list of agencies that can be contacted if the parent is in crisis (see section "Emergency contacts." Examples include Suicide and Crisis Lifeline (call 988 in the United States), family doctor or primary care physician (write down the phone numbers), or Samaritans (call 116 123 in the United Kingdom).

5. **Keeping the environment safe**

   Limit access to objects that the parent could use to act on suicidal ideation or thoughts of self-harm, such as sharps or medication.

   Encourage the parent to go somewhere with the baby where they aren't on their own.

Getting Professional Help

Calling the family doctor/primary care physician

Make sure the parent knows to call their family doctor or primary care physician directly if they have an urgent concern as clinical responsibility rests with their doctor. They may find it easier initially to seek help from others who know them well, as identified below.

Emergency contacts

In planning with the parent how to remain safe if they were to become actively suicidal or pose an active risk of serious self-harm or harm to another person (child or adult), it is helpful to identify who they would contact to seek help in that situation, someone who could ensure the parent's and others' safety. Often, this will be a member of their family (partner, parent, or sibling) or a health professional (family doctor, nurse practitioner, or primary care physician). It is important to identify with the parent who they would contact first and, if that person was unavailable, who they would turn to next (and so on). It is important to be clear with the parent that, if they felt uncomfortable with contacting their doctor or emergency services directly, someone else may have to do that on their behalf if there were serious risks to themselves or others. Figure 3.4 shows an example of a safety plan created with Mila.

Not every parent will need a safety plan; but you should be alert to risk issues throughout treatment, and you may need to create a safety plan later on in the treatment.

Emergencies During a Session

If you become concerned during a session that the parent is actively at risk of serious self-harm or suicide, or there is an active risk of harm to a child, it is important to discuss this without delay with a senior healthcare professional such as the family doctor/primary care physician or psychiatrist, in order to make an immediate plan of action to ensure the safety of the mother and her child(ren). This may involve ensuring that the parent puts into action their safety plan (with close monitoring) and contacts people who can support them, as well as

Think about	Actions
Triggers Skipping breakfast Going to bed too late	Make sure I have my breakfast before I feed Marta Give myself a deadline for going to bed
Warning signs Keeping to myself and not contacting friends	Make sure I contact someone each day
Helpful coping strategies Talking to my partner Talking to a friend Going out for a walk with my baby	Try one strategy, and if it doesn't work, try another
Helpful places to be if I don't feel well In a coffee shop Going for a walk around town	Make sure I get out of the house
Who can I talk to if I need help? My partner My mother	Lift the phone and speak to someone
Who can I contact in a crisis?	My doctor (phone number is . . .) My mom Crisis Lifeline (phone number is . . .)
How can I keep my environment safe?	Make sure I am with other people if possible

Figure 3.4
Mila's Completed Worksheet 5: Safety Plan.

contacting relevant support services yourself. However, in cases of extreme immediate risk, there may be a need to call emergency services to initiate a psychiatric admission or urgently involve the police and social services to consider how best to keep the parent and child(ren) safe.

Troubleshooting

Assessment and management of risk are clearly crucial in the first session, but you will need to be aware that this focus on risk may be difficult or triggering for the parent. It is important, therefore, to make sure that the emphasis at the end of this first long session is on practical steps and stressing the high likelihood of remission of the depression over the course of this program.

Home Practice

Toward the end of this session, you can discuss home practice to be done over the following week.

The main activity is for the parent to monitor their mood and situation on a regular basis so that you and they will begin to understand more about the depression. Worksheet 6: Mood Monitoring Record can be used for this. It is helpful to work through an example in session (thinking back on a couple of days) so that the parent understands exactly how to fill in the record during the week.

The parent will need multiple copies of Worksheet 6: Mood Monitoring Record so that they can complete a new worksheet as part of their home practice on different occasions. Feel free to photocopy the worksheet or direct the parent to the book website to print out their own.

Self-monitoring is most useful when it is done in real time rather than in retrospect. The record includes a rating of mood as this can be helpful in encouraging the parent to be specific about how they feel and helps them notice change. However, we acknowledge that some parents may find it difficult to rate their mood; encourage them not to obsess about the ratings and to be instinctive and approximate.

Figure 3.5 shows an example of part of a completed Mood Monitoring Record that Isabella completed in the first week.

You can also suggest to the parent that they reflect on their goals during the week and fill in Worksheet 8: Setting Goals for Therapy, to bring to the next session for further discussion. The parent may want to discuss this worksheet with their partner or with a friend. There will be a more detailed discussion of goals in the next session.

Summary of the Session and Feedback

The first session has been a long one, and a lot of material has been covered. It is important to summarize collaboratively with the parent what has been discussed in the session, what they feel their main concerns are, what they feel their strengths are, and what they want to change. It is helpful to think together about what the parent will take away from the session today. They may have found it difficult going through depressive symptoms, risk factors, and suicide risk, so it is important to focus on positive first steps and reiterate that if the parent engages with treatment, there is a high likelihood of remission of the depression. It is also important to make it clear that just because a person is feeling low and struggling doesn't mean they are not a good parent.

You can ask for feedback now on how the session has been, what has been helpful or unhelpful, and what might need to be different next time.

Key Points

- Deciding to do therapy is an important step.
- It's easy to get stuck in a vicious cycle of low mood after giving birth.
- Creating a safety plan can help to keep the parent safe and well.
- Setting goals helps focus on change.

Mood Monitoring Record—Isabella			
Completely overwhelmed 1 — 2	Low much of the time Frequent symptoms — 3 — 4	Low sometimes. Generally coping. Occasional symptoms — 5 — 6 — 7	Content much of the time Managing most challenges — 8 — 9 Enjoying life to the full — 10
Day	**Time**	**Rating**	**Note anything that has happened to change your mood**
Monday	AM	3	Didn't sleep well as Margarita teething and needing lots of cuddles.
	PM	6	Had a long conversation on the phone with my mom. She wants to help out and is going to visit soon.
	EVE	4	So tired. Argument with husband. Went to bed.
Tuesday	AM	3	Didn't sleep well, as worrying about all the things I have to do.
	PM	3	Felt too tired to make a proper lunch for myself.
	EVE	3	Margarita was crying a lot, couldn't get anything done.
Wednesday	AM	3	Sleep still not good.
	PM	6	A friend called and suggested we go out with our babies for a walk. It felt good to get out of the house.
	EVE	8	I was hungry after the walk and fixed a meal for myself and Jack. We had a relaxed evening as Margarita went to sleep more quickly.
Thursday	AM	7	Slept a bit better last night and had more energy.
	PM	4	Margarita was crying a lot again, and I couldn't settle her. I hate the sound of her crying. Stayed in all afternoon. I felt I must be a terrible mother.
	EVE	6	Jack made the meal so I could have a break once Margarita finally settled and went to sleep. I read my book and began to feel calmer.

Figure 3.5

Isabella's Partially Completed Worksheet 6: Mood Monitoring Record.

CHAPTER 4

Session 2: Values and Goal Setting

Aim of This Session

This session is the last part of the first module, which focuses on the foundations of therapy, including a comprehensive assessment, sharing a formulation with the parent of how low mood develops and how therapy can help, and finally looking at what is important to the parent and their values and using all of this information to set goals for your work together. Alongside discussing these foundations with the parent, the home practice on Worksheet 6: Mood Monitoring Record will provide you with additional information to tailor the therapy to what is happening for the parent in their daily life.

Outline

- Set agenda 82
- Review of mood and how things are going 83
- Review home practice 83
- Values 83
- Values as a parent 84
- Unhelpful beliefs about parenting 87
- Values as a family 89
- Values as an individual 90
- Setting therapy goals and weekly goals 93
- Troubleshooting 94
- Home practice 95
- Summary of session and feedback 97
- Key points 97

Postpartum Depression. Anne Stewart et al., Oxford University Press. © Oxford University Press (2026).
DOI: 10.1093/med-psych/9780197759707.003.0004

When to Conduct This Session

This session will come after the assessment session. It completes Module 1 in preparing the parent for the subsequent therapy sessions. It deepens the case conceptualization/formulation and understanding of low mood you have developed with the parent in the assessment session and reinforces the importance of having clear therapeutic goals.

Materials Needed

- Assessment Questionnaire (completed in the last session)
- Worksheet 7: Working Out Your Values
- Worksheet 8: Setting Goals for Therapy
- Worksheet 9: Weekly Goal Planner
- Worksheet 10: Weekly Goal Record

Worksheets appear in Appendix A at the end of this therapist guide and in Appendix A at the end of the parent workbook. Worksheets can also be accessed by searching for this book's title on the Oxford Academic platform, at academic.oup.com. Note that when more than one copy of a worksheet is required, you may photocopy the worksheets for the parent, ask the parent to make their own photocopies, or direct the parent to the book website to print their own.

Set Agenda

Setting the agenda for the session helps focus both you and the parent on how to best use your time together. From the session outline, explain to the parent what you would like to cover in the session. This will likely include the standard items as well as the specific topic for this session. Encourage the parent to add their own topics to the agenda. This collaborative stance helps promote a proactive and engaged approach to therapy. Discuss any practicalities for the parent or the baby that may impact on the session and agree how to manage these.

Review of Mood and How Things Are Going

Review how the parent's mood has been since the last session. Discuss what symptoms have been present and whether they have increased or decreased. You can also check out whether there have been any specific challenges or positives that have happened during the week.

Review Home Practice

Review the home practice task that was set with the parent in your last session together. If they have filled out the Mood Monitoring Record worksheet, look for patterns across the week of where the parent's mood was lowest or highest. Think with the parent about the triggers for their mood changing. If they haven't managed to complete the record, you can look together at how their mood has changed during the week.

Discuss what went well with the home practice and what the challenges were. Take a curious perspective on experiences, reinforcing that all learning is helpful, and encourage the parent to review the practice and further develop their understanding of what contributes to their low mood.

Another aspect to home practice was thinking more about goals for therapy. This will be covered as a separate item later in the session.

Values

This session will focus on helping the parent to think about what is important to them in their life: as a parent, in their family, and in their wider world. It is a way to individualize the therapy by really understanding what is important to the parent to set goals that will help them re-engage with a meaningful life, lift their mood, and help them to be more resilient to stress and challenges.

Most people become parents with an idea of what they would want their new family to be like. Parents have memories of their own childhoods, and these help them to know what they want to keep the same and what they would like to be different for their own children. As well as their own views and feelings about the way they were brought up, parents also have to manage other people's expectations of what having a new baby will be like, particularly from partners, their own parents, and other people who are important to them. We parent our children in a social world, full of baby groups, new parent friends, parenting books and courses, and lots of internet advice. As a parent of a new baby, it can be easy to lose sight of wider goals for life, including what is important in relationships, work, or their purpose in life.

Values as a Parent

Have a look together at Worksheet 7: Working Out Your Values. Begin with "Values as a parent." Explain to the parent that exploring their values—what is important to them—is helpful both in spotting what may have changed to make life feel less rewarding and in identifying what needs to be added in to make life feel worth living. Explain that together you can think about how the parent expected or would like life to be now and what differences there are from how it actually is.

Begin the discussion by asking the parent to talk about how they expected or would like life to be now and what differences there are from how it actually is. Ask them for three words that describe what is important to them about parenting their baby. Helpful prompts can be to ask them to think of any images that they had while trying for a baby or when pregnant of what life would be like now. Discuss whether there are key experiences from their own childhoods that are important to them, either positively or negatively, that influence how they feel they should parent. Ask the parent to think back to a time in the last week where they felt they were really getting it right or wrong as a parent, and explore exactly what they were doing. Think with them about what it was they were doing that told them this was important. Using the Mood Monitoring Record with this exercise can be really helpful in identifying these moments.

Let's see how Isabella got on exploring her values as a parent.

Isabella found it hard at first to think of three words to describe what kind of parent she wanted to be. When she talked to her therapist about what she had thought her life would be like with a baby it became easier to think about her values. She said she thought she would be in a good routine with her baby by now. They would play and relax together when the baby was awake, and after feeds when Margarita was sleeping, she would get some housework done or do some cooking for her and her partner. Talking about this, she and her therapist identified that she valued having a sense of personal satisfaction and competence about getting tasks done and her life being in order, as well as feeling loved and connected.

Once you have identified three values, begin to explore what the parent would be doing and how they would be behaving with these values present in their life. This is an important step as it starts to identify what the parent can do differently to feel that they are living in a way that they value. Helpful prompts for this include looking at one of the values they have named and asking: If they were parenting with this value, how would they know, or how would others know? Ask if there are any times in the day or week where they find themselves parenting with that value and what they are doing then. Explore whether there are behaviors they would like to do more of, or less of, to bring this value into their everyday life.

Useful questions for this part of the session include:

- *Can you find three words that would describe the way you want to be as a parent?*
- *What did you think becoming a parent would be like for you?*
- *How do you feel about yourself now that you are a parent?*
- *What sort of parent would you like to become?*
- *If you were a [insert value here] parent, what would you be doing?*
- *When do you do that now in your daily life? What helps you to do that?*
- *When would you like to do that in your daily life?*

Figure 4.1 shows Isabella's partially completed Worksheet 7: Working Out Your Values, with a focus on her values as a parent.

Working out your values	Three words to describe these values	What does this look like? What would you be doing? When do you do that now in your daily life? What helps you to do that?
Values as a parent	Feeling competent	Getting jobs done in the day, settling Margarita for her nap
	Feeling connected (love)	Having time to play with Margarita, sitting down to have dinner with Jack,
	Things in order	The house being tidy, dinner being on, clothes being wash ed
Values as a family		
Values as an individual		

Figure 4.1

Isabella's Partially Completed Worksheet 7: Working Out Your Values.

Unhelpful Beliefs About Parenting

You will find that thinking with the parent about what is important to them about their parenting is a useful opportunity to discuss with them how much they feel they are influenced by what people around them, and wider society, are telling them about how they "should" be parenting. For some parents, these influences can feel very invasive, and they may be aware of how much they compare themselves to others or feel criticized by their family. Other parents may be unaware of these influences and surprised by realizing that the negative way they are thinking is being shaped by those around them. Other parents may be less affected by these influences and aware of, but not struggling with, how the beliefs of those around them may conflict with their own.

Box 4.1 outlines some parenting beliefs that can negatively influence the way parents feel about how they parent. In discussing these with the parent, there may be others they are aware of that are particularly problematic for them.

Box 4.1 Unhelpful Beliefs About Parenting

Unhelpful Belief	Alternatives to Encourage
Super-parent	
The job as a parent is to do everything and do it all perfectly. Parents should have happy children, successful jobs, a clean house, homemade food, individual parent–child play time, play dates, baby groups . . . the list goes on. Often when parents see these messages in society, they can also be accompanied by a product that will help them "achieve it all." Emphasizing perfection can be a common way of helping parents feel that they are "good parents." They may particularly signal this to other parents when they feel worried that someone may "find out" that they also can find parenting tiring, frustrating, and boring at times.	Developing a more compassionate view of themselves that is less critical and less "achievement-driven" is key. Some parents can struggle with the switch from a goal-driven career to growing a human and building a relationship, which has less obvious objectives and no annual reviews. Encourage the parent to try and think of three things in the day that have fitted with their values rather than setting a goal of perfection in everything.

The Right Way

It can be easy as a parent to get pulled into believing there is one right way to parent our children. Believing there is one right answer to sleep difficulties, weaning, toddler tantrums, etc. can be a way of trying to cope with the worries and uncertainty that being a parent brings. Lots of conversations in baby groups and with other parents can be focused on how these common problems are being managed and the success or disasters of each method.	It is important to remember that all babies are different, and parents have different values about what is important to them about how they raise their children. Encourage the parent that when they are listening to advice and discussions it can be helpful to remember that no one way works for every family, and it is more important to parent in a way that fits with their values and their and their baby's needs at this stage in their lives.

No Crying

Parents can be surrounded by messages that their baby crying is a bad and even harmful thing to allow. Terms such as "no-cry", "gentle", and "attachment" parenting may be interpreted by parents to mean that bringing up a child should be peaceful and calm at all times.	It is important to soothe and nurture babies and help them manage their feelings. However, babies cry for important reasons; in their first 12 months of life, it's their primary way of communicating. It would be worrying if a baby didn't cry! It's also important to remember that parenting can be intensely stressful and that it is unachievable to always feel calm and peaceful.

Parents Shouldn't Get Angry!

Sometimes parents may have lots of difficult feelings such as anger, frustration, and panic. This doesn't mean they are bad parents. Parenting is challenging, and most parents will have difficult emotions. Having strategies to manage these feelings as a parent is key, but allowing themselves to have these feelings is also important.	Encourage the parent to build into their life a way of having time out to manage these difficult feelings. Sometimes this can be learning how to focus on breathing slowly and attending to the breath, taking time to have a cup of tea and a rest during naptime rather than tidying up, or placing the baby safely in their crib and walking away to count to 10 and take some deep breaths. Other times this can involve scheduled "time outs" such as going for a walk, doing the food shopping alone, or making time to see a trusted family member or friend.

You can discuss these beliefs with the parent and identify if any are playing a part in setting unrealistic expectations of themselves or being overly critical. Encourage them to consider whether holding these beliefs is helpful or unhelpful. Return to the values they have identified and consider again whether these are values they hold or whether these have been unhelpfully influenced by parenting beliefs.

Let's see whether looking at unhelpful parenting beliefs was helpful to Isabella.

Isabella found it useful to think about the parenting beliefs that were influencing her. She really related to the belief around "The Right Way". She was tearful when talking to her therapist about how she felt the other mothers in the parent and baby group often seemed to be following different sleep routines with their babies than she and her daughter were. Isabella said these conversations were really difficult for her and reminded her as well about her own mother's strong sleep advice. Isabella mentioned feeling puzzled when she spoke to another mom and they had different ideas about what a good sleep routine was. She and her therapist discussed how having different routines for different parents was very normal and it was better for everyone to have strategies that suited them and their values. They discussed how Isabella's routine worked for her and Margarita and that it was an ongoing process working out how best to help her baby sleep. Isabella talked about how having a baby felt for her as if there was a lot of information overload and this had been hard. Isabella and her therapist talked about how this time was about Isabella and Margarita getting to know each other and figuring out what worked for them both. Each parent and baby go through a similar process. Isabella felt reassured by the discussion and more confident as a parent.

Values as a Family

In this next section you will expand the discussion to think about how the parent's close relationships influence their values as a parent. In particular, it is important to think about the baby's other parent(s)/caretakers (whether or not the baby's parents are still in a relationship and whether or not the caretaker[s] is the baby's other parent, the baby's grandparents [whether they are regularly in the baby's life or not], or other close family [biological or not] member). These are the key people who may feel they have an opinion on what is important about how the baby is brought up.

Use Worksheet 7: Working Out Your Values, and the values already identified, to think with the parent about whether these values are the same as or different from those held by close family members. Discuss whether there are particular relationships where these values are important or relationships where these values feel downplayed or ignored. Consider whether there have been issues with ensuring these values are present in parenting and what this has been like for the parent.

Useful questions for this part of the session include:

- *Do you think you have much the same values as your partner/baby's other parent?*
- *Do you think you have much the same values as your family?*
- *How have these shared or different values shaped your family life?*
- *How do you resolve any differences between your values and those of your partner?*
- *How do you resolve any differences between your values and those of your family?*

Values as an Individual

In this last section of the values discussion, you will focus on the parent's wider values for themselves as an individual, before and after having their baby. This helps identify whether there are key values for the parent that have been significantly affected by the arrival of their baby and how important it is to focus on these as a contributor to their low mood.

You can use Worksheet 7 to consider what is important to the parent about having relationships with family and friends, the role the parent usually plays in these relationships, and whether this has changed. Explore what the parent was doing previously with their life, in education or in work, and what was important for them about this occupation. Discuss with them how they see their future and what values are important to retain from the life they had before their baby arrived.

Consider how difficult they may have found it since their baby arrived to keep these values going.

Useful questions for this part of the session include:

- *How important are family and friends for you, and have these relationships changed now that you have a baby?*
- *What's important to you about these relationships?*
- *What did you value about your work/career/studies before your baby was born (e.g., contributing, learning, achieving, building relationships, etc.)?*
- *Which of these values are present in your role as a parent? Has this changed?*
- *What do you want for yourself now?*
- *Are there other important interests you'd like to keep going or pick up again?*

Let's see how Lucy found exploring her values as a parent and those of her wider family.

Lucy found identifying her values as a parent and those of her wider family quite difficult. She described wanting her baby to feel loved, be healthy, and grow up with lots of time with family and felt her family would want the same. She found this discussion frustrating, and it didn't give the therapist much insight into how becoming a mother had led to low mood. However, when they began discussing Lucy's wider values for herself as an individual, her engagement in the conversation deepened and she became initially enthusiastic while describing what her plans had been prior to getting pregnant, before becoming very tearful at how these plans had changed. Her values for her wider life were to work hard, which she described as becoming a chef and learning different styles of cooking; to be active and fit; and to feel safe, which for her meant renting her own house. It was clear from this conversation that Lucy felt having a baby conflicted with all these values and that her low mood had developed as she felt restless and apathetic about her life. Her therapist reminded her that having resentful feelings about how having a baby changes our lives is very normal, and they began thinking about setting Lucy's goals for therapy.

Figure 4.2 shows Lucy's partially completed Worksheet 7: Working Out Your Values, focusing on her values as an individual.

Working out your values	Three words to describe these values	What does this look like? What would you be doing? When do you do that now in your daily life? What helps you to do that?
Values as a parent		
Values as a family		
Values as an individual	Hard work	Training in catering to become a chef, having a part-time job, earning my own money
	Being active and fit	Having time in my week for walks, swimming, feeling energized
	Feeling safe	Having my own place to rent, having somewhere to raise Jackson and for him to feel safe

Figure 4.2

Lucy's Partially Completed Worksheet 7: Working Out Your Values.

Setting Therapy Goals and Weekly Goals

Now that you have worked through the values exercise with the parent, the next step is to demonstrate how you can take one of these values and make it into a clear goal for behavior change. Goal setting is an important step in therapy in the Oxford Postnatal Programme and an essential part of cognitive behavioral therapy and helps you and the parent have a clear sense of what you are aiming for when you are working together. It helps measure progress and supports the parent to notice that each small change will add up over time. Parents with low mood can find it hard to imagine that their life will become rewarding and enjoyable again, and change can feel overwhelming. Setting a clear achievable goal at the end of each session is part of overcoming this sense of apathy.

You can begin this discussion by building on the ideas for goals that the parent gave you in the assessment session when you asked what they would like to work on in your sessions together. Some ideas may have already become clearer through exploring how their low mood developed or through discussing their values. Ask the parent to imagine that it is the end of therapy and their low mood has lifted: What would they be doing differently, and how would they or others know that the therapy sessions had been effective? Discuss what activities they might be enjoying or what they would be looking forward to if their low mood had gone.

To set useful goals, we can use the SMART acronym to help us (Box 4.2).

Box 4.2 The SMART Acronym

Specific—Define exactly what changes the parent will see in their behavior to reach this goal.

Measurable—Think about how you and the parent will know that the goal has been achieved.

Achievable—Make sure the goal is a small step toward wider change.

Relevant—Think about how this goal fits with the parent's values.

Time-based—Identify when the parent will meet this goal, on a daily or weekly basis.

Write the parent's goals on Worksheet 8: Setting Goals for Therapy. Setting out these goals clearly can be a useful starting point to think of smaller goals for each week of therapy. Once you have the goals for therapy worked out, think of the first small step toward this goal, and write this down as the weekly goal.

Let's see how Lucy found setting goals for therapy using Worksheet 8.

Working through Lucy's values led into setting Lucy's goals for therapy. From the completed Mood Monitoring Record, she and her therapist picked up that when Lucy took the baby out for a walk, or when she was able to get out walking by herself (when Lucy's mother looked after baby Jackson), Lucy's mood lifted. A first goal was therefore to work on her value of being active and fit, through going for daily walks, either outdoors, if weather permitted, or at a local community center with a walking track if the weather was bad. Lucy said she would also like to find a community center with a swimming pool and go swimming on a regular basis. A second goal was to work toward a part-time job in a local cafe or restaurant, once Jackson was taking a bottle, or to get re-enrolled in her training program in catering, which fit with her values of hard work and feeling safe. Lucy felt very despondent about reaching this goal; but it was important to write it down, and the therapist explained that each week they would work on small steps to bring this goal closer.

Figure 4.3 shows how Lucy and her therapist completed the goal-setting worksheet.

Troubleshooting

How easily the parent can access their values will depend on how much detail can be discussed in all three areas of the values. If the parent is finding it hard to access their values, it can be helpful to discuss in detail all three areas of values, getting concrete examples from the parent.

Goals for therapy	My goal is…	What does this goal look like? Remember, think SMART (specific, measurable, achievable, relevant, time-based)
Therapy goal 1	Get active and fit again	Go for a daily walk, outside if the weather is good or go to the walking track at the community center if the weather is poor. Find somewhere with a swimming pool, and go swimming once a week.
Therapy goal 2	Feel like I have opportunities for work or study	Get a part-time job in a cafe or restaurant or get re-enrolled in the training program in catering. Will need to help Jackson feel settled with a bottle and my mom looking after him and start looking for openings for a part-time job and scholarships to help pay for catering school, maybe get advice on all of this.

Figure 4.3

Lucy's Completed Worksheet 8: Setting Goals for Therapy.

Home Practice

Toward the end of this session, you can discuss home practice to be done over the following week.

You can ask the parent to complete another copy of Worksheet 6: Mood Monitoring Record, for the coming week. Or if the parent has kept the record over the past week, and there has been a simple trigger identified for mood dips, you could use Worksheet 9: Weekly Goal Planner to set a simple goal for the week to change behavior (see Figures 5.2 and 5.3 in both this therapist guide and the parent workbook; these are examples of completed Weekly Goal Planners in Chapter 5) and Worksheet 10: Weekly Goal Record to keep track of it over the week. The parent can also be encouraged to continue to think about their values and goals and perhaps discuss these with someone important to them such as their partner, parent, or close friend. Note that Worksheets 6, 9, and 10 will be used more than once, so feel free to photocopy the worksheets or direct the parent to the book website to print out their own.

Let's see how Lucy and her therapist used Worksheet 9: Weekly Goal Planner to set a weekly goal and Worksheet 10: Weekly Goal Record to keep track of it.

Lucy and her therapist used the Weekly Goal Planner to work out what small change Lucy was going to try out this week to work toward her therapy goal of being active and fit and going for daily walks or swims. Together they agreed that starting with a small walk would increase the likelihood of it being achievable on the days where Lucy was struggling with getting out of the house. They thought about where would be best to go for this walk. Lucy said there was a park just 5 minutes away by car, but on days where she felt low, she worried about meeting someone she knew and having to talk to them. Her therapist wondered whether there were other local places Lucy could go that were less busy, and Lucy remembered a walk that she enjoyed through a nearby neighborhood. Her goal for the week was therefore to go for a 10-minute walk on 4 out of the next 7 days through the neighborhood. Her therapist encouraged her to think through and write down what she would need to carry it out (coat and shoes for her and her baby by the back door), when she would carry it out (after lunch), what might get in the way of carrying it out (feeling low and having no energy), and how she could overcome these obstacles (remind herself it was just for 10 minutes, take a photo of something beautiful on the walk, and make herself a cup of tea or a refreshing drink when she got back). Lucy used the Weekly Goal Record to keep track of how this went.

Summary of the Session and Feedback

At this point you can check out what the parent has learned from the session and what they are going to do differently. It is also important to understand what they have found helpful in the session or unhelpful so that you can make modifications next time.

Key Points

- Understanding the parent's values—what is important to them—is a key step in helping you both understand what to change in their life to help lift their mood.
- Setting regular weekly goals with the parent, which are small enough to be achievable, will help them feel more in control of the things that are impacting their mood.
- Making a small change in activity can start to lift mood.

MODULE 2

Activating

Doing Things That Make You Feel Better

Module 2 covers the importance of doing things differently in order to feel better. There are four sessions that cover taking care of yourself (Chapter 5/Session 3), routines and social support (Chapter 6/Session 4), nourishing and depleting activities (Chapter 7/Session 5), and problem solving (Chapter 8/Session 6). It may not be necessary to cover all these topics; alternatively, some topics may require more than one session. The individualized assessment described in Module 1 will identify the key aspects that the parent may need to work on. It is also not essential to undertake these sessions in exactly the order described. For example, problem solving may be a key issue for a particular parent, and it may work best to cover this first so that the parent has the tools needed to manage other issues.

A helpful way to combat depression is to focus on setting small goals. Each session will end with a goal to practice over the following week. Each goal will be small because when making changes it is important to start with things that are manageable. It's easier to increase the goal than it is to fail it and be discouraged from changing at all. It will also be important to think through what obstacles might get in the way of achieving the goal so that there is already a plan to overcome these.

It is important to discuss with the parent at the start of the session what this module will entail and how you are going to work with them on it.

CHAPTER 5 Session 3: Looking After Yourself

Aim of This Session

The aim of Session 3 is firstly to introduce the parent to this overall module, which is about doing things to help improve mood. Session 3 is about helping the parent build in regular self-care and to be aware of how this can affect mood. You will explore either sleeping, eating, or physical activity, looking at the links in each of these areas between what we do and how this can affect our mood. For home practice you can ask the parent to practice setting a small goal in one of these areas to begin the process of change.

Outline

- Set agenda 102
- Review of mood and how things are going 102
- Review home practice 103
- General aspects of self-care 105
- Identifying what raises and lowers mood 106
- The importance of sleep *or* 106
- The importance of regular eating *or* 110
- How physical activity can help with low mood 113
- Troubleshooting 116
- Home practice 117
- Summary of the session and feedback 117
- Key points 117

Postpartum Depression. Anne Stewart et al., Oxford University Press. © Oxford University Press (2026).
DOI: 10.1093/med-psych/9780197759707.003.0005

When to Conduct This Session

This session comes first in the Activating Module as it focuses on the key physiological areas that are affected in postpartum depression: sleeping, eating, and physical activity. This session is usually completed after the Values and Goal Setting session; however, it can be useful to return to this self-care session at any point in treatment and can be extended to three sessions, each focusing on a different area.

Materials Needed

- Worksheet 6: Mood Monitoring Record
- Worksheet 9: Weekly Goal Planner
- Worksheet 10: Weekly Goal Record

Worksheets appear in Appendix A at the end of this therapist guide and in Appendix A at the end of the parent workbook. Worksheets can also be accessed by searching for this book's title on the Oxford Academic platform, at academic.oup.com. Note that when more than one copy of a worksheet is required, you may photocopy the worksheets for the parent, ask the parent to make their own photocopies, or direct the parent to the book website to print their own.

Set Agenda

Start by explaining what this overall module is about, and then go through with the parent the overview of the session; this will include the standard items as well as the specific topic for this session. Make a note of anything else that the parent would like to discuss in this session and work out an agenda together. Discuss any practicalities for the parent or their baby that may impact on the session, and agree how to manage these.

Review of Mood and How Things Are Going

Review how the parent's mood has been since the last session. Discuss what symptoms have been present and whether they have increased or decreased. Find out if there have been any significant events or challenges since the last session and how the parent coped.

Review Home Practice

Review the home practice task that was set with the parent in your last session together. If you are following this therapist guide and the workbook in chapter order, this task may have focused on self-monitoring of mood. You can look through Worksheet 6: Mood Monitoring Record together and draw out any patterns that have emerged. Figure 5.1 shows an example of Kenise's Mood Monitoring Record.

As you can see, Kenise has noticed that on days when she has very little structure and doesn't get out of the house, her mood drops. The lack of structure also links to not getting enough sleep and coping with the demands of Jayden and Serena. Kenise struggled even completing the Self-Monitoring Record during this week. However, she found that it worked best for her to do self-monitoring after lunch and before going to sleep. Doing the self-monitoring around the same time each day made it more likely that she would do it.

If the parent hasn't managed to do the self-monitoring, work out with them what the barriers might have been and brainstorm how to make it easier. Does it work best to complete the Mood Monitoring Record in their workbook, on a separate piece of paper, or on their phone or tablet/laptop? If necessary, feel free to photocopy the worksheet or direct the parent to the book website to print out their own copy so that they can carry these with them. You can remind the parent that it is easier to remember what they have done if they record it immediately after doing it. However, if they haven't managed to do it at all, you can discuss together what they remembered from the week and fill out the worksheet retrospectively together. This is not as useful as self-monitoring in real time, but it gives an indication to the parent of how important self-monitoring is and will provide some information on how the week has gone and what links there may be between mood and behavior.

Day	Time	Rating	Note anything that has happened to change your mood
Monday	AM	3	Didn't sleep much as Jayden and Serena require so much feeding.
	PM	3	Felt exhausted and didn't feel like doing anything. Missed lunch.
	EVE	6	Managed to watch a film with Demar once the twins went to sleep.
Tuesday	AM	3	Couldn't get back to sleep after feeding the babies, very tired.
	PM	5	A friend rang to ask how I was doing, which made me feel a bit better.
	EVE	4	Didn't do much in the afternoon.
Wednesday	AM	3	Sleeping still not great.
	PM	6	Decided to call my friend and suggested we meet up.
	EVE	7	My husband helped out with the meal, and we had a nice chat.
Thursday	AM	6	Slept much better and had more energy.
	PM	8	Took Jayden and Serena out for a walk in the local park.
	EVE	8	Cooked a nice meal while the twins were sleeping.
Friday	AM	7	Twins didn't feed as much in the night.
	PM	4	Twins very demanding, and I couldn't do anything else.
	EVE	5	Felt very tired.
Saturday	AM	3	Another bad night.
	PM	4	Didn't feel like going out.
	EVE	3	Went to bed early but couldn't sleep.
Sunday	AM	3	Tossed and turned all night thinking what a bad mother I am.
	PM	6	Demar persuaded me to go out for a drive with him and have lunch out.
	EVE	7	Felt better after having gotten out of the house.

Figure 5.1

Kenise's Completed Worksheet 6: Mood Monitoring Record.

As well as self-monitoring, you may have agreed to a simple goal with the parent, so you can check out how this went. Were there any challenges or difficulties in carrying out the goal, or have there been any positive outcomes? Was there anything the parent learned from carrying out the goal or not being able to carry it out?

Lucy's goal was to go for a 10-minute walk through the neighborhood 4 out of the next 7 days and look out for things to photograph. She managed this on 3 days and noticed that when she went on her walk, she became absorbed in the activity of looking for things to photograph, which helped her focus on the present moment and enjoy the activity.

The other part of home practice was reflecting on their values and goals, including perhaps discussing this topic with a friend, partner, or family member. Check out with the parent whether they have had any further thoughts about their values and what is important to them in life. If they have had further thoughts, would they like to revise their therapy goals in any way—either amend existing goals or add in new ones?

Having checked out the home practice, it is now time to focus on the main content of the session, which has to do with self-care, particularly focusing on sleep, eating, and physical activity.

General Aspects of Self-Care

Looking after ourselves is an important part of promoting our well-being. However, it is common in the postpartum period for the parent to focus on their baby and the rest of the family and neglect themselves. Using Worksheet 6: Mood Monitoring Record, the purpose of this session is to explore any disruptions in eating, sleep, or exercise and to use problem solving and goal setting to begin the process of change. The parent may not need to focus on all these areas of self-care if they are already managing to take care of themselves in one or more of these aspects.

The first step is to discuss the importance of self-care. Ask the parent to imagine being on an airplane. The flight attendant instructs the parent to put on their own oxygen mask first in case of an emergency before attending to their child. Discuss with the parent why this is important, and highlight that it is essential to look after yourself first before looking after your baby.

Identifying What Raises and Lowers Mood

While there are many factors that may affect how we feel and lead to low mood, how we look after our bodies is one of the most important. It is difficult for parents to get through a busy day, particularly if they are trying to manage low mood, if they haven't had enough sleep, aren't eating well, or are not exercising sufficiently. Having a baby means a lot of self-care routines change or are interrupted by the baby's needs. It is important to look at what might be affecting the parent's mood and to collaboratively set some small goals to help increase energy levels.

Useful questions for this part of the session include:

- *What changes have you noticed in your self-care routines since your baby was born?*
- *What are your priorities in terms of taking care of yourself?*
- *What would you like to be doing that has worked for you in the past?*
- *What are the current challenges that make it hard to care for yourself?*

Look again at completed Worksheet 6: Mood Monitoring Record together with the parent to identify any patterns related to self-care and discuss which area—eating, sleeping, or physical exercise—would be most useful to start with. If there is more than one, acknowledge this and choose which one feels the most important to start with. You may only have time to work on one area in this session.

The Importance of Sleep

Sleep is an essential way in which we can take care of ourselves, and it is often one of the things most affected by having a baby. Most parents find it a challenge to get enough sleep in the postpartum period. Their baby is likely to be waking up frequently for feeding during the night, and it can be hard to go back to sleep. The hormonal changes that occur during this period can also affect the circadian rhythm, leading to less sleepiness in the evening. If the parent is depressed, this can result in difficulty falling asleep or in waking early in the morning. Feeling tired and lacking energy can lead to low mood, and sleep deprivation can cause a significant number of physical side effects such as poor concentration and low energy.

Some parents have difficulty getting to sleep, wake up frequently in the night, or wake early in the morning and are not able to get back to sleep. Worrying about getting back to sleep can then keep them awake. Alternatively, some parents may feel they want to sleep all the time and could sleep for many hours and still feel they could sleep more. Either too little or too much sleep can affect mood and everyday life.

Useful questions for this part of the session include:

- *How is your sleep pattern currently? Is this different from how it was in the past?*
- *How is this affected by your baby's sleep patterns?*
- *What strategies have you tried to help your baby's sleep?*
- *How is this affected by your family's sleep pattern (partner/other children)?*
- *What is your sleep environment like?*
- *How easy is it for you to fall asleep at night and if you wake in the night?*
- *Do you wake early in the morning and have difficulty getting back to sleep?*
- *Do you have difficulty sleeping because you are worrying about things?*
- *What would you like to be different with your sleep at the moment?*
- *What strategies have you tried for your sleep?*
- *What has worked and what hasn't worked?*
- *What do you think might make a difference?*
- *What small step could you take to begin this?*
- *What challenges might get in the way of this?*
- *How could you plan to overcome these challenges?*

Go through with the parent the following suggestions for improving sleep, covering three main areas—where they sleep, what they do, and how they think. The parent has this same information in their workbook, which is why it is addressed to the parent here in the therapist guide. Identify a small change that the parent could try.

Where You Sleep

- Do you prefer to sleep in a light or dark bedroom? Think about sleeping with a light on or off, the door open or shut, or the curtains drawn or not.
- How warm do you like to be when you sleep? Think about whether you need more or fewer blankets or a window open or closed.
- Is it too noisy or too quiet for you to sleep? Think about sleeping with the radio or music off or on a very low level, or open or close your windows. If your baby is sleeping in the same room as you, having low-level noise going can help to mask the snuffles and sounds a baby makes at night (which can potentially wake you up).
- How comfortable are your bed, sheets, covers, or pillows? Think about whether you need to change them to help you to sleep better. Would a weighted duvet or more covers make you feel more snug at night and help to improve your sleep?

What You Do

- Just like children, adults need a wind-down routine to help them get off to sleep. Make sure you have enough time in the evening to relax immediately before you go to bed. This might involve having a relaxing bath, listening to music, reading, or some other activity that you find relaxing. Some parents start doing household chores when their baby goes to sleep, but if you are finding it difficult to sleep, you may find it helpful to switch to more relaxing activities.
- Turn off notifications on your phone during your wind-down routine.

- Try to avoid looking at your mobile/electronic devices immediately before bed—or if you do, try to avoid blue-light settings or use blue light–blocking glasses as blue light from electronics can disrupt sleep.
- Keep your bedroom a restful place; don't use it to watch TV, make phone calls, or use the computer. Try reading a book or magazine or listening to a podcast/music before going to sleep.
- Cut down on caffeine (tea, coffee, and other caffeinated beverages), nicotine (cigarettes), and alcohol in the evening: these are all stimulants that disturb sleep (see later in the chapter for advice on caffeine/alcohol if you are breastfeeding). Try a hot milky drink instead.
- Make sure you are eating well—if the body is hungry, it is hard to sleep.
- Don't eat or drink too heavily late in the evening—your digestion needs time to work before sleep.
- Try and fit in some exercise such as a brisk walk or stretching during the day—it will help you feel naturally tired. If it is too cold or hot to go out, you could try an exercise routine online.
- Try to avoid exercise just before bedtime, or keep it light, as vigorous exercise can make it harder to fall asleep.
- Try to get outside during the day, particularly in the morning, even if it is just a walk around the yard. This can stimulate production of the sleep hormone melatonin, which promotes sleepiness at night.
- If you need to nap during the day to catch up with lost sleep, try to make the nap short (20–30 minutes) as long naps in the day can disrupt sleep at night.

What You Think

- Worrying about not sleeping will keep you awake! Try telling yourself that worrying about it will not help. If you are worrying about a particular problem, write it down and tell yourself you will deal with it in the morning.
- If you can't sleep, don't lie in bed worrying. Get up and do a quiet relaxing activity such as reading or listening to quiet music until you feel sleepy/tired.

- Remember that you can't *get yourself* to sleep, but you are more likely to *fall asleep* if your mind is calm.
- Try to think of three things you are grateful for before you go to sleep.

Let's see how sleep deprivation is affecting Kenise's mood and what changes she made to help with this.

Kenise has found it difficult to get back to a normal sleep pattern after giving birth to Serena and Jayden. She wakes several times in the night to feed her babies and finds it hard to go back to sleep. During the day she feels exhausted and overwhelmed with the constant demands of the twins. She has become quite irritable with her husband, Demar, and is longing to have a deep sleep without interruptions. In discussion with her therapist, Kenise realizes that she could make some adjustments to her sleep routine that could increase the amount of sleep she has each day.

Kenise decides to go to bed earlier after the last feeding of the day and have a rest in the afternoon when her twins sleep. If Jayden and Serena aren't asleep at the same time, she at least makes sure that she sits down for a cuddle and some downtime with whichever baby is awake, with the television, an audiobook, or music on in the background to help her relax. During the night she develops a structure of feeding her twins together at regular times and leaving them for a little longer between feedings. Gradually, Kenise increases her sleep time and feels a little less exhausted during the day. She begins to go out of the house more, which also helps to increase her energy levels and improves her sleep.

The Importance of Regular Eating

Eating well during the postpartum period is important for parents, especially if they are breastfeeding. Individual calorie needs will vary according to body size, age, and activity levels, as well as whether the mother is breastfeeding. For example, a breastfeeding mother will need to consume around 400 calories more than usual alongside adequate levels of protein and healthy fats. Regularly eating a balanced healthy diet is also essential in helping one's mood stay steady and to keep energy levels up during this period of life. Eating too little or too much can lead to peaks or dips in mood, causing the mother to feel tired, drained, tense, or irritable. Adequate hydration is also important, particularly if the parent is breastfeeding.

In the postpartum period there is a focus on looking after the baby and making sure the baby is well fed and cared for. It can be difficult to fit in regular eating and healthy foods when working around an infant schedule and easy for the parent to neglect their own needs. In addition, parents may lose their appetite, or alternatively they may eat too much and gain weight, which can be distressing. Being on antidepressant medication can also affect appetite. Prioritizing normal eating may need a change in mindset to focus on one's own eating first.

Useful questions for this part of the session include:

- *How are your appetite and eating pattern currently? Are they different from how they were in the past?*
- *How does this fit in with your family's eating patterns? (Include breastfeeding if relevant.)*
- *Has your weight changed since having your baby? Is this something of importance to you?*
- *Does your appetite change with your mood, for example, when you feel low or stressed?*
- *Have you noticed any changes in mood with regular eating/not eating for long periods?*
- *Do your energy levels change in response to your eating patterns?*
- *Do you feel you have enough water to drink?*
- *Have you noticed any effects of alcohol or caffeine on your appetite or mood?*
- *What would you like to be different about your eating at the moment?*
- *What small step could you take to begin this?*
- *What obstacles might get in the way of this?*
- *How could you plan to overcome these obstacles?*

Read through with the parent the following suggestions for eating to support mood and identify a small change that the parent could try out. This same material appears in the parent workbook.

Drink Enough Water

Not drinking enough can lead to mild dehydration, which can affect our feelings and behavior, often leading to feeling restless or irritable. Try to drink eight glasses of water a day. Caffeinated drinks such as tea, coffee, or carbonated beverages may increase energy briefly but if drunk in large quantities can increase blood pressure, low mood, and anxiety. Try to limit your caffeinated drinks to three or four a day. If you are breastfeeding, the Centers for Disease Control and Prevention (CDC) recommends limiting caffeine to two to three drinks a day (less than 300 mg; www.cdc.gov).

Maintain a Healthy Weight

Weight loss deprives your brain and body of nutrients that you need to help your mood. Weight gain can lead to feeling out of control of your eating and may lead to yo-yo dieting. Try to eat regularly and healthily to help maintain a steady weight. Allow a least a year to lose the "baby" weight you may have gained.

Eat Regular Meals Throughout the Day

Eat three meals every day. Missing meals leads to low blood sugar, and this can lead to low mood, irritability, and tiredness. To make life easier for yourself, aim for simple meals or packaged meals with healthy ingredients; this will take away the burden of planning and prepping. Snack between meals on healthy foods such as fruit and nuts.

Eat More Whole-Grain Food and Less Sugary Food

Whole-grain foods, such as whole-grain cereals, whole-grain bread, fruit, and vegetables, are more filling than foods made with white flour, rice, and pasta; and the sugar from whole grains is absorbed slowly into your body, keeping your mood steady. Foods that are high in sugar such as cakes, cookies, and candy are absorbed quickly into your body, causing sugar "highs" that wear off and leave you feeling tired and low.

Limit Your Alcohol Intake

Alcohol can affect the brain by increasing low mood and reducing nutrients in the body through the effort it takes the liver to process. Alcohol consumption above moderate levels (one drink a day) can also impair judgment and the ability to safely care for the baby (CDC; www.cdc.gov).

Not drinking alcohol is the safest option for breastfeeding mothers. However, moderate alcohol consumption is not thought to be harmful to the infant if the mother waits at least 2 hours between drinking and before breastfeeding (CDC; www.cdc.gov).

Let's see how having a baby affected Mila's eating and what changes she is making to help with this.

Mila has started to skip meals because she is too tired to fix herself a meal. Her energy levels dip, and looking after her daughter, Marta, becomes a burden rather than a pleasure. Mila feels guilty about this and wants things to be different. In discussion with the therapist, she realizes the importance of regular healthy eating to give her the calories and nutrients that she needs to carry out all the tasks that are required each day as well as having time for herself. She decides to prioritize having a meal with her partner, Sophie, in the evening. They take turns cooking and focus on simple meals that are easy to prepare. If Marta needs attention, Sophie is happy to take over the cooking. Mila has also discussed with her therapist the importance of having breakfast first thing in the morning and has decided to set a goal around this.

Figure 5.2 shows Mila's completed Weekly Goal Planner for this week.

The final area to work on in this session is the link between physical activity and mood.

How Physical Activity Can Help With Low Mood

Keeping active and physically fit is an important strategy for boosting mood and helping one to feel energized and healthy. It may be helpful to have a discussion with the parent regarding research that shows that

Question	Notes
What is your goal for this week?	To make sure I eat breakfast by having a piece of toast and jam before I feed Marta
What do you need to carry it out?	Make sure a plate and knife are laid out and that bread, butter, and jam are available
When will you carry it out?	First thing in the morning when I get up
What might get in the way of carrying it out?	Having a difficult night with Marta, not sleeping, and feeling low
How will you overcome any obstacles?	Make everything ready the night before to remind me to do it and how important it is

Figure 5.2

Mila's Completed Worksheet 9: Weekly Goal Planner.

exercise can help to lift mood in people who feel low, as well as improve sleep, appetite, and energy levels. The increases in serotonin and endorphins with exercise contribute to this effect.

There are lots of reasons why making physical activity a regular part of the week can be more difficult after having a baby, including physical limitations after giving birth, lack of energy, tiredness, and finding the time to fit it in. However, learning to build in time for exercise can have big benefits in relation to energy levels and mood. Mothers who have recently had a C-section, will need to adhere to medical advice about returning to exercise.

Useful questions for this part of the session include:

- *Do you feel that your current physical activity level is how you want it to be?*
- *How is your current physical activity level different from how it was in the past?*
- *Have you noticed how your level of physical activity affects your mood?*
- *What would you like to be different about your level of physical activity at the moment?*
- *What small step could you put in place to begin this?*
- *What obstacles might get in the way of this?*
- *How could you plan to overcome these obstacles?*

Is important to emphasize that exercise can be beneficial even in small doses and does not need to be vigorous. Walking, swimming, and regular stretching can all help. You may find it useful to read with the parent the following suggestions, which also appear in the parent workbook, for fitting in physical activity and identify a small change that the parent could try out.

- Start slowly and build up gradually. Set short-term, realistic goals. Give yourself a reward when you have done your planned exercise.
- Try taking your baby out for short walks, perhaps to help them get to sleep or if they seem bored. Use a stroller or baby carrier and walk briskly.

- Try walking (if this is feasible) to places where you would usually take the car or bus, for example, to the local shops, to pick children up from school or childcare, to a friend's house, or to the park. This may not be possible due to the distance involved, but a short walk around the neighborhood can also work well.
- Try doing stretches on a regular basis.
- Talk to your partner, family, or friends about when they could watch your baby so that you could join an exercise class or go swimming. Take it in turns with a friend who also has children.
- Think of ways you could fit exercise into your daily routine indoors; stream an exercise program in the morning or put music on and do household chores such as vacuuming, gardening, or cleaning with lots of energy.

Let's see how beginning to prioritize physical activity has helped Lucy's low mood.

Lucy is struggling with being a single mother. She used to be very active, going to an exercise class at the local community center each week as well as swimming on a regular basis. However, it has been hard to make the time to get out of the house, see her friends, and do the things she used to. She has begun to realize the importance of building in some time to be active and has started to go out for a 10-minute walk around the neighborhood several times a week. While out walking one day she met a friend from her mother and baby group who has a baby the same age as Jackson. Her friend also values exercise, and they agreed to meet for regular walks together around the neighborhood. Lucy enjoys getting out for a walk and finds it supportive talking with her friend about looking after their babies. She has increased the length of her walks and has noticed that her mood has started to improve.

Troubleshooting

Even though eating, sleeping, and physical activity are the most fundamental activities to look at regarding changes to help with low mood, thinking about changes in these areas can be difficult for the parent. This session is placed first in this module to emphasize how much of an impact our physiological state can have on our mood. Encourage the parent to trust the process of therapy, and experiment with making just a small change in one of these areas.

Home Practice

Toward the end of this session, you can discuss home practice to be done over the following week.

You can ask the parent to use Worksheet 9: Weekly Goal Planner to set a specific goal to add a regular self-care activity into their week.

Remind them to make the goal concrete and specific, link it to values, and work through any potential obstacles. It is important to start small and make the goal practical and achievable. Worksheet 10: Weekly Goal Record can be used for a goal that is completed daily to record when it was completed and any comments about it.

Figure 5.3 shows Isabella's Weekly Goal Planner. She decided that it would be more realistic to plan some exercise at home rather than contemplate going out.

Encourage the parent to keep a record on their copy of Worksheet 10: Weekly Goal Record.

Summary of the Session and Feedback

At the end of the session, it is important to give the parent the chance to reflect on the key things they are going to take away from the session. You can then ask them for feedback:

- *Did they cover the things they wanted to?*
- *What was helpful about the session?*
- *Was there anything that was unhelpful?*
- *What could improve the session next time?*

Key Points

- Looking after yourself is really important when you have a baby.
- Getting enough sleep, eating well, and getting regular exercise can help to lift mood and give energy.

Question	Notes
What is your goal for this week?	To follow a DVD/YouTube exercise routine when Margarita is asleep during the day
What do you need to carry it out?	Make sure the DVD/YouTube link is ready and easily accessible Get comfortable clothes ready the night before
When will you carry it out?	As soon as Margarita goes to sleep
What might get in the way of carrying it out?	Feeling that I have too many other things to do
How will you overcome any obstacles?	Tell myself that exercise is important and that it doesn't have to be for very long. 10 minutes would be enough.

Figure 5.3

Isabella's Completed Worksheet 9: Weekly Goal Planner.

CHAPTER 6 Session 4: Routines and Social Support

Aim of This Session

The aim of Session 4 is to outline the concept of "acting from the outside in" and to introduce a daily or weekly routine to follow even when the parent is experiencing low mood. This will involve exploring the importance of acting according to plan rather than relying on mood or willpower and discussing how having a daily and/or weekly plan can be helpful to encourage activation. You will also discuss how important social support is for lifting mood and how to ensure that opportunities for this are fitted into the parent's daily or weekly routine. For home practice you will ask the parent to set a small goal to add an activity into their daily or weekly routine to help lift their mood.

Outline

- Set agenda 120
- Review of mood and how things are going 121
- Review home practice 121
- "Acting from the outside in" 122
- Identifying a daily and/or weekly routine 123
- Social support 125
- Troubleshooting 127
- Home practice 127
- Summary of the session and feedback 128
- Key points 128

Postpartum Depression. Anne Stewart et al., Oxford University Press. © Oxford University Press (2026).
DOI: 10.1093/med-psych/9780197759707.003.0006

When to Conduct This Session

Session 4 is a core session within the Activating Module and introduces the key concept of acting according to a plan rather than mood. This session is indicated when there are difficulties in establishing either a regular daily or weekly routine, including overactivity or inactivity, and when this is contributing to low mood.

Materials Needed

- Worksheet 9: Weekly Goal Planner
- Worksheet 10: Weekly Goal Record
- Worksheet 11: Weekly Routine *or*
- Worksheet 12: Daily Routine

Worksheets appear in Appendix A *at the end of this therapist guide and in* Appendix A *at the end of the parent workbook. Worksheets can also be accessed by searching for this book's title on the Oxford Academic platform, at academic.oup.com. Note that when more than one copy of a worksheet is required, you may photocopy the worksheets for the parent, ask the parent to make their own photocopies, or direct the parent to the book website to print their own.*

Set Agenda

Discuss the aim and overview of the session with the parent, and set the agenda together. This will likely include the standard items as well as the specific topic for this session. Make a note of anything else that the parent would like to discuss in this session. Discuss any practicalities for the parent or the baby that may impact on the session, and agree how to manage these.

Review of Mood and How Things Are Going

Review how the parent's mood has been since the last session. Discuss what symptoms have been present and whether they have increased or decreased. What might this have been linked to?

Has the parent been able to prioritize their self-care, particularly in the areas of eating, sleeping, and exercising? Review how this has gone with the parent, and discuss any difficulties or obstacles that have been present since the last session. What did they notice about trying to put this change into place?

Review Home Practice

Review the home practice task that was set with the parent in your last session together. If following this guide and the workbook in chapter order, then this task would have focused on making a small change to their self-care, using Worksheet 9: Weekly Goal Planner.

Discuss what went well with the home practice and what the parent found challenging. Reinforce that all learning is helpful, even small steps toward the weekly goal, and encourage the parent to review the practice and further develop their understanding of what contributes to their low mood. Celebrate when unexpected barriers and the parent's response to them perhaps led to unexpected benefits. If there were unexpected negatives that emerged from the situation, discuss the specifics of the actions and context with the parent and how that went for them. Empathize with them, and explore when moving forward if there might be other ways to think together about how to manage the situation (e.g., break down tasks, enlist someone for support, write reminders, plan to do task at a different time of day, or sandwich a tricky task between two other more pleasant tasks).

"Acting From the Outside In"

One of the most significant effects of low mood is that it can make us feel reluctant to do things. Sometimes we respond to this by not doing anything and then feel even lower because we are not getting things done. We may also respond by trying to do lots of things and feel distracted by how much there is to do and what a struggle it all seems. Having a baby means it can be difficult to get into a steady routine where there is enough time to do all the things we need to do. It can be difficult to prioritize things or get them in any kind of order, and some days the routine will be changed completely by the baby not sleeping or having a nap at a different time or becoming ill.

Useful questions for this part of the session include:

- *How do you view routines? Are they something you value/find helpful?*
- *Has your view of routines changed since having a baby?*
- *Did you value routines in the past? What about work routines?*
- *What do you think about routines for your baby? Is this a priority?*
- *Alternatively, do you see routines in a negative way?*
- *How do you find having a structure?*
- *Do you value being free to go with the flow or being spontaneous?*

A way to help manage the difficulty with balancing activities across the day and week to cope with low mood is called "acting from the outside in." This means planning our time and doing activities according to our goal- and value-related plans, rather than being derailed by how we feel in the moment. It means we don't have to rely on mood or willpower to motivate us. By changing what we do, in time our thoughts and feelings also change. This may feel like acting or being fake in the beginning; however, with time, mood catches up. As we engage in valued behaviors, we often feel a sense of competence and satisfaction.

Identifying a Daily and/or Weekly Routine

Decide with the parent whether it would be helpful to look at their daily or weekly routine. Looking at the daily routine is helpful if the parent finds that their low mood has typical dips at the same time each day. Looking at the weekly routine is helpful if the parent finds that they have some good days but other days when their mood can be low all day.

Use either Worksheet 11: Weekly Routine or Worksheet 12: Daily Routine. With the parent, write out their daily routine or their weekly routine. For the daily routine, it can be helpful to think about the parent's routine, their baby's routine, and their family's routine separately. Once you have these written out, think with the parent what they notice when they find their mood is low and how this might be related to the activities across that part of the day or week.

Discuss together what activities could be planned to help lift their mood at this tricky part of the day or week. It is also important to think about what backup plans could be used for these new activities so that there is some flexibility for changes or disruptions.

Useful questions for this part of the session include:

- *Beginning with your typical day, what happens for you and for your baby?*
- *Tell me about your week. Do you have regular activities scheduled in?*
- *What difference would it make to have a focus for morning, afternoon, evening?*
- *What activities would you value that would lift mood?*
- *What activities would it be helpful to do less often as these lower your mood?*
- *What could be alternatives on bad weather days or if the baby is sick (i.e., contingency plans that would be both manageable and meaningful)?*

See Figure 6.1 for an example of Zainab's weekly routine.

Day	Morning	Afternoon	Evening
Monday	Drop Layla off at preschool, Amir's nap, house chores	Pick Layla up from preschool, Amir's nap, house chores	Cook dinner, watch TV
Tuesday	Drop Layla off at preschool, Amir's nap, house chores	Pick Layla up from preschool, Amir's nap, house chores	Cook dinner, watch TV
Wednesday	Park with children	Amir's nap, watch TV, house chores	Cook dinner, watch TV
Thursday	Bounce and Rhyme at library	Amir's nap, watch TV, house chores	Cook dinner, watch TV
Friday	Play at home, Amir's nap, house chores	Attend mosque	Dinner at Tauseef's family's house
Saturday	Tauseef at gym, shopping in town	Amir's nap, watch TV, house chores	Dinner at Tauseef's family's house
Sunday	Tauseef at gym, house chores	Lunch out	Cook dinner, watch TV

Figure 6.1

Zainab's Completed Worksheet 11: Weekly Routine.

Social Support

It is well established that social support can influence health and well-being. Research has shown that in the postpartum period, encouraging parents to be part of social networks can help them to access appropriate care and develop positive behaviors (Adams et al. 2015). Low social support is known to increase the risk of postpartum depression. There are many advantages to social support including the sharing of tips between parents, encouraging parents to get out of the house, providing support to change behaviors, facilitating getting appropriate health or social services (such as parenting groups, family programming, and First Steps programs), and providing emotional support at a difficult time. However, in the postpartum period, it is all too easy to lose touch with friends and become isolated at home.

It is important therefore to help the parent take opportunities to build social support during this period of life. Their usual social support networks are likely to be disrupted, particularly if existing friends have not recently become parents, they've recently moved, or they struggle with social anxiety. However, meeting other parents at the same stage of life can be something that new parents really value as it reduces isolation, increases energy, and generally has a positive influence on well-being. Many new parents also receive social support from family members who may live close by. This may require building on existing relationships and developing the skill to ask for help. Building social support into daily or weekly routines can be a helpful way to make this a regular habit.

Look at the parent's completed daily or weekly routine worksheet and discuss with them what opportunities there are in their day or week for meeting or connecting with others. Think together about ways they could increase this and what type of activities might help.

Let's look at how Zainab and her therapist introduced more social support into her weekly routine.

Zainab used to go out regularly with friends, but since she had her baby, Amir, and her mood has dropped, she rarely goes out. She stays at home but finds she doesn't have the motivation to do anything other than the basic necessities of caring for Amir and looking after her older daughter, Layla. While Amir is sleeping, she spends a lot of time just sitting around and thinking what a bad mother she is. Her therapist asks her to think about routines that she used to have, and Zainab talks about the mother and baby groups that she used to go to with Layla. She found it helpful to get out and do something with other mothers and made some good friends through these groups. Her therapist discusses with her a small goal, which is to connect with one of the other mothers and suggest they go to a children's playground together. Zainab is initially reluctant to do this but agrees to text her friend to see how she is and whether she would like to catch up. Her friend immediately texts back and suggests a day and time they could meet.

Isabella had different challenges. Let's see what she worked out with her therapist.

Isabella tried taking Margarita to parent and baby groups, even though she was worried about meeting new parents because of her lack of confidence in social situations. Isabella found participating in these groups to be hard as it seemed that the other moms didn't relate to her struggles with motherhood. She found the interactions really tiring because she spent a lot of time trying to read their reactions and then worried that she was responding in the "wrong way." The gatherings were also very noisy, which was exhausting. Isabella found it stressful going to the groups but felt she needed to for the sake of her baby. She began to feel socially isolated, alone, and stuck; and her mood dropped further.

Isabella and her therapist looked at her weekly routine together along with her most recent Mood Monitoring Record, and they noticed that some of the groups were more difficult and more likely to lead to her low mood than others. Talking this through, Isabella realized she preferred groups with a set structure that helped her feel connected socially but didn't involve too many unstructured interactions. She and her therapist agreed that she would prioritize attending Baby Music and Swimming and replace going to a local parent and baby drop-in session with a regular walk around her neighborhood. She also arranged for a former co-worker with whom she got on very well to visit once a week in the late afternoon. Isabella found it reassuring knowing what was happening each day.

Troubleshooting

The parent may find the idea of changing their daily or weekly routine overwhelming, and it is important to normalize this (i.e., these are common problems that are experienced by many parents and are entirely understandable). Experiencing low mood can make it difficult to feel that fitting another thing into the day or week is possible. Focus on setting a very small goal and building up slowly, and encourage just taking the first step toward changing a routine.

It may be helpful to explore with the parent what their worries are about "acting from the outside in" and what they fear might happen. Talk about the idea of "If nothing changes, nothing changes," and revisit the understanding of how behavioral activation works and their individualized understanding of what is keeping their low mood going.

Although routines can be helpful because they can assist with staying on track and settling babies into a pattern that is more predictable, different people settle into routines differently. For some it can be more challenging than for others—both for parents and for babies. Encourage the parent to be gentle with themselves and their baby when trying routines, noting that all routines should be somewhat flexible; they just help to establish a general pattern.

Some parents may find it helpful to bring a partner or other family member to a session to discuss how the family can support the parent to make changes or at least to discuss their plan with the family to get maximal support.

Home Practice

Toward the end of this session, you can discuss home practice to be done over the following week.

Use another copy of Worksheet 9: Weekly Goal Planner to set a specific goal to add a new activity into the parent's daily or weekly routine.

Remember to make the goal small and specific and to work through any potential obstacles. Another copy of Worksheet 10: Weekly Goal Record can be used for a goal that is completed daily to record when it was completed and any comments on it.

Summary of the Session and Feedback

At the end of the session, it is important to give the parent the chance to reflect on the key things they are going to take away from the session. You can then ask them for feedback:

- *Did they cover the things they wanted to?*
- *What was helpful about the session?*
- *Was there anything that was unhelpful?*
- *What could improve the session next time?*

Key Points

- Changing what we do helps our thoughts and feelings to change.
- Having support from friends and family can improve our health and well-being.

CHAPTER 7

Session 5: Nourishing and Depleting Activities

Aim of This Session

The aim of Session 5 is to further develop the balance of activity in the parent's daily and/or weekly routine through exploring the balance of nourishing and depleting activities. The session explores the importance of balancing depleting activities in the parent's day or week with nourishing ones and how an imbalance of nourishing to depleting activities can contribute to low mood. For home practice, you will ask the parent to choose one small change they could make to their day or week to include a nourishing activity and try this out.

Outline

- Set agenda 130
- Review of mood and how things are going 131
- Review home practice 131
- Introduction to nourishing and depleting activities 132
- Balancing nourishing and depleting activities in a daily routine 135
- Troubleshooting 135
- Home practice 136
- Summary of the session and feedback 137
- Key points 137

Postpartum Depression. Anne Stewart et al., Oxford University Press. © Oxford University Press (2026).
DOI: 10.1093/med-psych/9780197759707.003.0007

When to Conduct This Session

Session 5 can be used when there are difficulties in engaging in nourishing activities that promote healthy mood and/or when the parent has difficulty in getting pleasure from daily life. This session naturally builds on the material in Chapter 6/Session 4: Routines and Social Support and links well into later sessions on compassion.

Materials Needed

- Worksheet 2: Motivational balance
- Worksheet 9: Weekly Goal Planner
- Worksheet 10: Weekly Goal Record
- Worksheet 13: Nourishing and Depleting Activities

Worksheets appear in Appendix A at the end of this therapist guide and in Appendix A at the end of the parent workbook. Worksheets can also be accessed by searching for this book's title on the Oxford Academic platform, at academic.oup.com. Note that when more than one copy of a worksheet is required, you may photocopy the worksheets for the parent, ask the parent to make their own photocopies, or direct the parent to the book website to print their own.

Set Agenda

As usual, start off by setting the agenda for this session together with the parent. If this session is at the mid-point of therapy, hopefully the parent will have become familiar with this task, and you can encourage them to make this a collaborative exercise. Discuss any practicalities for the parent or the baby that may impact on the session and agree how to manage these (e.g., baby needs feeding or is uncomfortable).

Review of Mood and How Things Are Going

Review how the parent's mood has been since the last session. Discuss what symptoms have been present, and encourage the parent to take a curious rather than judgmental view on this. If necessary, talk about how changes in patterns of low mood are not always straightforward, and there can be many ups and downs along the way.

Has the parent been able to:

- attend to their self-care: eating, sleeping, and exercising?
- plan a daily or weekly routine?

Review these skills with the parent, and discuss any difficulties or obstacles that have been present since the last session. Are they beginning to notice any patterns about their weeks where it is easier or harder to put skills into practice? What is this related to? It is important to model unconditional acceptance and positivity toward the parent in order to enhance engagement and reduce the fear of failure or resistance to taking small steps. The process skills—such as learning to be curious, gentle, and kind to yourself—are more important than the outcomes.

Review Home Practice

Review the home practice task that was set with the parent in your last session together. If following this guide and the workbook in chapter order, this task would have focused on building a daily or weekly routine using Worksheet 11: Weekly Routine or Worksheet 12: Daily Routine.

As in previous sessions, the parent may find there are challenges in putting the skills or their home practice into place, and it is important to spend time thinking these challenges through and reviewing them. It is essential at this early stage in therapy to familiarize the parent with taking an open and curious response to what has been hard as well as what has gone well. Celebrate all aspects of home practice—barriers, obstacles, small wins, and revelations—to help the parent see all change as learning. Remember also to warmly empathize with and accept the parent's experience of the home practice so that they feel listened to and understood.

Introduction to Nourishing and Depleting Activities

Following the session on routines and "acting from the outside in," this session focuses on helping the mother achieve a balance across the day and week. The balance is between activities that we have to do and activities that we enjoy doing, with equal attention given to those activities that are for other people and those for our self. This can be a good time to emphasize the importance of self-care, if this has proved difficult for the parent to prioritize. It is also a useful session to integrate with the later session on compassion as it focuses on being kind to oneself. This session is adapted from an exercise in mindfulness-based cognitive therapy (Williams & Penman, 2011).

Having a baby introduces many more things to think about and get done in the usual day. These can come on top of other demands already in the parent's life from their partners, other children, families, work, and general household tasks. When there is so much to think about, particularly if anxiety or low mood is dominating, there can be a tendency to choose those things that are more immediate and that will help manage the difficult feelings quickly, such as chores, doing things for other people, or going along with what other people want. In the short term this takes away low mood or worries through a quick fix of feeling effective and in control. In the long term, however, too much of this can result in feelings of being drained, undervalued, and bored and keeps low mood going. The parent may end up not having enough activities in their daily life that they value, such as time to play with the children, enjoying a cup of tea or coffee, or chatting with a friend. These are the things that can nourish and restore energy.

Discuss with the parent the balance in their day between doing things for others and doing things for themselves. Think together about whether this has changed since their baby has arrived and why. It can be useful to relate this discussion back to the parent's values discussed in previous sessions as these can provide important insights if the parent finds themself focusing on certain activities.

Useful questions for this part of the session include:

- *Think about your usual day. What do you feel the balance is between doing things for others and doing things for yourself?*
- *What do you feel the balance is between doing necessary activities, such as chores, and activities that are for pleasure?*
- *Has this changed since having a family?*
- *If you had time just for yourself and your baby, what would you find yourself doing?*
- *If you had time just for you, what would you find yourself doing?*
- *What activities are important to you to fit into your daily life?*

Let's see what Kenise noticed about the activities in her day.

Kenise and her therapist set a routine and self-care-focused goal from their last session that when her husband, Demar, was traveling for work and Kenise was on her own with the children, after her older daughter, Maya, was in in bed, and before the first nighttime feeding for Jayden and Serena she would go to her own bedroom with a relaxing drink and listen to a favorite podcast. Kenise was really looking forward to this as she and her therapist had talked about how this used to be an activity before she had her babies that she found very relaxing. However, when the children were finally asleep, Kenise found herself distracted by how much cleaning up there was to do, and by the time she finished that, there wasn't enough time to do anything else. The next two nights, Kenise felt so exhausted by all she had done during the day that she couldn't find the energy to make a drink and go to her bedroom and instead watched TV on the sofa. When she and her therapist reviewed the goal in their session, she described feeling really upset with herself that she hadn't been able to fit this important self-care activity in.

Look at Figure 7.1 with the parent as an example of the nourishing and depleting activities in Kenise's day. This figure appears in both this therapist guide and the parent workbook.

Time/Day	Activity	Nourishing or depleting
7am	Make breakfast for Maya. Feed Jayden and Serena.	Depleting
8am	Get children dressed and change twins' diapers. Make Maya's lunch. School run.	Depleting
9.30am	Come home. Feed Jayden and Serena. Put laundry in the washing machine.	Depleting
10am	Change twins' diapers. Twins nap. Tidy up from breakfast.	Depleting
11am	Hang washing out. Play with twins and read books.	Nourishing
12pm	Make lunch. Tidy up after lunch.	Depleting
1pm	Jayden and Serena play in baby gym and watch TV. Start making dinner and put in slow cooker.	Nourishing
2pm	Feed Jayden and Serena. Dress twins and change diapers. Write shopping list and pay bills to mail.	Depleting
3pm	School run. Twins nap. Go to shop, post office, and pharmacy.	Depleting
5pm	Finish making dinner. Feed children. Tidy up after. Run bath for children.	Depleting
6.30pm	Bathe and put children to bed.	Nourishing/depleting (depends on how tired children are)
8pm	Tidy up house. Put dishwasher on. Put breakfast things out. Clean and sweep floor. Bed.	Depleting

Figure 7.1

Kenise's Completed Worksheet 13: Nourishing and Depleting Activities

Developed from *Mindfulness: A practical guide to finding peace in a frantic world* (Williams & Penman, 2011).

Balancing Nourishing and Depleting Activities in a Daily Routine

Using Worksheet 13: Nourishing and Depleting Activities, ask the parent to think of a typical day and write down—for the morning, the afternoon, and the evening—a list of all the things that they do. Ask them to just write these in a list and not think or discuss too much the different things. After they have finished, go back through the list together, and decide whether each activity is nurturing (activities involving feeling fulfilled, energized, and/or living a valued life) or depleting (activities that are routine, boring, necessary, and/or unfulfilling). Look together at the balance of nourishing to depleting activities across the day. Are there any areas which suggest change?

Let's see how Kenise did with trying to balance her activities across her day.

Kenise's therapist noticed that she often spent the whole day focused on depleting chores, which led to her feeling exhausted by 8pm. Kenise agreed and said there were often tasks like straightening up the house still to be done when the children were in bed! Her therapist talked through the importance of balancing her day and how this could lead to having more energy and happier mood. Together they linked Kenise's focus on chores back to a core value of hard work and having a spotless house like her mother. Her therapist gently challenged the practicality of this thought at the moment with three young children. Kenise agreed to try balancing her day with making time in the morning and afternoon for 15 minutes to sit down with a cup of tea and read her book while the babies were napping and Maya was at school, rather than racing around trying to get everything done. Kenise and her therapist wondered if she would then have more energy for herself in the evening and whether she might try leaving the chores that weren't done by 8pm for another day. Kenise worried about how not doing all the chores would make her feel, but she agreed to give it a try.

Troubleshooting

As in Session 4 on routines, the parent may find it difficult and overwhelming to begin to think about how they could change how they do things within the day or the week. They may describe feeling that it is impossible to plan with a small baby who may have an unpredictable routine or a busy family who have frequent demands. Reinforce the idea that just trying out (small) new and different ways of planning their day or week can be useful, even if sometimes it takes a few attempts to find how it might work. Discuss the idea of "good enough" rather than "perfect" and that the new way of doing something might not work every day, but if it works more days than not, this can be counted as progress.

It is also important to be aware that this session may challenge some deeply rooted societal or cultural beliefs that are held by the parent or their family regarding parenting. It may therefore be useful to refer to Session 2 on values, particularly the section on unhelpful beliefs regarding parenting. If the parent continues to have difficulty with the idea that meeting their own needs should be as important as meeting the needs of others, you could gently explore with them where these ideas may have originated and what might be the advantages and disadvantages of challenging them. Going back to Worksheet 2: Motivational Balance to think about this with the parent may be helpful.

Home Practice

Toward the end of this session, you can discuss home practice to be done over the following week.

Use another copy of Worksheet 9: Weekly Goal Planner to set a specific goal to add a regular nourishing activity into the week. Problem-solve whether more nourishing activities can be fitted into the week or whether depleting activities can be made more nourishing. Discuss again the concept of "acting from the outside in" and the importance of planning nourishing activities into the day or week, rather than relying on mood or motivation to do them.

Remember to make the goal concrete and specific and to work through any potential obstacles. Another copy of Worksheet 10: Weekly Goal Record can be used for a goal that is completed daily to record when it was completed and any comments on it.

Summary of the Session and Feedback

At the end of the session, it is important to give the parent the chance to reflect on the key things they are going to take away from the session. You can then ask them for feedback:

- *Did they cover the things they wanted to?*
- *What was helpful about the session?*
- *Was there anything that was unhelpful?*
- *What could improve the session next time?*

Key Points

- When experiencing low mood, it is easy to fill our days with quick activities that push the feelings away immediately but keep us stuck in a cycle of low mood, rather than engaging in activities that feel more difficult to start but will help lift our low mood over time.
- Adding a nourishing activity into our daily routine will help balance out depleting activities and restore energy.

CHAPTER 8 Session 6: Problem Solving

Aim of This Session

The aim of Session 6 is to introduce a technique to identify and solve problems in order to encourage activation and setting of appropriate goals. You will explore with the parent how low mood can lead to avoiding problems that need to be dealt with and how avoiding dealing with problems can lead to getting stuck in a cycle of low mood. You will work through a current problem with the parent using an approach that looks at how to solve the problem in a structured way. For home practice you will ask the parent to brainstorm and select a solution to a small problem and then think through and plan a way to put the solution into action or to use the approach to solve other problems in a structured way during the week.

Outline

- Set agenda 140
- Review of mood and how things are going 140
- Review home practice 141
- Introduction to problem solving 142
- Tackling problems directly using a structured approach 143
- Troubleshooting 147
- Home practice 147
- Summary of the session and feedback 148
- Key points 148

Postpartum Depression. Anne Stewart et al., Oxford University Press. © Oxford University Press (2026).
DOI: 10.1093/med-psych/9780197759707.003.0008

When to Conduct This Session

Session 6 is useful when there are difficulties in making decisions or goal-orientated actions due to interrupted thinking or avoidance. This session is an extension of the other three activation sessions (Chapters 5, 6, and 7/Sessions 3, 4, and 5) or may be delivered after the later sessions on getting stuck in your thoughts (Chapters 9 and 10/Sessions 7 and 8).

Materials Needed

- Worksheet 9: Weekly Goal Planner
- Worksheet 10: Weekly Goal Record
- Worksheet 14: Problem Solving

Worksheets appear in Appendix A at the end of this therapist guide and in Appendix A at the end of the parent workbook. Worksheets can also be accessed by searching for this book's title on the Oxford Academic platform, at academic.oup.com. Note that when more than one copy of a worksheet is required, you may photocopy the worksheets for the parent, ask the parent to make their own photocopies, or direct the parent to the book website to print their own.

Set Agenda

Discuss the aims and overview of the session together with the parent and then set the agenda together. Again, if this session is midway through therapy, invite and encourage the parent to collaboratively set the agenda with you. Discuss any practicalities for the parent or their baby that may impact on the session, and agree how to manage these.

Review of Mood and How Things Are Going

As usual, review how the parent's mood has been since the last session. If this is midway through therapy, there may be established triggers for low mood or ways to lift mood that are becoming apparent every week. Emphasize these patterns to the parent to help them understand more about their individual formulation/case conceptualization.

Now move on to review how the parent is doing with their skills. Has the parent been able to:

- attend to their self-care: eating, sleeping, and exercising?
- plan a daily or weekly routine?
- balance depleting activities with nourishing ones?

Review these skills with the parent, and discuss any difficulties or obstacles that have been present since the last session.

If you have been following this guide in chapter order, then this session will be approximately halfway through therapy. Now is a good time to review the therapy as a whole with the parent. Useful questions include:

- *How do you feel about the therapy?*
- *Has it been helpful so far?*
- *What are the challenges?*
- *Are you able to be open about your difficulties?*
- *Do you feel understood?*
- *Is there anything you would like to be different?*
- *What are the main challenges to work on from here?*

This is a good chance to think about the therapy together and to put into place more helpful ways of working together if this is appropriate.

Having reviewed the therapy in general, you can now move on to thinking more specifically about the home practice for the last week.

Review Home Practice

Review the home practice task that was set with the parent in your last session together. If following this guide and the workbook in chapter order, this task would have focused on balancing depleting activities with nourishing ones using Worksheet 13: Nourishing and Depleting Activities.

Discuss what went well with the home practice and what were the challenges. Are the challenges experienced similar to ones that have happened before? What helped that time? To support learning from the home practice each week, encourage the parent to notice these patterns. A new challenge that hasn't occurred before provides new information and is something to be explored with curiosity and empathy. With practice, this approach can help the parent bring this non-judgmental inquisitiveness to their mood during the week and become able to take a step back from their mood becoming lower.

Introduction to Problem Solving

In this session, the focus is on developing a strategy to solve tricky problems when everything seems to be overwhelming to the parent. This may have led to the problem being avoided or to the parent being self-critical. The parent may have identified that they struggle to make decisions, that they tend to put off or avoid things, or that they struggle with coping with strong feelings; or there may be a specific and major problem in the parent's life that is important to focus a session on. Working methodically through a problem-solving sheet is in itself an activation strategy as it approaches the problem rather than avoids it. This is a core component of the behavioral activation approach that will have been emphasized in previous sessions, and therefore problem solving is a further application of this approach.

Discuss with the parent how sometimes we find ourselves putting off solving a problem or a tricky situation because we are not sure of what the solution is or because doing something about it brings up difficult thoughts or feelings. Explain that when we feel low and depressed, it is actually harder to think flexibly around a problem and find a solution, even if we are usually good problem-solvers when not feeling depressed. This can lead to us not doing anything to solve the problem and the situation getting worse or to finding ourselves thinking more and more about the situation and worrying more and more about it. It can mean that it is very hard to make changes in our lives, and we feel at a loss to know what to do. Writing down a problem can be very helpful as it can help us see it differently, encourage a logical approach, and make the problems feel more manageable.

Let's see why Sarah's therapist thought problem solving would be useful.

Over several sessions, Sarah's therapist had noticed that Sarah often identified thoughts or triggers about her return to work that lowered her mood. Sarah discussed worries about not knowing how she was going to manage her return to work and trying to avoid thinking about it. A baby group that a friend from work attended often triggered these thoughts, so Sarah had stopped going. She also struggled with putting in goals around routines as she didn't want to think about having to change these routines if she went back to work. After a difficult week in which she had received an email from her manager asking if she would like to have a meeting about returning to work, her therapist gently suggested that problem solving might help challenge some of Sarah's avoidance around returning to work. Sarah and her therapist talked through what her worries were, and Sarah described feeling guilty and sad about the thought of putting Chloe in daycare, having tried for such a long time to get pregnant. Sarah was tearful throughout this conversation, and she mentioned some fears that she hadn't shared with anyone else because she felt other people wouldn't take them seriously. For example, she worried that if something happened to Chloe at daycare, it would be her fault as she had decided to go back to work. She also worried about what would happen to her relationship with Richard (already under strain) when she returned to work and had less time to spend with him.

Tackling Problems Directly Using a Structured Approach

Along with the parent, look at Worksheet 14: Problem Solving, and ask them to identify a specific, concrete problem to be addressed. Sometimes the hardest part of problem solving is determining what the actual problem is. Ask the parent to write down their problem so that together you know exactly what it is the parent wants to think about and ask them to be as specific as they can—details of where, when, what time, how often, how it makes them feel, and what the short- and long-term consequences are. If this feels like a big step, encourage the parent to just make a start, and reassure them it is always possible to make changes later. Sometimes even the process of beginning to write down a problem can help define it and make the unknown more manageable, and this is all part of the problem-solving process.

Brainstorm all possible solutions to this problem, and encourage the parent to be open to all ideas without evaluation. Suggest relevant ideas in line with the parent's values openly and curiously if they struggle to think of solutions or if you think they have missed an important solution—but try not to lead the discussion too much. Encourage the parent to think creatively, from different perspectives, and without limitations as this can often help them to think of a solution that has previously been discounted and may provide helpful information. Ask the parent to write all ideas down in each box of the worksheet, under the "Possible solutions" column.

Work through each solution together, and identify the advantages and disadvantages for each solution, making sure each solution has at least one identified advantage and disadvantage. Often this process turns into a discussion about a few solutions, and through this process it becomes clearer which solutions are not viable and which solutions could be a possibility. Be patient during this discussion, and encourage the parent to think through each solution and come up with their own advantages and disadvantages.

Looking at the advantages and disadvantages of each solution helps us to understand that there are no perfect solutions and that all decisions involve some element of risk or difficulty. When experiencing low mood, even the smallest disadvantage can put us off acting to solve a problem. At the end of this exercise, the important step is therefore to decide on a solution (to be written down in the "Best solution" box) and commit to a small step forward to putting it into action.

Useful questions for this part of the session include:

- *Are there any solutions to this problem that you have tried before but which didn't work? It is important to write these down as well.*

- *Are there any solutions you have not written down because they seem impossible? Think about how you would solve this problem if money was no object or if you had all the time you needed. What would your solution look like then?*
- *How would the people who are important to you solve this problem? What would they suggest you do? Why?*

Let's see what happened when Sarah and her therapist tackled the problem, as she described feeling worried about using a structured approach.

After empathizing with how worried Sarah was feeling, her therapist identified that the specific problem was the worry that the daycare would be harmful for her daughter, Chloe, and the staff wouldn't take good enough care of her baby. Together they brainstormed all the potential solutions, including Sarah staying at home and giving up her job, hiring a nanny, talking to friends about which daycare they used, visiting local childcare centers to see what they were like, talking to Richard's mother about whether she could help out, and talking to Richard about whether he could reduce his hours to part-time. Having written all this down, Sarah was surprised by how many solutions they had found. Talking over each solution helped Sarah realize that she did want to go back to work as she enjoyed her job, and they wouldn't have enough money if she gave up her job.

She and her therapist identified two small goals for the following week that would help start to solve the problem. The first was to talk to her friends about which daycares they knew of and set up a visit to one or two of them to see what they were like. The second goal was to have a conversation with Richard about his ideas for whether he could reduce his hours or talk to his mother about helping. Sarah described feeling relieved after this conversation that she had a plan to begin to tackle this problem, even though she still wasn't sure what the solution would look like.

Sarah filled out Worksheet 14: Problem Solving, with her therapist, which we can see in Figure 8.1.

Problem	Possible solutions	Advantages	Disadvantages	Best solution
When? Going back to work	Stay at home and give up my job	I could look after Chloe myself and would have lots of time with her	We couldn't afford it. I would really miss my work and my colleagues.	No
What was happening? Feeling really worried about putting Chloe in daycare—what will it be like?	Hire a nanny	I could choose who would be looking after her and would feel less guilty	We couldn't afford it	No
	Find a good daycare	We could afford childcare fees. Chloe would have other children to play with.	Worries that the care would not be one on one. Would it be harmful for her?	Maybe. Could have a look at some daycares and talk to friends.
Who was involved? Haven't spoken to anyone about it yet	Ask mother-in-law to help out	Would help us save money. She loves spending time with Chloe.	Haven't talked to mother-in-law about this. It would be a 30-minute commute for her here and back.	Maybe. Need to talk to mother-in-law.
What were you doing? Nothing yet apart from worrying a lot and avoiding talking about going back to work!	Ask Richard to reduce his hours and work part-time	Would feel more that we were sharing childcare, and it would be lovely for Richard to spend more time with Chloe.	I don't know whether we could afford it. Haven't spoken to him about this.	Maybe. Need to talk to Richard.

Figure 8.1

Sarah's Completed Worksheet 14: Problem Solving.

Troubleshooting

The concept of problem solving using a structured approach is best demonstrated using an example, so maintain a clear focus on identifying a problem with the parent and work through it using Worksheet 14: Problem Solving. This exercise may feel uncomfortable for the parent, particularly if it is a problem they have been putting off addressing or one that leaves them feeling upset or stuck in how they think about it. Use engagement skills to be warm and playful, and encourage the parent to think creatively and play around with ideas. Writing down a solution that is outrageous can often be a good way to release some tension and initiate imaginative thinking.

Home Practice

Toward the end of this session, you can discuss home practice to be done over the following week.

Use another copy of Worksheet 9: Weekly Goal Planner to choose the best solution for solving the problem and together decide on a small, manageable goal to put into practice over the next week to begin.

Discuss again the concept of "acting from the outside in" and the importance of planning activities into the day or week, rather than relying on mood or motivation to do them. Encourage the parent to use the problem-solving exercise to tackle other problems that come up during the week.

Remember to make the goal *concrete and specific* and to work through any potential obstacles. Another copy of Worksheet 10: Weekly Goal Record can be used to record on which days the goal was completed and any comments on it.

Summary of the Session and Feedback

At this point in the session, you can discuss with the parent how it has felt thinking about a problem and working through it systematically. Has it been hard to face up to the problem? Has it been a relief? Does the parent have ideas to move forward? What are they going to take away from today's session to manage other problems? Is there anything further that they want to discuss today?

Key Points

- Avoiding solving problems can cause them to grow and seem even more overwhelming.
- Thinking through the problem and possible solutions in a clear and balanced way helps tackle the problem head on.
- Deciding on small steps to start taking back control of issues that trouble us and bring our mood down can help us feel more in control and lift our mood.

✓ MODULE 3

Thinking

Helping Your Mind to Help You

The focus of Module 3 is on helping the parent to understand how different thinking styles can impact their mood.

There are two themes for this overall module:

- The first two sessions (Chapters 9 and 10/Sessions 7 and 8) focus on how getting stuck in unhelpful thinking, or rumination, can contribute to low mood and what to do about it. These sessions cover the key skills of being able to recognize when we are getting stuck in our thoughts, understanding why we are getting stuck, and finally identifying alternative strategies to change this thinking style.
- The second two sessions of this module (Chapters 11 and 12/Sessions 9 and 10) focus on how the way we talk warmly to ourselves, or the way we are compassionate toward ourselves, can help us exit unhelpful patterns of thought and lift our mood. They cover the key skills of noticing the warmth of our self-talk, understanding the meaning of compassion, using a compassionate image to increase the warmth of our self-talk, and how to use self-compassion in daily life.

During this module, hold in mind that you are encouraging the parent to develop what is known as a *meta-cognitive* perspective. This is the understanding that we are separate from our thoughts and that we can view our thinking as an action much as any other of our actions. In this way, you can help the parent to link the action of their thinking to their mood, and in changing this action, lift their mood.

CHAPTER 9

Session 7: Understanding How We Can Get Stuck in Our Thoughts

Aim of This Session

The aim of Session 7 is to help the parent recognize the process of getting stuck in their unhelpful thoughts and when they do it. You can explore in detail when and how this might happen, what keeps it going, and how it impacts their mood. For home practice ask the parent to notice when they are becoming stuck in their thoughts and to write this down.

Outline

- Set agenda 152
- Review of mood and how things are going 153
- Review home practice 153
- What is meant by getting stuck in our thoughts? 154
- Comparing unhelpful and helpful repetitive thinking 155
- Understanding how we get stuck in our thoughts 156
- Troubleshooting 157
- Home practice 159
- Summary of the session and feedback 159
- Key points 159

Postpartum Depression. Anne Stewart et al., Oxford University Press. © Oxford University Press (2026).
DOI: 10.1093/med-psych/9780197759707.003.0009

When to Conduct This Session

Session 7 is a core session within the Thinking Module. It helps the parent to understand how their thinking patterns may be contributing to their low mood. These skills are helpful when a parent frequently becomes stuck in cycles of negative thoughts that impact their mood, lower their self-esteem, and lead them to avoid engaging in activities they find meaningful. It is particularly useful if a parent has difficulty engaging in therapy due to feeling quickly overcome by their worries and negative thoughts or feeling that the therapy won't make any difference.

Materials Needed

- Worksheet 15: Understanding How We Get Stuck in Our Thoughts
- Worksheet 16: Getting Stuck in Your Thoughts Record

Worksheets appear in Appendix A at the end of this therapist guide and in Appendix A at the end of the parent workbook. Worksheets can also be accessed by searching for this book's title on the Oxford Academic platform, at academic.oup.com. Note that when more than one copy of a worksheet is required, you may photocopy the worksheets for the parent, ask the parent to make their own photocopies, or direct the parent to the book website to print their own.

Set Agenda

As usual, set the agenda collaboratively with the parent. You can first go through the overview of the session with the parent and write down the key topics for this session, then note down anything else that the parent would like to discuss in this session. Check out whether there are any practical issues for the parent or their baby that may impact the session, and work out with the parent how to manage these. Make sure that there is time at the end of the session to discuss the key points and get feedback from the parent.

Review of Mood and How Things Are Going

Review how the parent's mood has been since the last session. Have they experienced any symptoms of depression? If so, have these increased or decreased since the previous week? What positives have there been during the week? Were there any links between their mood and activities?

Review with the parent how they have got on with practicing their skills. Has the parent been able to:

- attend to their self-care: eating, sleeping, and exercising
- plan a daily or weekly routine
- balance depleting activities with nourishing ones
- address problems directly using a structured approach

Review these skills with the parent and discuss any positive impact experienced from carrying out these skills, as well as any difficulties or obstacles they have encountered when practicing these skills.

Review Home Practice

Review the home practice task that was set with the parent in your last session together. If following this guide and the workbook in chapter order, this task would have focused on a small goal to help the parent put problem-solving skills into practice.

Discuss what went well with the home practice and what were the challenges. Emphasize the importance of problem-solving the challenges with completing the home practice. At this point in therapy, the parent may have become familiar with this exercise of treating achievements and challenges with home practice just the same; all change can help us understand more about ourselves and how we may be susceptible to low mood. If the parent is confident with this approach, extend the discussion by helping them to also practice acceptance by describing what has happened without judgment or criticism. This is key for this module of being able to view our thoughts with a neutral, curious, and warm attitude.

What Is Meant by Getting Stuck in Our Thoughts?

Getting stuck in our thoughts, also known as *rumination*, is when we find ourselves thinking about something over and over (repetitively), but our focus is on the big, abstract, unsolvable parts of the issue (e.g., asking ourselves, "why" things are "always" this way). This pattern of thinking typically does not result in resolving or acting on what we are thinking about. It is usually accompanied by negative feelings such as worry, sadness, or frustration; and even when the thoughts are dismissed, they tend to recur.

Researchers have found strong links between ruminating and depression. Susan Nolen-Hoeksema defined rumination as "the tendency to focus repetitively and passively on one's symptoms of depression and on the possible causes and consequences of those symptoms without taking action to relieve them" (Nolen-Hoeksema, 1998, p. 237). Ed Watkins has worked extensively on translating our understanding and managing of rumination to specific intervention skills, and the material in these sessions is adapted from his work (Watkins, 2016).

First, discuss with the parent whether they recognize what getting stuck in their thoughts looks like. Useful terms that people might use when describing this thinking style include "lost in my thoughts," "I can't stop thinking about it," "being in my head," or "it's always on my mind." Encourage the parent to label this thinking style with a term or a phrase that means something to them.

Explain to the parent that this style of thinking about a problem, where the person goes over it again and again (repetitively) in their mind while focusing on the unsolvable "why's" in the problem, is known as rumination. Explain that it is often accompanied by negative feelings and that there is a strong link between getting stuck in our thoughts and low mood. Discuss with the parent whether they have noticed that when they are stuck in their thoughts in this way, there is an impact on their mood and their ability to fully engage what is happening around them.

Useful questions for this part of the session include:

- *Have you noticed that sometimes you think so much about something that it preoccupies you?*
- *What do you* not *notice when this is happening?*
- *What does this feel like?*
- *Do you find yourself thinking about it so much that it is difficult to notice what is happening around you?*
- *Does it prevent you from enjoying daily life?*
- *How hard is it to stop thinking about whatever is preoccupying you?*

Let's see how Sarah responded to this concept.

Sarah's therapist noticed that in previous sessions their conversations could often become one-sided as Sarah would talk at length and repetitively about something that was bothering her. It could be difficult for the therapist to stay on task with the session content or use the conversation to develop change. When Sarah's therapist introduced the material on unhelpful repetitive thinking, Sarah recognized this thinking style instantly. She described it as her "self-destructive thinking" and that she would go over and over a difficult situation in her head, wondering why she had behaved the way she had and why others had done what they did and what that might mean about who they were or how they felt about her. She would become irritable and worried, struggling to think about or attend to anything else.

Comparing Unhelpful and Helpful Repetitive Thinking

It is important to normalize that everyone engages in repetitive thinking from time to time as it is a natural reaction to being faced with something we need to understand or when we need to make a plan or solve a problem. We may think over and over about a situation or event when we feel there is a difference between how things are and how things should be: our expectations of life. However, there are important differences between repetitive thinking that is helpful and repetitive thinking that is unhelpful.

Table 9.1 appears in both this therapist guide and the parent workbook. Look at the table with the parent, and discuss what style of repetitive thinking they recognize themselves using when they need to think something through.

Table 9.1 Repetitive Thinking

Unhelpful repetitive thinking	Helpful repetitive thinking
Narrow focus on either self or other without integration	Focuses on all aspects of a situation: self, others, context
Negative, critical, angry, evaluative, or judgmental	Balanced, neutral, warm, curious
Focused on past or future events	Focused on the present
Lengthy, circular, unresolved, abstract	Short-term, resolved, concrete, specific
Questions focus on why?	Questions focus on how? when? what next?
Rehearsal of events or responses	Reflective about events or responses

Understanding How We Get Stuck in Our Thoughts

Using Worksheet 15: Understanding How We Get Stuck in Our Thoughts, choose an example with the parent of a time when, in the last week, they have found themselves stuck in their thoughts.

Begin by noting down, under "Brief description of situation," a quick description of what is getting stuck in the parent's thoughts. Be careful not to get too involved in the content; this needs to be a description of it such as "worries about breastfeeding" or "had an argument with my partner" rather than a detailed account.

Work through the prompts on the worksheet that enable you and the parent to complete a functional analysis of how they get stuck in their thoughts using the acronym CUDO: **C**ontext, **U**sefulness, **D**evelopment, and **O**ptions. You will come back to this exercise in the following session once the parent has used the home practice to notice more aspects about how they get stuck in their thoughts.

Useful questions for this part of the session include:

- *What does this exercise tell you about why you might get stuck in your thoughts?*
- *Is it an attempt to solve the situation?*

- *Is it a way to avoid acting on the situation?*
- *Is it a habit, a learned behavior from someone else?*
- *Is it an attempt to better understand why you or others might be feeling a certain way?*

Kenise initially found it hard to understand the concept of rumination.

Kenise wasn't sure what her therapist meant by getting stuck in her thoughts or how this was linked to her low mood. However, when she and her therapist reviewed her week together, she described forgetting to give Maya her art project homework to take to school as when her mood had taken a real dip. When she looked at this with her therapist, Kenise described getting caught up in her "I'm a bad mom" thoughts, and her therapist suggested they use this as an example for unhelpful repetitive thinking.

Figure 9.1 shows Kenise's completed worksheet.

Troubleshooting

Parents may sometimes become stuck in unhelpful repetitive thinking as you start to talk about this together. You may notice that you are finding it hard to break into a conversation or realize you are moving away from noticing the *process* and getting into the *content* of the parent's thoughts. Gently notice this with the parent, and name it together: "losing focus," "sticky thinking," or "going round and round" are all handy terms. When it occurs again, name what is happening warmly and clearly, and redirect the conversation to noticing what triggers are present for this style of repetitive thinking.

Parents may also struggle to identify the context of when they are getting stuck in their thoughts. Sometimes repetitive thinking and rumination can be very habitual and hard to notice. Discuss how the parent might notice they are stuck in their thoughts over the next week (e.g., a sense of losing time, being unable to get a certain thought out of their heads, or the family noticing that they are preoccupied), and then move on to collaboratively setting the home practice.

Brief description of situation where I can get stuck in my thoughts	Forgot Maya's art homework project for school. Saw all the other children in her class with art projects when she was on her way to the bus stop.
Context Where, when, who with, what, and how does it happen?	Trying to get everything right for school is often a trigger, so much to remember. Also happens at baby group. All the other moms look like they have it all together—why can't I?
Usefulness How did it help? How did I feel? What did it avoid? What are the consequences?	Felt awful, really low. Started thinking I was a bad mom and then beating myself up for not being able to cope and thinking that my daughter deserves better. Couldn't face the housework so watched TV, felt worse. Avoided actually doing something about it or just accepting I'd made a mistake.
Development When did it start? Where did I learn this from? Who did I learn this from?	My Dad was a hardworking businessman and would get really upset if he thought my Mom didn't do something "right" for us kids or around the house. I remember that. He was worried about us looking bad as a family. But that's not true now.
Options Are there times when I don't get stuck in my thoughts? What is different when my thoughts feel helpful?	My good friend Veena can make me laugh at myself, and I don't ruminate as much when I've been with her. She forgets stuff too and doesn't seem to mind. I'd like to be able to be more forgiving of myself like her. I'd be more fun as a parent and more relaxed, which is important to me.

Figure 9.1

Kenise's Completed Worksheet 15: Understanding How We Get Stuck in Our Thoughts.

Developed from Rumination-*focused cognitive behavioral therapy for depression* by Ed Watkins (2016).

Home Practice

Using Worksheet 16: Getting Stuck in Your Thoughts Record, ask the parent to fill it in over the next week when they notice they are getting stuck in their thoughts. Use the key points from discussing with the parent where, when, who with, what, and how rumination happens (the context) to highlight to the parent how they might notice they are stuck in unhelpful repetitive thinking.

Summary of the Session and Feedback

As usual, it is helpful to ask the parent what the main things are they have learned from the session. This is a good opportunity to check out whether they have understood the concepts and found them helpful and whether they felt the ideas about rumination applied to them. You can also ask whether there are any aspects of the session that they find unhelpful or topics that they don't feel are addressed adequately.

Key Points

- Getting stuck in our thoughts, also known as rumination, is when we find ourselves thinking about something over and over (repetitively) but without resolving or acting on what we are thinking about.
- Everyone engages in repetitive thinking from time to time as it is a natural reaction to being faced with something we need to understand or when we need to make a plan or solve a problem. However, there is a difference between unhelpful and helpful repetitive thinking.
- Keeping a record of our thoughts and thinking about the Context, Usefulness, Development, and Options for when we get stuck in our thinking can help us start to identify alternative strategies.

CHAPTER 10

Session 8: Finding Alternatives to Getting Stuck in Our Thoughts

Aim of This Session

The aim of Session 8 is to develop and practice alternative strategies to challenge unhelpful repetitive thinking. As in Session 7, Ed Watkins has worked extensively on translating our understanding and managing of rumination to specific intervention skills, and the material in this session is adapted from his work (Watkins, 2016). The first part of the session focuses on reviewing the parent's record of when they have found themselves stuck in their thoughts (Worksheet 16) and uses that information to add to the understanding from last session (Worksheet 15) of why this can happen. The second part of the session looks at identifying alternative strategies the parent could use to getting stuck in their thoughts (Worksheet 17) and opportunities to practice these.

Outline

- Set agenda 162
- Review of mood and how things are going 163
- Review home practice 163
- Unhelpful thinking as a form of avoidance 164
- Identifying strategies for getting stuck in unhelpful thinking 165
- Troubleshooting 167
- Home practice 169
- Summary of the session and feedback 169
- Key points 169

Postpartum Depression. Anne Stewart et al., Oxford University Press. © Oxford University Press (2026).
DOI: 10.1093/med-psych/9780197759707.003.0010

When to Conduct This Session

Session 8 is a follow-up to Session 7, which covered understanding how we can get stuck in our thoughts. In that session, you helped the parent notice and understand when they might get stuck in their thoughts and explore why. This session extends that exploration, further deepening the parent's understanding of why they might get stuck in their thoughts and helping them to develop alternative strategies to this thinking style.

Materials Needed

- Worksheet 9: Weekly Goal Planner
- Worksheet 10: Weekly Goal Record
- Worksheet 15: Understanding How We Get Stuck in Our Thoughts
- Worksheet 16: Getting Stuck in Your Thoughts Record
- Worksheet 17: Alternative Strategies to Getting Stuck in Our Thoughts

Worksheets appear in Appendix A at the end of this therapist guide and in Appendix A at the end of the parent workbook. Worksheets can also be accessed by searching for this book's title on the Oxford Academic platform, at academic.oup.com. Note that when more than one copy of a worksheet is required, you may photocopy the worksheets for the parent, ask the parent to make their own photocopies, or direct the parent to the book website to print their own.

Set Agenda

Start off by discussing the aims of the session together with the parent, and then set the agenda together based on these aims. This will include the standard items as well as the specific topic for this session. Ask the parent if they have anything else they want to discuss in today's session, and add this to the agenda. If the agenda is getting too long for the time available, you may need to discuss how to prioritize. If there are any current issues for the parent or their baby that might impact the session, discuss how to manage this, if appropriate using the problem-solving skills that have been discussed earlier in the program.

Review of Mood and How Things Are Going

As usual, check out how the parent's mood has been over the last week and whether there have been any symptoms of depression. Find out if these symptoms are improving or getting worse.

For this session, review with the parent if they have been able to:

- attend to their self-care: eating, sleeping, and exercising?
- plan a daily or weekly routine?
- balance depleting activities with nourishing ones?
- address problems directly using a structured approach?
- notice when they might be stuck in unhelpful thoughts?

Review these skills with the parent, and find out what has been going well, before inquiring about any difficulties or obstacles that have prevented practicing the skills.

Review Home Practice

Review the home practice task of completing Worksheet 16: Getting Stuck in Your Thoughts Record that was assigned to the parent this past week. Add what the parent noticed about this thinking style to the previously filled out Worksheet 15: Understanding How We Get Stuck in Our Thoughts. Discuss together what the parent has learned about when this thinking style can happen, why it has continued, and how it developed.

Discuss what went well with the home practice and what were the challenges. It may be relevant to gently notice with the parent if they become stuck in unhelpful thinking about the home practice. Take time to explore this a little using the skills discussed in Session 9. Is this a common pattern? When does this occur elsewhere? Discuss with the parent whether the unhelpful thinking led to avoiding doing the home practice, which leads directly into the first topic to be discussed this session.

Unhelpful Thinking as a Form of Avoidance

Often, we can get stuck in our thoughts because thinking over something is easier than doing something about it, otherwise known as *avoiding* rather than *approaching*. Repetitive thinking can feel as if we are acting to resolve the situation when actually we are avoiding acting. This may be due to worries about what would happen if we did act, such as conflict with someone we love, judgment from others, or facing into the loss or reality of a situation. Low mood can also make acting to solve a problem feel overwhelming. Avoiding acting may feel more helpful in the short term but can often make things worse in the long term.

Discuss with the parent whether they feel that sometimes getting stuck in their thoughts might be a way of avoiding acting on something they feel worried about. Are there examples they can think of where repetitive thinking has meant they have avoided acting on something they are worried about? What was the consequence for the situation? What was the impact on their mood? Add this information to Worksheet 15: Understanding How We Get Stuck in Our Thoughts.

Let's see how considering unhelpful repetitive thinking as a form of avoidance was useful for Lucy.

When Lucy and her therapist reviewed her Getting Stuck in Your Thoughts Record (Worksheet 16), they noticed that when Lucy spent time with her mom, this could trigger lots of unhelpful thinking. Lucy described her mother as wanting to help, so she often tried to give Lucy lots of advice about how to parent baby Jackson. Lucy felt frustrated with this and found herself having endless angry conversations in her head with her mom, which affected Lucy's mood for the rest of the day. Lucy and her therapist talked about what she was avoiding by doing this, and Lucy realized she was worried about telling her mother that she found her advice upsetting because she really valued her mom's practical support. Lucy and her therapist used the problem-solving worksheet (Worksheet 14) to think through ways Lucy could address this issue directly with her mother.

Identifying Strategies for Getting Stuck in Unhelpful Thinking

Identifying alternative strategies to getting stuck in unhelpful thinking is in line with the focus of Module 2: Activating: Doing Things That Make You Feel Better, by encouraging the parent to use skills that involve acting in a situation rather than avoiding. Use Worksheet 17: Alternative Strategies to Getting Stuck in Our Thoughts to help structure these ideas with the parent.

Research has shown that unhelpful repetitive thinking can interfere with our ability to notice and enjoy our activities and experiences and to be able to engage in effective problem solving. One of the first steps to unwinding unhelpful repetitive thinking can therefore be helping people to step outside of this pattern of thinking and directly engage in their experiences.

Focus on "Right Now"

Explain to the parent that focusing on what they can do in the here and now will help shift their focus from their thoughts back into the present. Changing the questions they are thinking about from "why" to "what" and "how" is often helpful. It can shift thinking from going over past events or worrying about future events into what is happening around the parent then and there. A good prompt for this is the question "What is the next thing I need to do *right now*?"

Focus on Action

Target the avoidance by moving toward action. Help the parent to decide whether they can act on a solution to what they are thinking about—for example, is it a problem, a conflict, or a task that can be addressed? Action moves the parent toward *doing* rather than *avoiding*, which will help to lift their mood. Integrate the skills here from Module 2, such as "acting from the outside in" and problem solving.

Focus on Distraction

At times, repetitive thinking can be so preoccupying or distressing that helping the parent to find strategies that distract them from these thoughts can be a useful option. This is particularly true when the parent cannot act on the thought—for example, if it is an upsetting memory, a catastrophic worry, or an intrusive thought—and therefore needs to distract from it. Knowing what activities really engage our attention is helpful and unique to each person; this distraction could be an engrossing TV show, a good book, or phoning a friend. Activities that meet our values in some way, or provide a sense of satisfaction or competence, can also be good for distraction; this could be checking something off the to-do list, finally putting all the clean laundry away, or sorting out a corner of the yard. Talk about what activities really engage the parent's attention, and problem-solve how the parent may be able to use the activity when they find themselves stuck in their thoughts.

Focus on Absorption

Anchoring ourselves to the present moment can be a helpful strategy to change our focus from inside our thoughts and back to the world around us. It is particularly useful for parents when they find themselves stuck in unhelpful thinking without an easily available distraction, such as in the middle of a feeding or during a baby group. Encourage the parent to practice ways they can become absorbed in their immediate experience. This could be focusing on their senses by deeply noticing what they can see, hear, touch, or smell, *at this moment*. Examples can be noticing the way the light is streaming through the open window, listening to the murmuring chatter of the cafe, smelling the aroma from the cup of coffee, and enjoying the way the cup feels warm to the hand. It could be becoming absorbed in their baby, focusing on the tiny details such as the baby's hands or eyes, what they are looking at, or what their facial expression may be conveying. Focusing on a calm, long breath is also useful during this practice and helps bring a sense of stillness.

Let's see what strategies Mila thought she would like to try as alternatives.

Mila has found breastfeeding her daughter Marta difficult and finds herself worrying constantly about Marta's weight gain. Her therapist has noticed that this is a frequent topic of conversation in their sessions, and on reviewing Mila's home practice, they notice Mila spends time every day thinking over why breastfeeding is not going well, comparing herself to her friends and going over all the things she feels she has done wrong. Together, Mila and her therapist work through understanding why she is getting stuck on these thoughts, and Mila realizes it helps her to avoid how bored and frustrated she feels with breastfeeding and the guilt associated with this. Mila and her therapist work through alternative strategies and make a small goal of Mila watching her favorite TV program while nursing to help distract her from her thoughts.

See Figure 10.1 for Mila's completed worksheet.

There is another example of this worksheet in Figure 12.1 in Chapter 12.

Troubleshooting

Sometimes it can be difficult to work out with a parent why a past memory or future worry is getting stuck in an unhelpful way. There are two options here:

1. If the memory or worry is linked to an intrusive or traumatic thought or image, it may be helpful to work through Optional Session 13: Understanding and Managing Intrusive Thoughts, Images, and Urges or 14: Understanding and Managing Traumatic Images or Memories. This will provide specific strategies that are helpful when the parent's thinking has become stuck due to a traumatic experience.

2. The second option is to link the memory or worry back to the core values discussed in Session 2. This can help pinpoint what it is about the memory or worry that is challenging the parent's values and what the parent could do to move toward action.

Brief description of situation where I can get stuck in my thoughts	When I am breastfeeding Marta, I end up totally lost in worries about how much weight she is gaining and feeling useless and hopeless about whether I am feeding her in the right way.
Right Now: Move toward a focus on the "here and now." What is the next thing you need to do right now?	Take some deep breaths. Notice that I am getting stuck in my thoughts. Remind myself that this won't help with feeling low. Focus on what I could do differently with my thoughts.
Action: Move toward action. What could you do to act on what you are thinking about?	This is hard. Keeping going with breastfeeding and telling myself I am doing okay is probably the most helpful.
Distraction: What activities really engage your attention that you could use to distract? Or those that give you a sense of satisfaction?	Put on my favorite TV show. It lifts my mood and stops me worrying. Make sure I have a drink of water and something healthy to snack on. Remind myself that I need to take care of my own needs as well.
Absorption: Practice absorbing yourself in your immediate experience to change your focus of attention. What could help remind you to do this?	Focus on my breath and relaxing my shoulders and my back. Every time there is a commercial break, make sure that my body is relaxed and take a drink of water.

Figure 10.1

Mila's Completed Worksheet 17: Alternative Strategies to Getting Stuck in Our Thoughts.

Home Practice

Using another copy of Worksheet 9: Weekly Goal Planner and another copy of Worksheet 10: Weekly Goal Record, decide with the parent on a specific alternative strategy to try when they notice they are stuck in their thinking.

Summary of the Session and Feedback

At the end of the session, you can check out with the parent what they have learned in the session and what they have found helpful. There may be things the parent did not fully understand, so now is the opportunity to clarify. The parent may feel that some issues haven't been discussed enough, so this is something you may want to come back to in future sessions. As always, it is really productive to give the parent the chance to provide feedback so that sessions can be as helpful as possible.

Key Points

- Often, we can get stuck in our thoughts because thinking over something (avoiding) is easier than doing something about it (approaching). Repetitive thinking can feel as if we are acting to resolve the situation when actually we are avoiding acting.
- Identifying alternative strategies to getting stuck in unhelpful thinking can help develop strategies to act in a situation rather than avoid. Focusing on "right now" and moving toward action can help approach the cause of the unhelpful thinking rather than avoid it. Focusing on distraction and absorption is a way of acting to address the unhelpful thinking when it is not possible to change or problem-solve the thoughts directly.

CHAPTER 11

Session 9: Understanding the Importance of Self-Compassion

Aim of This Session

The aim of Session 9 is to introduce self-compassion, work through an exercise to create a compassionate image, and set a home practice of bringing this image to mind daily.

Outline

- Set agenda 172
- Review of mood and how things are going 172
- Review home practice 173
- Introducing self-compassion 174
- Using an image to practice self-compassion 176
- Troubleshooting 180
- Home practice 181
- Summary of the session and feedback 181
- Key points 182

When to Conduct This Session

Introducing self-compassion to the parent is helpful when their low mood is related to persistent self-criticism, feelings of failure, or meeting the needs of others before their own. Such thoughts often get stuck in unhelpful repetitive patterns, and therefore this session is a natural follow-up to the sessions on rumination. The skills in self-compassion are also focused on connecting with feelings of love, safety, and self-acceptance, which can support engaging with meaningful and valued

Postpartum Depression. Anne Stewart et al., Oxford University Press. © Oxford University Press (2026).
DOI: 10.1093/med-psych/9780197759707.003.0011

behaviors. These sessions are therefore helpful for parents who may engage well with the technical aspects of therapy but struggle to connect with their feelings in sessions.

Materials Needed

- Worksheet 9: Weekly Goal Planner
- Worksheet 10: Weekly Goal Record
- Worksheet 16: Getting Stuck in Your Thoughts Record
- Worksheet 18: Using an Image to Practice Self-compassion

Worksheets appear in Appendix A at the end of this therapist guide and in Appendix A at the end of the parent workbook. Worksheets can also be accessed by searching for this book's title on the Oxford Academic platform, at academic.oup.com. Note that when more than one copy of a worksheet is required, you may photocopy the worksheets for the parent, ask the parent to make their own photocopies, or direct the parent to the book website to print their own.

Set Agenda

At this later stage in therapy, you may want to encourage the parent to take a lead on the agenda. Explain the key topics you would like to cover, and then build the order of the session together. Use this opportunity to gently notice with the parent any topics they may be ruminating on (wanting to focus the agenda on just one issue) or, in contrast, avoiding (not mentioning an issue that has seemed important or painful previously). Discuss any practicalities for the parent or their baby that may impact the session, and agree how to manage these.

Review of Mood and How Things Are Going

Review how the parent's mood has been since the last session. Discuss what symptoms have been present and whether they have increased or decreased.

Review with the parent how they are getting on with their skills. Has the parent had the opportunity to:

- attend to their self-care: eating, sleeping, and exercising?
- plan a daily or weekly routine?
- balance depleting activities with nourishing ones?
- address problems directly using a structured approach?
- notice when they might be stuck in unhelpful thoughts?
- use action or distraction as an alternative to getting stuck in unhelpful thoughts?

Review these skills with the parent, and discuss any difficulties or obstacles that have been present since the last session.

Review Home Practice

Review the home practice task that was set with the parent in your last session together. If you are following this guide and the workbook in chapter order, this would have been coming up with a small goal to use as an alternative action or distraction strategy when getting stuck in unhelpful repetitive thinking.

Discuss what went well with the home practice and what were the challenges. Session 9: Understanding the Importance of Self-Compassion and Session 10: Putting Self-Compassion into Action build on the work you have focused on in previous sessions with the parent on developing a curious, warm, non-judgmental, and accepting attitude to the achievements and obstacles of home practice. These qualities are foundational to being able to take a compassionate attitude to the process of setting goals and trying to achieve them. If you have noticed in previous sessions that the parent finds this difficult, particularly if self-criticism gets in the way, then these sessions on compassion are especially important. Take time to gently notice with the parent what their internal self-talk is regarding home practice and what qualities it may have.

Kristin Neff, a leading researcher on self-compassion, describes the concept as follows: "self-compassion entails treating oneself with kindness, recognizing one's shared humanity, and being mindful when considering negative aspects of oneself" (Neff, 2011, p. 1).

Self-compassion focuses on the tone and approach of how we talk to ourselves. Our internal voice can significantly impact our mood. If we talk to ourselves with a harsh, critical voice, it is difficult to feel uplifted, encouraged, and positive, especially when facing challenges. However, if we can learn to talk to ourselves in a warm, wise, and understanding voice that accepts we are human and encourages us to keep going, it can help lift our mood and focus on moving forward. Being self-compassionate is a way of approaching problems and difficult situations with a gentle and forgiving stance, involving acceptance that we are human and can make mistakes.

Research has investigated how increasing our self-compassion can benefit our mental health. Therapeutically, Paul Gilbert developed the idea of a "compassionate mind" approach in compassion-focused therapy (Gilbert, 2010; Gilbert, 2014). The material in these sessions is adapted from his work and the work of Deborah Lee on the links between self-compassion, trauma, and attachment (Lee & James, 2012).

Discuss with the parent what the word *compassion* means to them and how compassionate they feel they are toward themselves. It can be useful to compare how compassionate they are to others with how compassionate they are to themselves. Often, we are much better at being warm, encouraging, and empathic to other people than we are to ourselves; and in fact, we can be overly negative and self-critical. Table 11.1 provides a comparison of negative self-talk with compassionate self-talk.

Table 11.1 Comparing Negative Self-Talk and Compassionate Self-Talk

Negative, critical self-talk	Compassionate self-talk
Oh, I forgot my mom's birthday! How could I be so stupid? She's going to be upset with me. This is awful! What am I going to do? It's such a disaster. Why am I always doing things like this? I can't seem to remember things anymore. What's wrong with me?	Oh, I forgot my mom's birthday! I was so busy rushing around when the kids were sick. I wonder what I can do? Poor mom, but maybe I could call her or send flowers? I'll call her. This is a wake-up call. I think I need to slow down a bit and give myself time and space. She'll understand.
Wow, I just sat down, and the baby has woken already from his nap! I knew I shouldn't rush around so much and should've given him more time to settle before I left the room. I was so distracted. I'm just not catching his signs of tiredness. Why didn't I do it right? This is all my fault. I'm so tired. Why don't I get a break? Every day is like this. It's so horrible.	Wow, I just sat down, and the baby has woken already from his nap! And I so need a rest from how much we did this morning. I wonder what woke him? I'll get his pacifier and see if he wants to snuggle on the couch. Then I can finish my sandwich, and we can rest together. Oh, this is so tough, and I'm tired too! This is being a mom, right? I've got to remind myself I'm doing okay and sometimes naps just don't go to plan. We're doing okay. We'll get there.

Useful questions for this part of the session include:

- *What comes into your mind when you hear the word* compassion?
- *Are there any people who embody compassion for you?*
- *How are you with feeling compassion toward other people?*
- *How are you with feeling compassion toward yourself?*

Let's see what compassion meant to Zainab.

Zainab could see that her internal voice was negative and critical, and through talking with her therapist, she was surprised to realize how this extended to all aspects of her life—how she looked, parented, did domestic chores, and thought about what she had achieved in life. Zainab made the link quickly with how this would impact her low mood and described that when she felt low she would be even more critical of herself, telling herself she was wrong to feel sad, criticizing herself for being depressed, and berating herself for being too weak to overcome it. Her therapist asked if this internal voice changed or helped how Zainab was feeling, and she tearfully replied that she knew it made her feel worse but that she couldn't see an alternative.

Using an Image to Practice Self-Compassion

Introducing the concept of compassion to the parent through the use of an image helps in several ways. It is important that the parent has a quick way to practice being compassionate to themselves as, like with any other skill or habit we want to do more often, it takes repeated practice. In the beginning, it can be hard to even imagine saying compassionate things to ourselves, and using imagery is a helpful way to link compassionate feelings to a familiar and quickly available image. With the repeated practice of using the image to connect to feelings, a compassionate image can help the parent feel warm, encouraged, and relaxed.

Using Worksheet 18: Using an Image to Practice Self-Compassion, explain to the parent that developing self-compassion is a skill that takes practice. Explain that one of the features of low mood is that people tend to blame themselves for things that go wrong, and so it takes some work to counter that and develop their compassion.

Ask the parent to first allow an image to come to mind that best represents compassion to them. Remind them that the key qualities of compassion are warmth, strength, wisdom, and acceptance. Encourage the parent to take their time when thinking through what comes to mind and not to worry if they feel blank or uninspired but to stay with the task.

Discuss with the parent that the image may be a color, a shape, a place, something from nature, or a person. There are some examples for inspiration in Figure 11.1, which appears in both the therapist guide and parent workbook. These examples have been chosen from nature, but there is a wide range of images from which the parent may choose. If the selected image is a person, it is best that this is not someone who the parent knows currently as this relationship will be vulnerable to stresses that can affect any relationship, and this may impact the safety of the image.

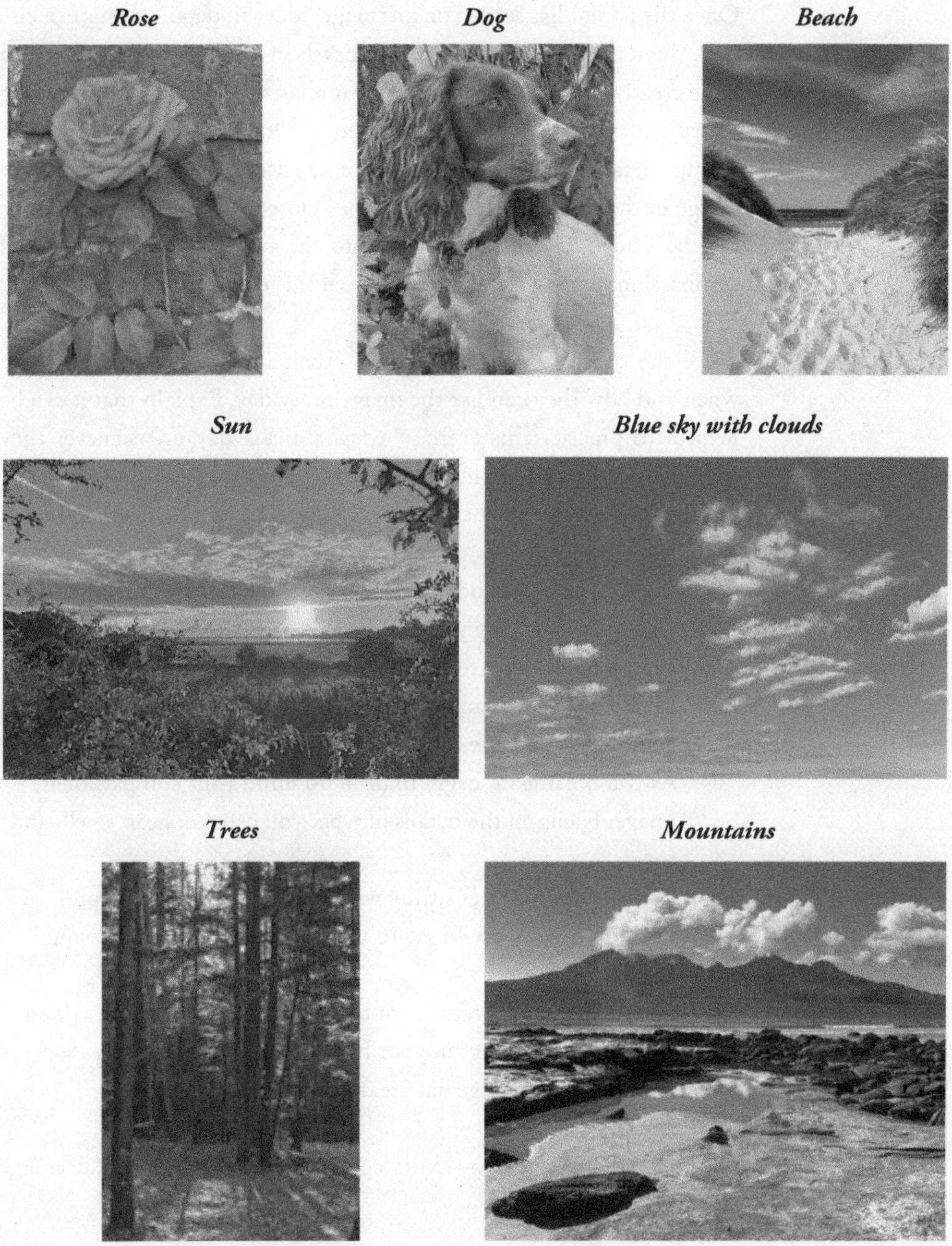

Figure 11.1

Examples of Compassionate Images

Once the parent has settled on an image, focus in detail on this exercise with them using the questions on Worksheet 18. Encourage the parent to be creative and to play with ideas, emphasizing that this is something to try and to learn from the experience. Once you have developed a strong, detailed image with the parent, encourage them to hold the image in their mind (it may help if they close their eyes) and to breathe deeply. Encourage them to hold onto the image and the feelings of compassion in their mind and stay with this experience.

Once the parent is comfortable with their image, discuss with them when and how they can use the image every day. Explain that it can be helpful to practice this exercise a few times a day or whenever they notice themselves becoming self-critical or stuck in unhelpful thinking. The following steps can be helpful actions to bring the image to mind:

- Try to relax your body, whatever position you are in, and notice where in your body you are tense or constricted. Uncross your legs and arms, and relax your shoulders and neck.
- Breathe in deeply, and breathe out slowly. It may help to close your eyes if it is safe to do so.
- As you breathe in, begin to bring to mind your compassionate image. Focus on the details of what you can see, hear, smell, and touch.
- Spend a few minutes sitting with your image, and if helpful, imagine what it would say to you right now and how it would like you to feel.
- Gently and slowly return yourself to your surroundings, taking with you the feelings in your body and mind that your compassionate image has created.

Figure 11.2 illustrates how Mila completed her compassionate image worksheet.

	Describe in detail (hold in mind the qualities of strength, wisdom, warmth, and acceptance)
My compassionate image is:	My church
Where are you?	I am sitting at the back of the church. My eyes are closed, and my head, neck, and shoulders are relaxed. My hands are loose in my lap, and my feet are firmly on the floor.
What can you see in your image? *(e.g., color, shape, movement)*	I can see myself walking in through the light white front door and sitting down at the back of the church. No one else has arrived yet, and it feels familiar and comfortable. There is sunlight coming through the door behind me.
What can you hear in your image? *(e.g., voice, other sounds)*	It is completely still and silent. I enjoy how calm and quiet it is.
What does your image want you to feel?	Peaceful, calm, and held. I feel a sense of space, stillness, and freedom. I know that no one will disturb me, and I can take a moment to be quiet and serene.
What does your image want to say to you?	It tells me that I am doing my best, even when things are difficult. It tells me that other people are doing their best, even when it doesn't seem that way.
What does your image want you to know?	It wants me to know that I am enough, and I need to take care of myself. I am safe, and everything will be okay.
What else is important to you about this image?	The peace and the stillness allow me to feel calm about whatever I am facing, my daily tasks, a worry, or a problem. I feel able to take a moment to focus and think clearly.

Figure 11.2

Mila's Completed Worksheet 18: Using an Image to Practice Self-Compassion.

Developed from compassion-focused imagery work by Paul Gilbert (2010).

Troubleshooting

The parent may find this type of creative visualization exercise difficult. If this is the case, then you can begin by asking them to bring a positive memory to mind and focus their attention on what in the memory they can see, hear, and feel. Once the parent can describe this, move on to asking them to visualize a safe place, bringing to mind a place where they feel calm and at ease. This can be either a real place or an imaginary place. Encourage them to allow the image to materialize in their mind, and then ask them to describe what they can see, hear, smell, and feel. Once they have practiced this visualization, ask them to move on to building the compassionate image.

It can also help to focus on concrete cues for compassionate feelings if visualization is difficult, for example, thinking of a key phrase to repeat to encourage self-compassion, such as "I am doing the best that I can" or "I am enough." Asking the parent to record when they notice they are being self-critical over the next week using another copy of Worksheet 16: Getting Stuck in Your Thoughts Record can also help to identify this style of thinking and consider alternative phrases to try out.

It is not unusual when first trying to think of a compassionate image to have self-critical thoughts about not deserving the compassion that comes to mind. It may be useful in these instances to normalize these experiences and then guide the parent toward images that are less related to a person or specific experience. Some parents might also find it difficult to let go of their self-critical voice and move into a compassionate mind. If this is the case, return to the work on understanding when we get stuck in our thoughts from Session 7/Chapter 9, and explore the meaning of this thinking style to them. Is it a way of motivating them? Often a critical inner voice can be a way of trying to ensure that feared or disliked attributes such as laziness, silliness, or untidiness are prevented. Look at both the advantages and disadvantages of this style of thinking. The disadvantage is the impact on the parent's low mood. Explore the attributes of compassion that relate to strength and wisdom and how these attributes might help motivate the parent instead. Return to developing an inner voice that encourages and praises, rather than one that judges and criticizes.

Home Practice

Using another copy of Worksheet 9: Weekly Goal Planner and another copy of Worksheet 10: Weekly Goal Record, the home practice for this session is for the parent to practice bringing to mind their compassionate image daily for 5–10 minutes. Problem-solve what will remind them to do this; good reminders include putting a photo of a favorite place on the fridge; a small, colored dot on the TV remote or phone; or a symbol of nature on their keychain. Writing a compassionate phrase on an index card or Post-it and placing this somewhere easily visible can also be a helpful reminder.

Let's see how the compassionate image exercise was useful to Lucy.

Lucy initially struggled with finding a compassionate image, feeling uncomfortable and unable to settle on any one thing. Her therapist asked her to visualize a safe place, and she described sitting in a park she liked. This gave her the idea of using a maple tree as her compassionate image. She and her therapist took time to work through this image in detail, imagining precisely where Lucy would be in relation to the tree, what the weather would be, and what Lucy was wearing. Lucy described sitting under the tree with her back against the trunk. It was early morning in springtime, and she was wearing a soft, warm shirt. She was looking up at the tree and could see the sunlight playing through the green leaves. Lucy imagined the tree talking to her in a deep, low, warm voice, reassuring her with its age and strength; and she felt relaxed and peaceful. The tree repeated to her "This too shall pass," which Lucy found comforting. Lucy felt pleased with the final image and interested in trying out the exercise. She decided to collect some maple leaves to dry and put in her kitchen as a reminder, and she also wrote "This too shall pass" on Post-it notes to put in her bedroom and bathroom.

Summary of the Session and Feedback

Compassionate mind may be a new concept to the parent, so it is important to check out what they are taking away from the session as well as what has been helpful or unhelpful. You can ask them for specific feedback on how the session went and what might be improved for next time. In particular, it might be worth checking what they understand of the concept. By this stage in therapy the parent should feel relaxed about giving you feedback as their therapist. Making it a routine part of each session helps with this.

Key Points

- How we talk to ourselves with our internal voice can significantly impact our mood. If we talk to ourselves in a harsh, critical voice that always tells us we must do better, it is difficult to feel uplifted, encouraged, and positive.
- However, if we can learn to talk to ourselves in a warm, wise, and understanding voice that accepts we are human and encourages us to keep going, it can help lift our mood and focus on moving forward.
- Being self-compassionate is a way of thinking helpfully about problems and difficult situations, involving accepting that we are human and can make mistakes.
- It can be easier to feel compassionate if you have an image in your head that links with this feeling. Images are good at helping us link to the feelings that go with them, so practicing visualizing a compassionate image helps us feel warm, encouraged, and relaxed.

CHAPTER 12 Session 10: Putting Self-Compassion Into Action

Aim of This Session

Session 10 aims to reinforce the importance of self-compassion and brainstorm ways to integrate this into the parent's daily life. At this stage in the treatment program, you will start to bring together the different skills the parent has learned in preparation for creating the "Staying Well Plan" (Worksheet 19) in the next two sessions, which highlights all the learning that has been achieved.

Outline

- Set agenda 184
- Review of mood and how things are going 185
- Review home practice 185
- Combining self-compassion with behavioral activation 186
- Combining self-compassion with a daily nourishing activity 187
- Combining self-compassion with problem solving 188
- Combining self-compassion with alternative strategies to getting stuck in unhelpful thinking 190
- Troubleshooting 193
- Home practice 193
- Summary of the session and feedback 193
- Key points 194

Postpartum Depression. Anne Stewart et al., Oxford University Press. © Oxford University Press (2026).
DOI: 10.1093/med-psych/9780197759707.003.0012

When to Conduct This Session

This session is a follow-up to Session 9: Understanding the Importance of Self-Compassion. Take time in this session to review with the parent the daily home practice of bringing to mind their compassionate image, and troubleshoot any difficulties that may have arisen.

Materials Needed

- Worksheet 9: Weekly Goal Planner
- Worksheet 10: Weekly Goal Record

One of:

- Worksheet 13: Nourishing and Depleting Activities
- Worksheet 14: Problem Solving
- Worksheet 17: Alternative Strategies to Getting Stuck in Our Thoughts

From previous session:

- Worksheet 18: Using an Image to Practice Self-Compassion

Worksheets appear in Appendix A at the end of this therapist guide and in Appendix A at the end of the parent workbook. Worksheets can also be accessed by searching for this book's title on the Oxford Academic platform, at academic.oup.com. Note that when more than one copy of a worksheet is required, you may photocopy the worksheets for the parent, ask the parent to make their own photocopies, or direct the parent to the book website to print their own.

Set Agenda

Collaboratively set the agenda with the parent. In particular, Session 10 includes topics that can be focused on where the parent would like to integrate self-compassion skills into everyday life. Use your formulation/case conceptualization of the parent that you developed through previous therapy sessions to think about which topics would be most relevant. Discuss any practicalities for the parent or their baby that may impact the session, and agree how to manage these.

Review of Mood and How Things Are Going

Review how the parent's mood has been since the last session. Discuss what symptoms have been present and whether they have increased or decreased. Check out how they are getting on using their skills. Has the parent had the opportunity to:

- attend to their self-care: eating, sleeping, and exercising
- plan a daily or weekly routine
- balance depleting activities with nourishing ones
- address problems directly using a structured approach
- notice when they might be stuck in unhelpful thoughts
- use action or distraction as an alternative to getting stuck in unhelpful thoughts
- use their compassionate mind to be kind to themselves

Review these skills with the parent, and discuss any difficulties or obstacles that have been present since the last session.

Review Home Practice

Review the home practice task that was set with the parent to practice visualizing their compassionate image daily. Use Worksheet 18: Using an Image to Practice Self-Compassion, completed in the last session, to integrate the learning from the home practice.

At this stage, take time if needed to adapt the image according to what worked and what didn't. You may need to add the challenges that occurred to the agenda and think through with the parent what it was that made certain aspects difficult. Notice with the parent when the compassionate image was helpful and when it wasn't, when it came to mind easily and when it didn't, and other specific triggers that may have affected using it—such as the time of day, people the parent was with, or how well rested they were. How the parent managed the achievements and obstacles created by the home practice presents an opportunity to practice in-the-moment compassionate self-talk and model a warm, non-judgmental, open, and curious attitude to the discussion.

Combining Self-Compassion With Behavioral Activation

You can choose one of the already introduced skills with the parent to combine with self-compassion skills to work on in this session. This has the effect of rehearsing and adapting both sets of skills and integrating them further into the parent's everyday life. It emphasizes the importance of action and how to make self-compassion a regular, lived practice, rather than a passive image or thought.

Choose one of the following skills to combine with self-compassion:

- daily nourishing activity
- problem solving
- alternative strategies to getting stuck in unhelpful thinking

Choosing which skill to combine with self-compassion in this session may depend on several factors. These include:

1. which previously introduced skill may be most helpful in addressing the parent's low mood
2. which skill could do with more practice
3. which skill is being impacted the most by self-critical or judgmental thoughts

Collaboratively make this decision with the parent through using your understanding of their formulation/case conceptualization of their low mood, and therefore what would be the most effective. Reviewing the qualities of compassion from the last session with the parent may be helpful at this point.

Combining Self-Compassion With a Daily Nourishing Activity

It is important when discussing self-compassion to emphasize that it is a skill just like any other that must be scheduled and rehearsed. All too easily we can say, "I must be kinder to myself" or "I must look after myself" without really making the effort to plan it into a routine to practice, practice, practice. It simply becomes another "should" on a long list of things that are hard to get done. Making self-compassion an act, rather than simply a thought, is key to changing how we think and feel toward ourselves.

For this part of the session, use another copy of Worksheet 13: Nourishing and Depleting Activities. Ask the parent to think of a typical day and write down a list of all the things that they do. Review the list together, and decide whether each activity is nurturing or depleting. Ask the parent to bring their compassionate image to mind and use this to look at the balance of nourishing to depleting activities across the day. While using this worksheet in previous sessions helped focus on self-care skills and reminding the parent to meet their own needs as well as everyone else's, in this session the focus is on developing and holding a self-compassionate stance to really connect with how it might feel to practice meeting one's own needs every day. Self-compassion practice can strongly connect us with feelings that might be getting in the way of self-care, which previously may have been hard to express. Challenging these feelings affectively as well as cognitively can be very useful and bring new perspective.

Useful questions for this part of the session include:

- *When is the hardest or most depleting part of the day?*
- *When do you notice yourself becoming self-critical?*
- *Bring your compassionate image to mind. What would your compassionate image say about the balance of nourishing to depleting activities in your day or week?*
- *How would it feel to be self-compassionate and meet your own needs every day?*
- *What would remind you to be self-compassionate when you are most self-critical?*
- *What would your compassionate image say to encourage you?*
- *What would your compassionate image say to thoughts about self-care not being important?*

Let's see how using self-compassion while balancing nourishing and depleting activities across the day helped Lucy.

Lucy had found a compassionate image of a maple tree that she liked and tried it out a few times during the week, which she had found comforting. However, she added how tired she was feeling to the session agenda as she was concerned that this was still a problem she worried about and therapy was nearing the final session. Her therapist suggested they write down the balance of nourishing to depleting activities in Lucy's day again. Lucy and her therapist noticed that she was working hard to do so many different things for the house and for baby Jackson during the day.

The therapist asked Lucy to bring her compassionate image of the maple tree to mind and to look again at the balance of activities in her day using this self-compassionate feeling. To her surprise, Lucy became immediately very tearful and described her image as reminding her that "You are enough." Her therapist explored gently why this felt painful to hear, and Lucy described strong feelings of guilt as Jackson's father was not in his life and wanting to do everything herself to make it up to him and show everyone that they were just fine. Her therapist empathized and accepted how difficult these feelings were and reminded Lucy to stay with the feelings and use her compassionate image to soothe herself. Lucy began to feel calmer, and she and her therapist looked again at the balance of activities in her day and made a small goal for Lucy to let her family help with some of the housework during the following week and notice how this made her feel.

Combining Self-Compassion With Problem Solving

An important art of developing self-compassion is understanding how it combines warmth with strength and acceptance with wisdom. It is not simply empathy or letting things go but also involves maintaining boundaries, choosing difficult solutions, and saying no. A helpful way to demonstrate this can be to use the parent's compassionate image during structured problem solving. This can be particularly effective if a parent is struggling to see the usefulness of self-compassion or frequently gets into "shoulds" and "musts."

Use another copy of Worksheet 14: Problem Solving to explore a current problem that the parent has. Encourage the parent to hold their compassionate image in mind and listen to what it is suggesting when writing possible solutions to problems. Ask the parent what the self-compassionate response would be to this problem. Work through the advantages and disadvantages of each solution with the same self-compassionate perspective. Notice with the parent how taking this perspective changes their thinking during the exercise and what this is like.

Let's see how Sarah used self-compassion to help with problem solving.

Sarah is struggling with using her compassionate image, which is a childhood pet, and has difficulty connecting to a warmer, accepting internal voice. She has often used a critical voice to motivate herself to overcome difficulties in her life. Her therapist suggests that they problem-solve a situation that Sarah is ruminating about—whether she should take Chloe to a friend's party some distance away this weekend. It's a baby shower for a close friend of Sarah's who she would really like to see and introduce her to Chloe, but she worries how she will cope with managing Chloe's needs at the same time. Sarah works through the solutions, and her therapist encourages her to use her compassionate image.

Sarah finds connecting with her self-compassion easier when engaged in a practical exercise. She is surprised that it encourages her to go to the party and to focus on taking care of her own needs as well as Chloe's. She notices that her self-compassion encourages her to drive to the party during the baby's naptime, stay just a few hours, and buy a cake rather than make one. This feels like a much more balanced option, and Sarah is pleased with this solution. She talks to her therapist about her relief in realizing her compassionate image can help her make wise choices as this is something she values.

Combining Self-Compassion With Alternative Strategies to Getting Stuck in Unhelpful Thinking

Developing a self-compassionate voice is a natural extension to the skills developed in noticing and addressing unhelpful repetitive thinking. If the parent is very self-critical in their repetitive thinking, it is important in this session to focus on using their compassionate image as an alternative strategy to address this self-criticism.

Use another copy of Worksheet 17: Alternative Strategies to Getting Stuck in Our Thoughts to work through a recent or frequent situation with the parent where they became stuck in unhelpful thinking. Encourage the parent to bring to mind their compassionate image and practice combining self-compassion with using the strategies on the worksheet.

Figure 12.1 is an example of Zainab's completed Worksheet 17.

Useful questions for this part of the session include:

To focus on Right Now:

- *What are the ways to bring your compassionate image into the present?*
- Can you focus on the different senses that you have described in your compassionate image—what you can hear, see, touch, or smell?\
- *Can you find a picture of your image, a smell from it, or a sound to place around your home?*
- *What will remind you to use your compassionate image when you are stuck in unhelpful thinking?*

To focus on Action:

- *What activities does your compassionate image encourage when you feel you are stuck in your thoughts?*
- *What could you do to take care of yourself?*
- *How could you do something that is different while taking care of yourself?*
- *How could you pair a self-care activity with something that is unpleasant?*

Brief description of situation where I can get stuck in my thoughts	Tauseef is late home from work, and I have had the children all day. I end up having an imaginary argument with him in my head and get irritable with the children.
Right Now: Move toward a focus on the "here and now." What is the next thing you need to do *right now*?	Put on a TV show for the children and give them a quick snack. Use my compassionate image to help me with my mood.
Action: Move toward action. What could you do to *act* on what you are thinking about?	Make myself a cup of tea, sit down, take some deep breaths. Bring my compassionate image to mind. Make some notes on my phone about what to calmly discuss with Tauseef about how I feel when he is late.
Distraction: What activities really engage your attention that you could use to distract? Or those that give you a sense of satisfaction?	Call a friend. Fold clothes from the dryer as I talk to her. Share how I am feeling, but also get all the clothes folded, which always makes me feel calmer and gives me a sense of achievement!
Absorption: Practice absorbing yourself in your immediate experience to change your focus of attention. What could help remind you to do this?	Take more deep breaths. Focus on the taste of my favorite drink, my children's laughter at their favorite TV show, the softness of my favorite chair. Repeat my compassionate image (my grandmother's comforting phrase), "You're doing fine, keep going, you'll get there."

Figure 12.1

Zainab's Completed Worksheet 17: Alternative Strategies to Getting Stuck in Our Thoughts with Compassion.

To focus on Distraction:

- *What activities help distract you and help you look after yourself?*
- *What stops you from engaging in an activity that distracts you and that you enjoy?*
- *Can you use your compassionate image to help you schedule in this activity?*

To focus on Absorption:

- *Can you distract yourself from your stuck thoughts by deepening and immersing yourself in your compassionate image? For example, take a breath, look at the image, and then focus on the details including noticing the different colors.*
- *What breathing exercises can you use to connect to your experience of your compassionate image?*

Let's see how Sarah used self-compassion to manage unhelpful thinking about the upcoming party.

When Sarah was driving to the party, she found herself suddenly lost in overwhelming self-critical thinking about everything that might go wrong. She worried about how she would find being with the other parents because at a baby group the previous week, Chloe became grumpy and agitated when there were lots of other moms and babies. Sarah worried that other parents at the party might think Chloe was a demanding baby and Sarah would be judged for being a bad parent. Noticing how self-critical she was being, she took a deep breath and brought her compassionate image to mind. Slowing her breathing helped her focus on the compassionate feelings, and she was able to find her self-compassionate voice. This reassured Sarah that all the other parents would have had times when their babies were cranky, and they would know how this would feel. She remembered that her good friend Jess had messaged to say she would be there as well, and Jess was always a good support when Chloe was restless. Sarah decided she would ask Jess for help to distract Chloe if needed or to come with her to the yard if Sarah felt it was getting to be too much, and then she felt much calmer again.

Troubleshooting

When combining self-compassion with previous skills it can be tricky to keep the focus on self-compassion. Frequently bring the parent's attention back to keeping their compassionate image in their mind throughout the exercise. This is a helpful rehearsal for keeping the image in mind while also doing a task and using it for a practical purpose. Keep a playful, creative attitude during this time to discourage self-consciousness and to help the parent play with ideas and try out what works. Compassionate images can be emotive and leave the parent feeling vulnerable and exposed, so creating a safe therapeutic space to explore these ideas is essential.

Home Practice

Using another copy of Worksheet 9: Weekly Goal Planner and another copy of Worksheet 10: Weekly Goal Record, the home practice for this session is to choose a small goal to practice self-compassion in combination with one of the previously learned skills. Again, problem-solve with the parent how they will remember to use their compassionate image or self-compassion practice as it is a new and different thinking style that will take time to develop into a habit. It would also be helpful to discuss with the parent that, as the next two sessions will focus on staying well after therapy ends, it may be useful to arrange for a partner or other supportive person to attend one or both of these sessions. Discuss with the parent whether they would find that helpful and emphasize that choosing to have someone attend these sessions is their decision.

Summary of the Session and Feedback

You can now check out how the parent found this session and what they are going to take away from the discussion. Has it been challenging to incorporate self-compassion into the skills they have learned through this program? Has it been helpful? How has the discussion changed the way the parent views things?

Key points

- All the previously introduced skills in this treatment program can be combined with self-compassion. This helps rehearse and adapt the skills and integrates them further into the parent's daily life.
- Self-compassion is a skill just like any other that needs practice. It is all too easy to say, "I must be kinder to myself" or "I must look after myself" without really making the effort to practically plan when we do it. Making self-compassion an act, rather than simply a thought, is key to changing how we think and feel toward ourselves.

✓ MODULE 4

Heading to the Future

Planning How to Stay Well

The focus of Module 4, the final module in this treatment program, is on reviewing the parent's progress and what they have learned throughout the therapy, discussing how to consolidate changes already made, identifying goals for the future, and developing a relapse prevention plan including coping strategies for the inevitable challenges that will occur.

The aim of this module is to develop a collaborative narrative with the parent as to why therapy began and how to continue to stay healthy after it has finished. This module is split into two sessions (Chapters 13 and 14/ Sessions 11 and 12), although some parents may benefit from an additional session if there is a lot to cover.

For some parents, it can be helpful to space out these sessions so that therapy will finish gradually. For others, the option of booster sessions following the end of therapy will help to consolidate the learning and provide the opportunity to try things out for a few weeks before the therapy finally comes to an end. This option is discussed in Session 11.

Some parents may like to invite their partner or other family member to join one or both sessions so that the family member is aware of the plan and can support it. You can discuss this possibility with the parent and make a collaborative decision as to whether to do this.

CHAPTER 13 Session 11: Preparing to Finish Therapy

Aim of This Session

The main aim of Session 11 is to discuss the ending of therapy and how to prepare for it. A draft relapse prevention plan (also referred to as a *Staying Well Plan*) will be developed in this session, to be finalized in the next.

Outline

- Set agenda 198
- Review of mood and how things are going 198
- Review home practice 199
- What this module involves 200
- Finishing therapy 200
- Developing a relapse prevention plan (Staying Well Plan) 201
- Booster sessions 208
- Troubleshooting 208
- Home practice 209
- Summary of the session and feedback 209
- Key points 209

When to Conduct This Session

All parents will need to undertake these two final sessions after the completion of Module 3 (Sessions 7 to 10/Chapters 9 to 12).

Postpartum Depression. Anne Stewart et al., Oxford University Press. © Oxford University Press (2026).
DOI: 10.1093/med-psych/9780197759707.003.0013

Materials Needed

- Worksheet 10: Weekly Goal Record
- Worksheet 19: Staying Well Plan

Worksheets appear in Appendix A at the end of this therapist guide and in Appendix A at the end of the parent workbook. Worksheets can also be accessed by searching for this book's title on the Oxford Academic platform, at academic.oup.com. Note that when more than one copy of a worksheet is required, you may photocopy the worksheets for the parent, ask the parent to make their own photocopies, or direct the parent to the book website to print their own.

Set Agenda

By now, the parent will be confident about bringing topics for the agenda. The important topic for this session is preparing for the end of therapy. However, the parent may have other topics to discuss, particularly as they are aware that they only have two sessions left. As usual, discuss any practicalities with the parent for managing the session.

Review of Mood and How Things Are Going

As always, it is important to check out mood early in the session. It is not uncommon for mood to dip at this stage of treatment, particularly as the parent is aware that they will soon be managing on their own without therapy. You can help the parent to see dips in mood as normal fluctuation rather than a setback.

As therapy is now almost complete, it is helpful to check with the parent how they are doing with the skills they have been practicing. Has the parent:

- attended to their self-care: eating, sleeping, and exercising
- planned a daily or weekly routine
- balanced depleting activities with nourishing ones
- addressed problems directly using a structured approach

- noticed when they might be stuck in unhelpful thoughts
- used action or distraction as an alternative to getting stuck in unhelpful thoughts
- used their compassionate mind to be kind to themselves

Review these skills with the parent, and discuss any difficulties or obstacles that have been present since the last session. It is particularly important at this stage to check out if the parent has been able to develop more compassion for themselves. This is a core skill that will help them to keep going following the end of therapy. See the next section for helpful questions to check this out.

Review Home Practice

The previous session covered work on developing self-compassion. You can check with the parent if they have been using their compassionate image and how this worked for them. You should also review their Weekly Goal Record (Worksheet 10). In the previous session you will have asked them to practice self-compassion in combination with one of their previously learned skills. See how this practice went for them. There may have been times during the week when things didn't go so well, and it is important to look at these instances and discuss what happened and what ideas the parent has for doing things differently.

Useful questions for this part of the session include:

- *Have you been using the compassionate image that you worked on?*
- *How has this gone?*
- *Is there anything that made it difficult to use?*
- *What impact does it have on your life and those around you when you are more compassionate to yourself?*
- *Have you been able to work toward using compassion with your other skills?*
- *How did you manage the times during the week when things didn't go so well?*

You can remind the parent that it takes time to develop the habit of self-compassion, particularly if this is a new idea for them.

What This Module Involves

Now is a good opportunity to describe what will be covered in the final two sessions. You can explain to the parent that these sessions give an opportunity to review what they have learned in therapy, to think about any challenges that lie ahead and how they will cope, and to plan for the future, including working out how they can continue to stay healthy.

Finishing Therapy

The parent will have been working with you for 10–12 sessions, and hopefully you will have built a strong working alliance. It may be daunting, therefore, for the parent to consider finishing therapy and progressing further on their own. You can introduce this topic by inviting the parent to think about how therapy has been, what has been useful, and what they would like to continue working on in the future. This is a good chance to allow the parent to express any feelings about ending therapy, for example, sadness, fear, apprehension, frustration, or relief.

Having discussed how the parent feels, you can look again at the goals that were set at the start of therapy (this will have been written on the parent's completed Worksheet 8: Setting Goals for Therapy) to see how far they have come on their journey toward recovery.

Useful questions for this part of the session include:

- *How have you got on working toward these goals?*
- *How have your goals been changed or refined?*
- *What do you feel you have achieved?*
- *What issues/challenges have made the goals difficult to work toward?*
- *What has supported you to work toward your goals?*
- *Which goals still need further work?*

It is likely that the goals have not been entirely met, so you can consider with the parent how to continue working toward meeting these goals following the end of therapy.

It is helpful at this stage to ask for feedback on the therapy overall. This helps the parent reflect on what has been achieved and may identify any remaining gaps in their progress through the therapy that need to be addressed either in the session today or in the final session.

Given that the parent has continued attending therapy up to this stage, you can let them know that it is positive that they have kept going despite the therapy being challenging at times.

There may be some parents who are still experiencing difficulties with low mood at the end of therapy. If this is the case, you may need to discuss referring to another healthcare provider, for example, a psychiatrist specializing in postpartum depression, who can consider other forms of treatment. It is important to frame this suggestion as part of the journey toward getting better and to help the parent not feel that they are a failure or to be blamed for the chronic nature of their depression. Even if the parent needs referral to another provider, it is still important to review what has changed during this therapy and to develop a Staying Well Plan.

Let's see how far Zainab had come at this point in the treatment program.

Zainab had made considerable progress during therapy, and her functioning had improved. However, she was still taking medication for her depression, and given the recurrent nature of her depression, it was agreed that she should continue to see her psychiatrist for monitoring of her mood and medication as well as have regular check-ins with her primary care provider.

Developing a Relapse Prevention Plan (Staying Well Plan)

Having discussed the parent's goals and obtained feedback on therapy, the rest of the session is devoted to developing the relapse plan, which is called a *Staying Well Plan*. It is helpful for the parent to have a written record that they can look at again after therapy has finished. This plan will include:

- how the depression began and got stuck
- what changes have been made

- what has been helpful
- what will be the next steps
- who can support the parent to do this
- what could lead to setbacks
- how to overcome them

This is a useful process of consolidation and will give the parent something tangible to look back on.

You can use Worksheet 19: Staying Well Plan and begin to fill it in with the parent during session.

How Did Your Low Mood Come About?

Useful questions for this part of the session include:

- *Let's first talk about what led to this episode of low mood. When did your low mood begin?*
- *What were the initial problems that led to your low mood developing?*

What Kept Your Low Mood Going?

- *After you initially felt low, what kept this going?*
- *Were there further difficult times that made the low mood worse?*
- *Did how you feel about being low make a difference to how much the low mood affected you?*
- *Did the low mood change how you felt about yourself as a parent?*

What Have You Learned That Has Been Helpful to You in Dealing With This?

- *What did you learn during therapy that has helped to lift your mood?*
- *What has been most useful?*
- *What have you been doing that has helped?*

Let's see how Zainab made sense of how her depression began and how the therapy helped.

Zainab was able to look back to the start of the depression. It seemed to come unexpectedly like it did in her first pregnancy, and she felt a loss of control. She found therapy hard to start as she felt guilty that she had become depressed again and needed therapy. She got caught up in negative thinking that just went around in circles and prevented her from sleeping at night. However, Zainab stuck with the therapy, and bit by bit she began to feel better. She felt the breakthrough came when she made some progress getting on top of the negative thinking and began to focus on things outside herself. She took an interest in the garden when her daughter, Layla, was at school and baby Amir was napping, and she began to enjoy seeing things grow. Zainab's doctor prescribed an antidepressant for her, but she was reluctant to take this as she didn't feel she needed it. The therapist discussed with her the pros and cons of taking medication, and she decided to take it and found it helpful.

How Can You Build on What You Now Know to Continue to Make Changes?

It is important to convey that change is a continuous process and that it is normal to realize at this point in treatment that the changes made already could be expanded or developed. It is also the case that life is changing too, and the parent may need to build up confidence to do other things, for example, to get back to employment. Many parents are still working on getting the right balance between self-care and looking after their baby and their family. Some parents still need to do further work on being compassionate toward themselves. It is useful to have a detailed discussion with the parent about the areas that still need attention and how they might build this into their plan for the future.

This step is partly about continuing to work toward goals and about consolidating progress already made and working out how to maintain this progress.

Useful questions for this part of the session include:

- *Considering how much you have achieved already, let's think about what would be helpful to put in place or work toward next. Which strategies would you like to continue working on and developing?*
- *What are your goals for the next month in making changes?*
- *What can you do to maintain a healthy mood?*

Who or What Can Support You to Continue Living in a Way That Lifts Your Mood?

The success of the Staying Well Plan will depend very much on who or what is able to support the parent to keep going. It is helpful to discuss in detail with the parent who might be available to support them now that therapy is finishing. It is worth clarifying what sort of support would be helpful, practical (if so, what?), or emotional (how can this be given?). If the parent's partner or other family member is present in this session, this is a good opportunity to brainstorm how they can help. Support from others is an important part of the Staying Well Plan.

Useful questions for this part of the session include:

- *When thinking about making these changes, it is also important to think about who around you will support you in this progress. Who has been helpful over the last few months in supporting you to make changes?*
- *What is it that they do?*
- *How can you ask them for help?*
- *Who provides emotional support, for example, who do you talk to about how you feel?*
- *Who provides practical support?*

There might also be activities the parent is currently doing that can support them to keep well, such as engaging in regular exercise.

What Challenges Lie Ahead, and What Would the Signs Be That You Are Becoming Increasingly Stressed or Low?

There are inevitably going to be challenges. Life is never perfect, and there may be significant stresses or challenges that threaten to destabilize the parent. It is helpful to think about these possibilities in advance so that the parent can plan how to deal with these challenges. Examples of challenges might be:

- coping with their baby's next stage of development, particularly if there are difficulties with feeding or sleeping
- feeling isolated
- managing demanding behaviors in the parent's other children, which might threaten their confidence as a parent
- getting overwhelmed with tasks

The first step of this part of the process is to identify what these challenges might be before moving on to a discussion of what the early warning signs might be of the low mood returning.

Useful questions for this part of the session include:

- *It is important to think about whether there are times when you might notice your mood start to drop again and what might trigger this. What is coming up that may be challenging?*
- *How might your baby's next stages of development present challenges?*
- *What would be a sign that things are starting to get difficult again?*
- *What are the early warning signs?*
- *How would you know if your mood was dropping?*
- *What could you look out for?*

How Can You Cope With These Challenges and Look After Yourself Well?

Now you can think very specifically with the parent about what they could do when faced with challenges or stresses in the future. They may experience early signs of low mood in relation to these challenges, for example, not sleeping well or withdrawing from friends or family. It can work well to get the parent to imagine the challenge and the early signs of low mood and how they would deal with it. You can help the parent to draw on things they have learned throughout the therapy, for example, the importance of self-care and having routines.

Useful questions for this part of the session include:

- *Finally, let's think about what you could do to manage early signs that your mood is getting low and what strategies would be helpful to use at these times. How can you handle these early signs quickly to reduce or prevent any further low mood?*
- *How could challenging times be prepared for in advance?*
- *What else might be helpful?*
- *What could you do differently?*

Let's see what Lucy discussed when she was working on her Staying Well Plan.

Lucy has had 12 sessions with her therapist and found them helpful. She looked back on what exactly had helped. With her therapist's encouragement she had started swimming regularly at a local community center and was seeing her friends more. This was made easier by being more prepared to ask her mother for help with Jackson and prioritizing getting out over keeping her house perfect. These changes had a noticeable effect on Lucy's mood, which she was able to reflect on in this session.

She also reviewed what she had done to get herself out of the vicious cycle of getting stuck in her negative thoughts. Lucy felt much more confident now to use strategies to address the triggers to this thinking and deal with them (such as being angry with her mother). She learned to be more compassionate toward herself and prioritize looking after herself, which meant making sure that she had time to go swimming and meet up with her friends.

Lucy acknowledged that she is going to miss her therapist as she valued the support each week and the chance to talk things over, particularly as she does not have a partner. She is aware that life will continue to be challenging as a single mother. She is planning to go back to her catering program in the next few weeks, and she is aware that it will be difficult fitting everything in around her son, Jackson, and still finding time to go swimming and see friends. Lucy realizes that she can't do everything, so socializing and exercise may need to be fitted around her catering classes.

Figure 13.1 shows an example of Lucy's completed Staying Well Plan.

Question	Notes
How did your low mood come about?	I found it hard to cope with the restrictions that happen when you have a baby. It was very hard having to focus on Jackson, and I lost contact with my friends. I started withdrawing into myself and couldn't be bothered to make meals for myself.
What kept your low mood going?	I became really tired and exhausted, and the more exhausted I became, the more I kept to myself and stopped going out. So my mood kept going down, and all I wanted to do was curl up under my covers.
What have you learned that has been helpful to you in dealing with this?	When I feel low, I need to get support from my friends and accept their offers to help me. I am much more aware of the triggers for my negative thinking and can get myself out of the negative spiral by focusing on the present. I have noticed that keeping active and having contact with friends keep my mood up.
How can you build on what you now know to continue to make changes?	I need to make sure I let my mom help me so I can have a night out with my friends. I feel better and sleep a whole lot better if I have regular exercise. I go swimming regularly at the local pool. Mom looks after Jackson while I am there.
Who or what can support you to continue living in a way that lifts your mood?	Once I start the catering program again, I will have less time to swim so will need to get some exercise by doing stretches or an online exercise program at home. I am looking forward to meeting new people in the program. Hopefully, I will make friends, and socializing will help to keep my mood up. I also need to make sure I don't skip meals when I am busy. My mom lives close by, and I know she will keep an eye on me.
What challenges lie ahead, and what would the signs be that you are becoming increasingly stressed or low?	The big challenge for me is starting my course. I would notice that my sleep has gotten worse again and I am really tired during the day.
How can you cope with these challenges and look after yourself well?	I need to make sure I keep active and make time to chat with my friends. I am lucky to have my mom living nearby and need to be prepared to ask her for help more often. I need to prioritize my sleep.

Figure 13.1

Lucy's Completed Worksheet 19: Staying Well Plan.

Booster Sessions

At this point in the treatment program, it is important to discuss the opportunity for booster sessions. Parents who have been through this program have found it helpful to have a chance to be in contact with their therapist again and review how things are going after the end of therapy. We recommend offering two booster sessions at around 4–5 months after the formal end of therapy. It is helpful to encourage the parent to see the time from the end of therapy to the first booster session as a "testing ground" in which the parent can try out the strategies they have developed during therapy. The option of booster sessions and what might be included in them is discussed more fully in Chapter 17.

Troubleshooting

It is common for parents to find the idea of finishing therapy daunting and to present new problems for discussion in order to prolong the therapy. There is some flexibility in this program to plan additional sessions. You may also, as noted just above, be offering booster sessions after a few months (this will be discussed in detail in the final chapter). However, it is still important to have a clear finishing date. This provides a sense of urgency and a need to work hard to make the best use of the sessions. It also gives the message that you are confident that the parent has the skills to continue working on problems. It is unlikely that the parent will have addressed everything—there will still be issues to work on—but by now the parent should have the confidence to do this themselves. It is also important to have a detailed discussion regarding the key support people for the parent following discharge.

As mentioned earlier, in situations where the parent is still very unwell at this point in therapy, it is important to consider whether the parent needs referral to another provider, for example, to a medical practitioner experienced in postpartum depression.

Home Practice

The home practice for Session 11 is to encourage the parent to reflect on the discussion and finetune their Staying Well Plan (Worksheet 19) so that it can be completed next session. It is important that the parent brings their plan to the next session, so make sure you mention this. You may also want to make a copy so that you have it available the next time you meet.

Summary of the Session and Feedback

As usual, you will ask the parent to describe the main things they learned in this session and what has been helpful or unhelpful. You can remind them that the next session is the last session and that it will be an opportunity to think further about ending therapy and to have any final discussions.

Key Points

- It is helpful to reflect on what has changed over the course of treatment and why.
- Any changes can continue to be built on after therapy has finished.
- It is an achievement to have kept going throughout therapy despite the challenges.
- Working out who can be a support in the future can maximize the chance of further progress.
- It is helpful to have a specific plan as to what to do to remain well.

CHAPTER 14 Session 12: Finishing Therapy

Aim of This Session

The aim of Session 12 is to finalize the parent's Staying Well Plan, summarize the principles of therapy, and agree on arrangements for finishing therapy.

Outline

- Set agenda 212
- Review of mood and how things are going 212
- Review home practice 213
- Finalizing the Staying Well Plan 213
- Review the key principles of therapy 213
- Saying goodbye 215
- Troubleshooting 215
- Arrangements for the end of therapy 216
- Summary of the session and feedback 217
- Key points 217

When to Conduct This Session

This is the final session of therapy and will be a chance to consolidate what has been achieved in therapy and finalize plans for the future. Some parents may have booster sessions in a few months, but it is still important to properly complete the therapy at this stage.

Postpartum Depression. Anne Stewart et al., Oxford University Press. © Oxford University Press (2026).
DOI: 10.1093/med-psych/9780197759707.003.0014

Materials Needed

- Worksheet 19: Staying Well Plan *(started last session)*

Worksheets appear in Appendix A at the end of this therapist guide and in Appendix A at the end of the parent workbook. Worksheets can also be accessed by searching for this book's title on the Oxford Academic platform, at academic.oup.com. Note that when more than one copy of a worksheet is required, you may photocopy the worksheets for the parent, ask the parent to make their own photocopies, or direct the parent to the book website to print their own.

Set Agenda

This will be the final agenda of the last session of therapy. It is important to include items that the parent wants to discuss before finishing therapy as well as the main planned items for this session.

Review of Mood and How Things Are Going

As usual, it is important to check how the parent has been since the last session. It is not unusual at this stage of therapy for the parent to feel some anxiety about finishing, and they may experience a dip in mood that can be reframed as an understandable blip in progress.

By this stage of therapy, the parent will hopefully have made a number of changes. Has the parent:

- attended to their self-care: eating, sleeping, and exercising
- planned a daily or weekly routine
- balanced depleting activities with nourishing ones
- addressed problems directly using a structured approach
- noticed when they might be stuck in unhelpful thoughts
- used action or distraction as an alternative to getting stuck in unhelpful thoughts

- used their compassionate mind to be kind to themselves
- started to develop a blueprint for the future (Staying Well Plan)

Review these skills with the parent and discuss any difficulties or obstacles that have been present since the last session.

Review Home Practice

The main task from the previous session was to reflect on and complete Worksheet 19: Staying Well Plan. If the parent has not been able to do this, there is time in this session to go through it carefully together and ensure that the parent is happy with it.

Finalizing the Staying Well Plan

The main aim of Session 12 is to go through the Staying Well Plan again and ensure there is sufficient detail for it to be useful for the parent. They may have had further thoughts since the last session. Zainab has worked on her Staying Well Plan, which is depicted in Figure 14.1.

Review the Key Principles of Therapy

An important part of the last session is summarizing the principles of the Oxford Postnatal Programme as shown in Box 14.1. More detail is provided earlier in Chapter 2 regarding these principles.

Useful questions for this part of the session include:

- *Let's have a look at the principles together. What do you think were the most important for you and that you'd like to remember for the future?*
- *What would help to remind you to look at these principles and your Staying Well Plan?*
- *Where could you keep them so they are readily accessible?*

Question	Notes
How did your low mood come about?	I was very depressed after my first baby, Layla, was born, and I felt anxious that this was going to happen again. I began to have negative thoughts about being a bad mom and just couldn't get them out of my mind. I felt guilty about not spending enough time with Layla and found it difficult to sleep at night, and my mood just spiraled down.
What kept your low mood going?	I stopped eating well and began to lose weight, and my energy levels went down. It was hard to cope with everything, especially with a baby and a preschooler, which made me feel inadequate. My mood just stayed low.
What have you learned that has been helpful to you in dealing with this?	Just because I am depressed doesn't mean I am a bad mother. Looking after myself is really important if I'm going to look after the children, and I need to make time to relax too.
How can you build on what you now know to continue to make changes?	Have confidence in my ability as a parent. Realize that I can do something to lift my mood. Continue to be kind to myself.
Who or what can support you to continue living in a way that lifts your mood?	Make sure I eat regular meals. Do something relaxing before I go to sleep. Meet up with my friends regularly. Have a regular date night with Tauseef while his parents look after Amir and Layla.
What challenges lie ahead, and what would the signs be that you are becoming increasingly stressed or low?	A continuing challenge is coping with two children. The negative thoughts about being a bad parent starting to return. Neglecting my family and friends.
How can you cope with these challenges and look after yourself well?	Use the strategies I have learned to manage my negative thoughts: - Distraction - Seeing the thoughts as part of the depression and not me - Making sure I get enough rest so that I have the energy for two children

Figure 14.1

Zainab's Completed Worksheet 19: Staying Well Plan.

Box 14.1 Key Principles of the Oxford Postnatal Programme

- **What we do and think influence how we feel.**
  Remember we can lift our mood by doing things differently.
- **Becoming more active can lift mood.**
  Getting out, exercising, and meeting with friends can all help us feel better.
- **Taking small steps, one at a time, is important.**
  It can be overwhelming trying to do too much all at once; just take it one step at a time, and you will make progress that way.
- **Dealing with unhelpful thinking can break the vicious cycle of depression.**
  It is easy to get caught up in unhelpful thoughts that go round and round and make us feel worse. However, we can take control and manage these ways of thinking.
- **Scheduling in routines can help you take control.**
  When things seem out of control, setting a schedule for yourself can be a way of taking charge and feeling back in control again.
- **It is important to look after yourself first.**
  Unless you take care of yourself, it is hard to look after other people.
- **Becoming your own therapist is key.**
  Going through this program teaches you life skills that you can put into practice long after you have finished therapy.
- **Continuing with helpful strategies can help you stay well.**
  It's important to keep going with the things that you have found helpful in keeping you well. These are skills for life.

Saying Goodbye

Coming to the end of therapy involves acknowledging what has gone on in therapy and the mixed feelings that the parent may have, such as relief, sadness, fear, thankfulness, anxiety, joy, and anger. It is important to end well, acknowledging the journey that the parent has been on; the challenges they have encountered; their hopes, fears, and expectations for the future; as well as the therapeutic relationship that has been created and will come to an end.

Troubleshooting

Some parents will find it hard to cope with the end of therapy, and it is important to give them space to express their feelings and to acknowledge them.

Arrangements for the End of Therapy

Given the common feelings of anxiety felt by many parents at the end of therapy, an important part of the discussion is to identify who can support the parent after therapy is over. You can also direct the parent to the Resource List at the end of the parent workbook, which may be helpful following therapy.

It is important to discuss practical arrangements for ending therapy, ensuring that the parent has a plan for who to contact should they experience low mood in the future and how to access appropriate services. It's often worth writing this information down because if the parent experiences a crisis, it might be difficult to remember what to do and who to contact.

As discussed in Session 11, some parents may need to be referred straightaway to another provider/service, but it is still important to discuss the ending of this therapy and who will support the parent with the transition.

Having a couple of booster sessions following the end of therapy, as also discussed in the previous session, can help with the process of ending therapy and provide the parent with the opportunity to try things out on their own for a few months. Not all parents decide to participate in booster sessions, and those who do not should be encouraged to meet with their primary care provider 3–4 months after therapy has finished. Worksheet 22: Booster Session Review (discussed in Chapter 17) provides a structured framework for reviewing progress. Chapter 17 includes details on what might be covered in the booster sessions.

Let's see what ideas Mila had for getting support following the end of therapy.

Mila felt anxious finishing therapy as her parents live in Poland and her partner, Sophie, is often busy with work. Mila had found the therapy supportive and was not sure how she was going to continue to get support. In discussion with the therapist, she identified that she could continue to meet with a friend who has a baby the same age as Marta. They could exchange ideas on parenting, which they both found helpful, and do some fun things together to relax. Sophie also expressed a willingness to help, and though it was sometimes tricky, with some persistence, the two of them are figuring out ways to ask for support and who can do what and when. Mila is keen to attend a booster session in 4 months to review how things are going.

Summary of the Session and Feedback

It is helpful to summarize the session together and then ask the parent to give feedback on the session, in particular whether there are additional things that need to be discussed before the session ends and therapy is complete. It is worth emphasizing that although this is the end of therapy there are likely to be ups and downs in the future. Life will bring stresses from time to time that can throw us off balance. The important thing is having the skills to deal with stressful situations and fluctuations in mood and to get back on track so that life feels meaningful and of value.

Finally, it is important to give the parent plenty of positive affirmation for having kept going with the treatment program right to the end and for the hard work they have done.

Key Points

- Having a written plan can be helpful for the parent to look back on.
- It is important to check out sources of support—both informal and formal—that the parent can access following therapy.
- Booster sessions can help to consolidate change.

[illegible]

Summary of the Session and Feedback

[illegible]

[illegible]

Key Points

- [illegible]
- [illegible]

Additional Sessions

In addition to the standard four modules covered in this treatment program (Module 1 Preparing: Finding Out What Is Going On for You, Module 2 Activating: Doing Things That Make You Feel Better, Module 3 Thinking: Helping Your Mind to Help You, and Module 4 Heading to the Future: Planning How to Stay Well), there are two optional sessions that can be used with some parents as needed. These sessions aim to help the parent develop additional skills in dealing with intrusive thinking and traumatic memories, where this is relevant. These sessions can be used flexibly at any point throughout the program following Module 1. Prior to the session on traumatic memories, you may wish to discuss with the parent the option of recording the session so that they can listen to it again afterward (which parents have found very helpful). The recording may be done either on the parent's cell phone or on a device belonging to the therapist.

CHAPTER 15

Session 13: Understanding and Managing Intrusive Thoughts, Images, and Urges

Aim of This Session

Session 13 focuses on intrusive thoughts, one of the "additional skills" chapters that might be helpful for some parents. We will explain what intrusive thoughts are and then how to assess and then address these together with the parent.

Outline

- Set agenda 222
- Review of mood and how things are going 222
- Review home practice 223
- Introducing intrusive thoughts, images, and urges 223
- Developing a shared understanding of intrusions with the parent 225
- Addressing intrusive thoughts 231
- Troubleshooting 235
- Home practice 235
- Summary of the session and feedback 236
- Key points 236

When to Conduct This Session

Please see the section below on what intrusive thoughts are and are not. You can use this additional skill session if you have identified, or the parent has shared with you, that they experience problematic intrusive thoughts (commonly about deliberately harming their baby). You can

Postpartum Depression. Anne Stewart et al., Oxford University Press. © Oxford University Press (2026).
DOI: 10.1093/med-psych/9780197759707.003.0015

conduct this session at any point during the course of therapy (after Module 1). The choice of when to conduct this session is based on the impact the intrusions are having on the parent's mood and well-being or whether it is disrupting treatment. If the impact appears to be greater than a feature addressed in Sessions 3–10 (such as rumination, Sessions 7 and 8), then you might choose to conduct this session early in therapy.

Materials Needed

- Worksheet 9: Weekly Goal Planner
- Worksheet 10: Weekly Goal Record
- Worksheet 20: What Can Keep Intrusive Thoughts Going?

Worksheets appear in Appendix A at the end of this therapist guide and in Appendix A at the end of the parent workbook. Worksheets can also be accessed by searching for this book's title on the Oxford Academic platform, at academic.oup.com. Note that when more than one copy of a worksheet is required, you may photocopy the worksheets for the parent, ask the parent to make their own photocopies, or direct the parent to the book website to print their own.

Set Agenda

As usual, discuss with the parent the aims for the session and what will be covered. Make a note of anything else that the parent would like to discuss in this session, and agree on the agenda. You will need to check whether there are any issues for the parent or their baby that might have an impact on the session, such as their baby needing to be fed or changed or the parent needing to take a call, and agree how to manage these.

Review of Mood and How Things Are Going

At the start of this session, you can review how the parent's mood has been since the last session. Discuss what symptoms have been present, whether they have increased or decreased, and how this has impacted on the parent's day-to-day functioning.

Now you can move on to see how the parent is doing with their skills. Which skills have been covered already will depend on the timing of this session. However, it is likely that the parent has covered self-care, routines, and problem solving, so you can check whether the parent has been able to:

- attend to their self-care: eating, sleeping, and exercising
- plan a daily or weekly routine
- balance depleting activities with nourishing ones
- address problems directly using a structured approach

If this session is undertaken later in the therapy, then you may need to check if the parent is using alternatives to getting stuck in unhelpful thoughts or is using their compassionate mind to be kind toward themselves.

Review the relevant skills with the parent, and discuss any difficulties or obstacles that have been present since the last session, as well as how they have coped with challenges in putting these skills in place.

Review Home Practice

Review the home practice task that was set with the parent in your last session together. (This chapter focuses on additional skills and may be given flexibly at different points in the program; therefore, the focus of your previous session will depend on the timing of the session.) Discuss what went well with the home practice and what were the challenges. As usual, emphasize with the parent that all learning is helpful, and encourage them to review the home practice, taking into account their understanding of what contributes to their low mood.

Having reviewed home practice, you can now move on to the main focus of this session, which is identifying and managing intrusive thoughts.

Introducing Intrusive Thoughts, Images, and Urges

It is important that you, as the therapist, have a clear understanding of intrusive thoughts—especially that by addressing them you are likely to help parents feel relieved and understood and that asking about intrusive thoughts will not increase the likelihood of acting out their content. The concern that some therapists might feel about this is similar to the concern that asking about self-harm or suicidal ideation could increase the risk of a person seriously harming themselves or taking their own life. In both cases, the evidence indicates that talking about these thoughts does *not* increase the possibility of them being acted out (Lawrence et al. (2017).

Background Information for Therapists

The term *intrusive thoughts* is actually shorthand for a range of cognitive phenomena, including verbal thoughts/cognitions, images, and urges. We will use *intrusion* to refer to this broad range and will describe the specific type of intrusion (e.g., intrusive image).

Intrusions are any type of mental event that are recurrent, spontaneous, and unwanted and often inconsistent with a person's conception of themselves (or egodystonic). Intrusions typically interrupt a person's focus of attention and are accompanied by intense negative emotions. The negative emotion relates to the content of intrusions, and this is because the content often focuses on forbidden (e.g., stripping naked in public), morally unacceptable (e.g., racist abuse), and/or taboo (e.g., audible flatulence in public) behaviors.

The fact that intrusions are unwanted and frequently inconsistent with a person's conception of themselves distinguishes them from other types of thoughts that are accompanied by an intention to act on the content of the thought. For example, thoughts of harming one's baby that happen repeatedly and unexpectedly and are very much unwanted (and often horrify the parent) are different from thoughts involving deliberate planning for harming one's baby or oneself.

It is important to recognize that intrusions are an almost universal but unwelcome experience in adults. Studies in Western non-clinical samples suggest that the majority of adults experience them (Belloch et al., 2004). Furthermore, they are very common in new parents; and as the content of intrusions may often center on what is most relevant and important to the individual, some of the most frequently occurring thoughts include distressing images related to possible, even deliberate harm to the baby (Fairbrother & Woody, 2008). The presence of such content does not imply intent or predict the parent will act out its content.

Perhaps the single most important fact to share with parents about intrusions is that people *don't* act out their content. This distinguishes intrusions from parents' thoughts of deliberately harming babies, for example, in the context of psychosis, where the thoughts might be command hallucinations (and not intrusions). There are useful questions to ask (see section in this chapter headed "Differentiating intrusions from thoughts posing a primary risk to the parent or others") to differentiate intrusive thoughts from thoughts that include intention or plans to deliberately harm their baby.

Parents are often fearful of the content of intrusions about harming their babies and may be particularly worried that if they share these thoughts, their baby may be taken away. Parents can find it safer to address such thoughts if the therapist first establishes that intrusions are common, harmless, and meaningless and tell us nothing about the person experiencing them.

Developing a Shared Understanding of Intrusions With the Parent

As with many problems you will address in this treatment program, it is helpful to begin by developing a shared understanding of what the problem *is*. This has three stages:

1. The first stage is providing psychoeducation to help the parent understand what intrusive thoughts are and how common they are.
2. The second stage is identifying the intrusive thoughts that the parent is experiencing and confirming that these are intrusive thoughts. This may be done by taking a graded approach to assessing their experiences of intrusions—starting with a focus on intrusions *un*related to their babies and only then focusing on their intrusions about their babies. (This graded approach is used in order to progress at a pace that is safe and manageable for parents.)
3. The final stage is working out with the parent how the response to the intrusions may be maintaining their depression.

Then, with a shared understanding in place, you can plan with the parent how to address the intrusive thoughts about deliberately harming their babies and then practice this in the session.

Stage 1: Psychoeducation

Having first explained what an intrusive thought/intrusion is, you can discuss with the parent that intrusions are experienced by most people, whether or not they have ever experienced any mental health problems. They are especially common in parents of babies (studies suggest that almost 100% of new parents experience them). This might be because of the stresses that accompany being a new parent and/or the increased responsibility of being a baby's parent. So, by themselves, intrusions are something that nearly all parents experience.

In discussing this with the parent it can be helpful to find out what they think it says about a person when they have such thoughts. It is then important to discuss the fact that many people have such thoughts, and it doesn't mean they are bad for having such thoughts.

Useful questions for this part of the session include:

- *Have you heard the term* intrusive thoughts*?*
- *Most people experience intrusive thoughts. Did you experience intrusions before becoming a parent?*
- *What is your reaction to knowing that these thoughts are very common, even thoughts that are distressing or weird?*
- *These kinds of thoughts don't say anything about the person's character. What do you think?*

Stage 2: Parents' Experiences of Intrusions

The *content* of intrusions is only clinically important when the person experiencing them believes it to be so. By implication, people who view the intrusions they experience as meaningless or strange but harmless are relatively unaffected by the intrusions. In your work with parents, it is those intrusions that parents experience as *meaningful* that will need to be addressed.

We have found it helpful to use a graded approach to assessing the parent's intrusions about harming their babies. This means that we begin by discussing intrusions that do not relate to their baby.

Normalizing intrusions

For example, you could ask the parent whether they have experienced common intrusions such as:

- Jumping from a dangerous high place
- Insulting a stranger
- Leaving their home unlocked or with the stove on
- In drivers, swerving their own vehicle into traffic or off the road

The aim of normalizing intrusions is to help the parent see intrusions for what they are—strange mental experiences that need have no bearing on reality nor on how the person responds to them. So, if a parent identifies with one of the common types of intrusions above, you can discuss with them what happened when they had the intrusion. For example, if they had an intrusion about insulting a stranger, did they go on to insult a stranger? If not, how come that didn't happen? If they have had an intrusion about jumping off a dangerous or high place, how come they didn't do *that*?

A common feature of people's responses to examining intrusions is to state that they did not *want* to act out the content of the intrusion, and *that* is why they did not do it (for example, insult a stranger or jump from a high place). It is crucial to note that intrusions, by definition, are unwanted, and typically the content is something a person does not want. This distinguishes them from thoughts and intentions about self-harm. People can, of course, *want* to jump from a dangerous and high place in order to harm or kill themselves.

Differentiating intrusions from thoughts posing a primary risk to the parent or others

When thoughts are accompanied by an *intent* or a *desire* to act out their content, they are *not intrusions*. In such cases, you would assess the risk of harm to the self or others, especially the baby and then manage that risk following local clinical guidelines (see Chapter 3 on managing risk).

By the end of this discussion, you and the parent should have a shared understanding that intrusions:

- are experienced by almost everyone (and therefore a normal experience)
- often occur involuntarily
- are often unpleasant
- are unwanted
- are *not* a sign of wanting the content to occur

Taken together, this means that intrusions are not a sign that the parent has any sort of secret desire to act out the content of an intrusion.

Intrusions about the baby

With that established, you can assess the parent's intrusions about harming their baby and encourage them to talk about the intrusions. The groundwork that you have done with the parent will mean that you have a shared understanding of what intrusions are (i.e., "normal," unpleasant, unwanted, and without bearing on what type of parent they are), and that allows you to discuss the content and other features (frequency, triggers, responses) in a way that a parent can find safe.

The following are examples of common types of intrusions that parents experience:

- walking or driving away from their baby
- hitting the baby too hard while burping them
- letting the baby, in the stroller, roll into traffic
- puncturing the soft skin on the top of the baby's skull
- sexually assaulting their baby
- shaking their baby
- smothering their baby during feeding or with a pillow
- throwing their baby to the ground or against a wall
- drowning their baby in the bath

Therapist Note

The parent workbook does not include a list of examples of intrusions relating to the baby. This is because providing examples might, in itself, make some parents more distressed. So, the example(s) that you choose to share with the parent you are working with will depend on your detailed understanding of their psychological state. (For example, if feeding the baby is a sensitive issue for a parent, sharing an example *un*related to feeding their baby might be easier for the parent to hear and understand.)

Having discussed some possible examples of intrusive images, you can check with the parent whether they experience intrusive thoughts and what they are. It is helpful to encourage the parent to be open about their thoughts. You will need to check how frequent the thoughts are, what the triggers are, and how the parent responds to them.

Intrusive thoughts can be distressing, are very common, and—although they are upsetting—are not harmful and, on their own, indicate no primary risk of harm to the parent or their baby.

When some parents are under enormous stress—such as when their baby is persistently crying and the parent is sleep-deprived—they may feel at risk for impulsively harming their baby. Very rarely, some parents make plans to hurt themselves and/or their babies because it can feel like doing so is the only logical thing to do—that it is difficult to avoid. In both cases, this is *different from having an intrusive thought.* It is essential to assess whether the parent finds that acting on such a thought feels unavoidable or whether they feel at risk from impulsively harming their baby when under stress. This is so you can assess whether there is really any risk of harm to the parent and/or baby and take action.

In order to clarify that these thoughts *are* intrusions, it is helpful to address the following questions:

- *Is the parent indifferent to the intrusions?*
- *Is the parent emotionally unaffected by the intrusions?*
- *Does the parent try to trigger the intrusions?*
- *Does the parent decline help to manage the intrusions?*
- *Does the parent intend to act out the intrusions/plan to harm their baby?*
- *Has the parent ever intentionally harmed their baby?*

If the answer is "yes" to any of these questions, then the thoughts might not be intrusions, and it is important to assess risk to self and others, especially the baby, and, if required, take appropriate action to address such risk. This may involve getting in touch with other professionals in order to help keep the parent and their baby safe (see Chapter 3).

It is useful to have a discussion with the parent about the fact that they may be very bothered by the intrusions. If you have already ascertained that there is no intention to harm the baby, you can discuss how the thoughts might be troublesome because, in fact, the parent is very concerned about the safety of their baby and on the lookout for any possible dangers or risks. The thoughts are not a sign that they are at risk of harming their baby.

Stage 3: The Role of Intrusions in Maintaining Depression

To identify how intrusions might play a role in maintaining the depression a parent experiences, it is helpful to refer to the formulation/conceptualization of their depression that you developed earlier in therapy with the parent. The meaning of an intrusion and a ruminative response to intrusions are typically the crucial ways in which intrusions contribute to the maintenance of the depression.

Cognitive processes

One key way that intrusions can maintain depression is by narrowing a parent's focus of attention on the intrusions or associated negative thoughts or rumination about them. This will limit a person's ability to engage in their environment and derive an important sense of achievement, enjoyment, or closeness.

Behavioral processes

Avoidance behaviors can often contribute to the maintenance of the problems that arise from a parent's intrusions. This is especially so if parents try to avoid the triggers for their intrusions or avoid behaviors related to the content of their intrusions. This might be, for example, avoiding giving their baby a bath because of an intrusive thought of drowning the baby. Avoidance behaviors are an entirely understandable response to experiencing intrusions when we consider how aversive they are to experience and the fear a parent might have about acting out the content of the intrusion. However, avoidance behaviors can increase a person's worry about intrusive thoughts and contribute to continuing low mood.

Let's see what Mila and her therapist identified about Mila's intrusions.

Mila's therapist has identified that she has been experiencing extremely distressing intrusions about harming her baby, Marta. The content of these intrusions is usually either Mila holding Marta at the top of the stairs at home and then launching herself and Marta down the stairs or holding Marta under the bath water so that she drowns. The therapist explained to Mila what intrusive thoughts are by normalizing them with a focus first on intrusions whose content was unrelated to harming infants, and then on the particular intrusions Mila experienced about harming Marta. The therapist and Mila identified two particularly important issues about Mila's intrusions. First, Mila often ruminated on the intrusions (often asking herself what they meant about her as a mother and telling herself that she was a terrible parent because she had the intrusions). Second, Mila tried to avoid going into situations that would trigger the intrusions (for example, bathing her baby, Marta).

Use Worksheet 20: What Can Keep Intrusive Thoughts Going to guide your discussion with the parent. Figure 15.1 demonstrates Mila's experience, which you can talk through with the parent.

Addressing Intrusive Thoughts

Having spent time developing a shared understanding of intrusions and what keeps them going (which is a key step in helping the parent to think differently about them), you can now move on to addressing the intrusions more directly. It is helpful to think about cognitive and behavioral approaches.

Cognitive Approaches

Whether or not intrusions occur is not in our control—they can occur spontaneously and be unwanted. However, *how* we respond to them *is* under our control.

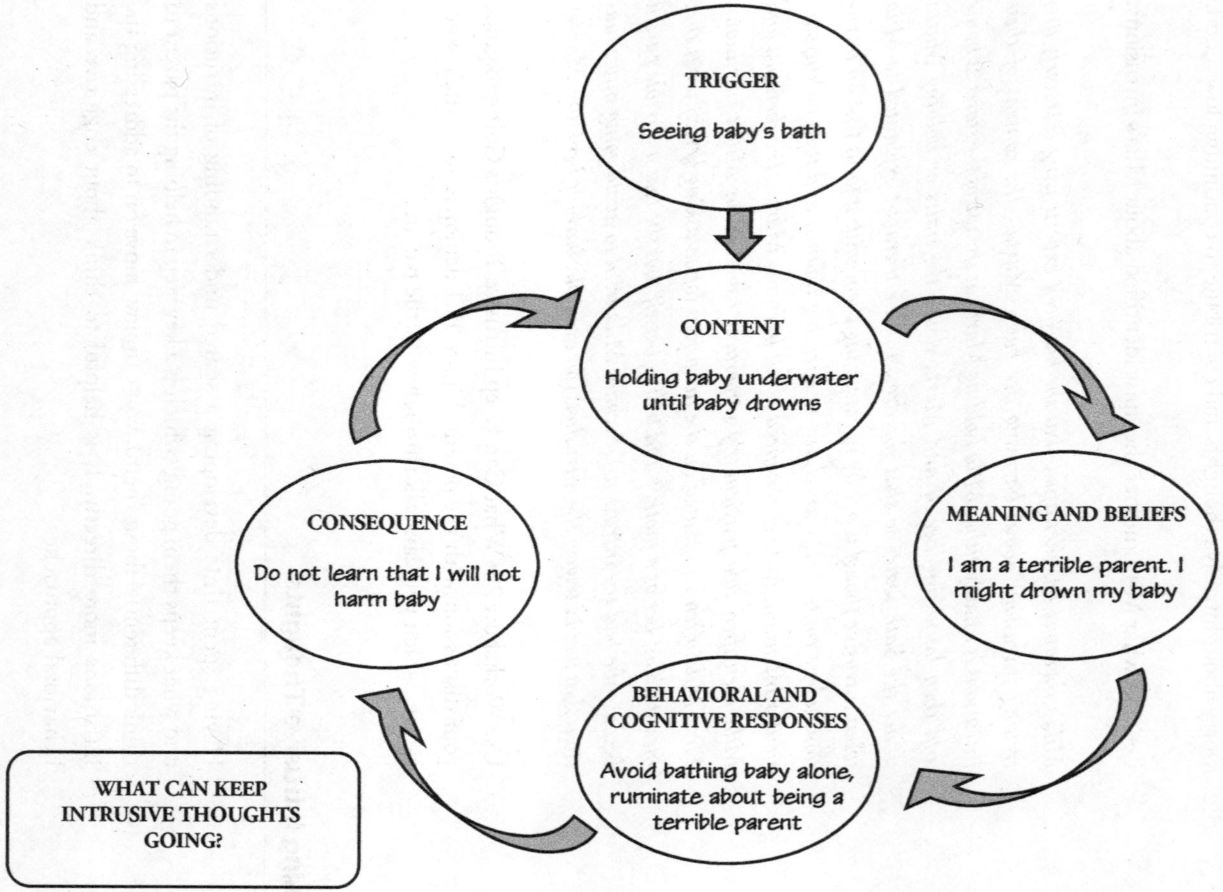

Figure 15.1

Mila's Completed Worksheet 20: What Can Keep Intrusive Thoughts Going?

The essence of effectively addressing intrusions is in understanding their nature. So, once a parent understands that their intrusions about harming their baby, however horrific their content is, are just the same as the intrusions almost everyone experiences on a day-to-day basis, these intrusions are likely to become less frequent and cease to have a negative impact on the parent.

It is important to check with the parent whether they have any cognitive responses or rituals to their intrusions. For example, do they do something "in their head"—such as trying to push the intrusion away—that helps them to feel "safe" or to believe that they will not act out the content of their intrusions? These responses can increase the focus on the intrusions and keep them stuck. If this is happening, you can use the strategies from Chapter 10/Session 8 (which help the parent *focus* on right now: action, absorption, and distraction) to plan how the parent can cope with intrusions in a way that does not keep them going in the longer term.

Alternatively, do the intrusions trigger judgmental thoughts, such as "I am being a bad parent?" If so, it is important to emphasize how common these sorts of thoughts are, with the implication that, if most parents have them, most parents are "bad parents," which, of course, they are not.

Some parents may find it helpful to externalize the intrusions as a way of distancing themselves from them. For example, they might say to themselves, "There is another one of those intrusive thoughts; everyone has them, they are only thoughts, not facts, and they mean nothing about me or what I will do."

Other parents may find it helpful to ground themselves in the present and notice what is going on around them rather than focusing on the intrusion. It may also be helpful for them to engage themselves in enjoyable or interesting activities (for example, Mila engaged her attention by watching her favorite TV program), which can act as an effective way to diminish the intrusions.

Behavioral Approaches

As described earlier, safety behaviors can often accompany intrusions. For example, where the content of a parent's intrusion is about stabbing their baby, they might remove sharp knives from their kitchen, or where the content is about drowning their baby, they might avoid giving their baby a bath. This avoidance makes the intrusive thoughts more powerful, just as avoidance can increase anxiety. Once the parent understands this, they can be helped to engage in the behaviors they are avoiding.

Some parents find it helpful to be fully in the present when these thoughts occur and notice what is going on around them rather than focusing on the intrusion—for example, noticing what their baby is doing, how they look, how they sound, or how they feel.

Once the parent is aware of the intrusion, they can also be taught how to use it as a cue to do something different, in particular the strategies introduced in Chapter 10/Session 8 (*focusing* attention on action, right now, absorption, and distraction). Some examples might be focusing on what is going on around them (as described above), making themself a cup of coffee, texting a friend, or even just telling themself out loud that this is an intrusion, is quite normal, and does not mean anything bad about them. Use another copy of Worksheet 17: Alternative Strategies to Getting Stuck in Our Thoughts.

To summarize, here are some steps for the parent to manage intrusive thoughts:

1. Notice the intrusion, watch it, and let it come and go. Do not try to push it away.
2. Remind yourself that having these thoughts is very common and doesn't mean you are a bad parent. Be kind to yourself.
3. Notice your feelings (e.g., fear or anxiety), and recognize that this is a natural response.
4. Take some deep breaths.
5. Ground yourself in the present situation, noticing what is going on around you.
6. If you are getting caught up in ruminating in response to the intrusions, engage in something that absorbs your attention.
7. Make sure that you are not avoiding situations that might trigger an intrusion, such giving your baby a bath. Avoidance just makes it worse because it prevents you from learning that you never act on the intrusions.

Let's see how responding to intrusions in different ways was helpful for Mila.

In response to the discussion about intrusive thoughts, the therapist firstly helped Mila understand that these thoughts are very common and not a sign that she is a bad parent. Then they used the focusing strategies (from Chapter 10) to help Mila; they planned what absorbing *and* distracting *activities Mila could try out when she ruminated on an intrusion. Regarding the avoidance of bathing Marta, the therapist helped Mila to understand that, while this avoidance is entirely understandable, it actually keeps the intrusions going. So, the therapist and Mila created a plan to gradually have more contact with Marta at bath time until she felt confident (even though not 100% comfortable) to bathe Marta by herself. This involved initially running water into the bathtub, then undressing Marta, and finally being able to put Marta in the bath and wash her. Mila's partner, Sophie, got involved in this plan, too, so that she could help with the gradual approach toward Mila bathing baby Marta alone.*

Troubleshooting

The parent may find it difficult to make the transition from experiencing intrusions as meaningful mental events to dismissing them as unfortunate but meaningless. This will often be because of the horrifying content of their intrusions. If this is the case, it can be helpful to spend more time with the parent focused on their (absence of) intention to harm their baby. This focus often helps the parent to recognize the "what if" type of worry/ruminative processing they become stuck in and that this is similar to pressing a car's accelerator pedal when in neutral gear.

The parent may find it hard to stop avoiding the triggers for intrusive thoughts. A gradual approach can be taken, as with Mila having a graded exposure plan.

Home Practice

It is unhelpful to ask the parent to monitor the intrusions as this can make them more troublesome.

If the parent experiences intrusions between sessions, it will be helpful for them to re-read Chapter 15/Session 13 in their workbook and remind themselves what intrusions are, in particular that they are normal. The parent can also practice responding differently, for example, focusing on the present, rather than on the intrusion.

You may also work out with the parent goals for this week to include behaviors that help to consolidate progress that they have made in other areas (using Worksheet 9: Weekly Goal Planner) and ask the parent to complete another copy of Worksheet 10: Weekly Goal Record during the week.

Summary of the Session and Feedback

This may have been a difficult session to conduct because parents can be highly anxious about their experience of intrusive thoughts, particularly those relating to harming their baby. It is important to check out how the session has been for them and how the parent feels now. You can encourage them to give you feedback on the session. Has it been helpful? Is there anything they still don't understand? Is there anything further they would like to cover regarding intrusive thinking? Do they now have strategies for dealing with these unwanted thoughts?

Key Points

- Intrusions are an almost universal but unwelcome experience in adults.
- Intrusions about deliberately harming their baby are common in parents and can be very frightening.
- Parents might believe that there is something wrong with them for having these thoughts or images.
- It is important to ask about intrusions and give permission for parents to talk about them.
- Experiencing intrusions does not mean that your baby is at risk.
- How parents respond to the intrusions is crucial.
- Intrusions can be addressed by psychoeducation and reducing the cognitive and behavioral responses that keep the worry about the intrusions going.

CHAPTER 16

Session 14: Understanding and Managing Traumatic Images or Memories

Aim of This Session

Session 14 focuses on traumatic images; it is one of the Additional Skills chapters that might be helpful for some parents. We will explain what traumatic images and memories are and how to assess and then address these collaboratively with the parent.

Outline

- Set agenda 239
- Review of mood and how things are going 239
- Review home practice 240
- How to structure the work on traumatic images 240
- Psychoeducation regarding traumatic images and their impact 241
- Assessment of traumatic images 243
- Transforming traumatic images 246
- Debrief 250
- Troubleshooting 251
- Home practice 251
- Summary of this session and feedback 251
- Key points 252

When to Conduct This Session

It is important to consider carefully whether to work with traumatic images in this short-term therapy, where depression, not trauma, is the main focus of the intervention. In cases where the trauma symptoms

Postpartum Depression. Anne Stewart et al., Oxford University Press. © Oxford University Press (2026).
DOI: 10.1093/med-psych/9780197759707.003.0016

are moderate to severe (i.e., the parent meets the criteria for a diagnosis of post-traumatic stress disorder [PTSD]), it may be more helpful for the parent to receive a medium- to long-term specific trauma-focused therapy, for example, trauma-focused cognitive behavioral therapy or eye movement desensitization reprocessing for PTSD, which may mean referral to a practitioner experienced in those approaches. This is particularly indicated where the traumatic images and symptoms are related to "developmental trauma" such as childhood sexual abuse, child maltreatment, and domestic violence.

The components this treatment program outlines for traumatic images are suitable when:

- The traumatic event has been experienced within the last 12 months, particularly if related to becoming a parent (e.g., difficult pregnancy or birth, life-threatening illness for parent or baby, baby being endangered or thought to be endangered).
- You have established a therapeutic relationship with the parent and completed at least four therapy sessions with them.
- The parent's trauma symptoms are mild and, while distressing to them, cause no significant impediment to their daily life or suicidal ideation.
- Basic "grounding" techniques can be established with the parent to manage distress (this will be discussed with the parent early in the session).
- The parent agrees, following a clear and explicit discussion, that talking about the traumatic image in a safe and containing relationship would be beneficial for them (this will be discussed with the parent in the session before embarking on the detailed work with images).

You can choose when to conduct this session based on the impact the traumatic images are having on the parent's mood and functioning and whether the images are interfering with treatment. Ideally, you will have completed Modules 1 and 2 before embarking on this work, so you may choose to conduct this session before Module 3 if the impact is greater than any of the features addressed in Module 3.

Materials Needed

- Worksheet 10: Weekly Goal Record
- Worksheet 21: What Can Keep Traumatic Images Going?

The parent might benefit from having an audio recording of the session to help them recall the changes you make with them to their traumatic image(s). This needs to be discussed in advance with the parent and decided whether the parent will record on their device or the therapist will record for them and send it to them following the session.

Worksheets appear in Appendix A *at the end of this therapist guide and in Appendix A at the end of the parent workbook. Worksheets can also be accessed by searching for this book's title on the Oxford Academic platform, at academic.oup.com. Note that when more than one copy of a worksheet is required, you may photocopy the worksheets for the parent, ask the parent to make their own photocopies, or direct the parent to the book website to print their own.*

Set Agenda

As usual, you may start with reviewing together the outline for this session. Make a note of anything else the parent would like to discuss in this session, and set the agenda together. Discuss any practicalities for the parent or their baby that might have an impact on the session, and agree how to manage these.

Review of Mood and How Things Are Going

At the start of this session, you can review how the parent's mood has been since the last session. Discuss what symptoms have been present, whether they have increased or decreased, and how this has impacted the parent's day-to-day functioning.

For this session, signs of progress will depend on the focus of your previous session. It is likely that the parent will have started incorporating antidepressant activities into their daily schedule, be engaged in self-care, and have learned the skills of problem solving.

You can review the relevant skills that the parent has learned and discuss any difficulties or obstacles that have been present since the last session.

Review Home Practice

As usual, review the home practice task that was set with the parent in your last session together. This chapter focuses on additional skills, so we cannot predict the focus of your previous session.

Discuss what went well with the home practice and what were the challenges. Reinforce that all learning is helpful, and encourage the parent to review the practice taking into account their understanding of what contributes to their low mood.

How to Structure the Work on Traumatic Images

It is important that you, as a therapist, have a clear understanding of what traumatic images are and especially that, by addressing these, you are likely to have to support a parent through relatively acute emotional distress. You will need to discuss with the parent that they may feel initially more distressed when talking, or even thinking, about traumatic images. It is important to discuss early in the session a range of grounding techniques for helping the parent cope with any distress that may occur in bringing up their image(s). Some examples of grounding are given later in the chapter.

As with many problems you will address in therapy, it is helpful to begin by developing a shared understanding of what the problem *is*. Regarding traumatic images or memories, there are three steps:

- First, discuss with the parent the nature of traumatic images in general and the rationale for working with them.
- Second, identify what the parent's traumatic image(s) is/are, their importance to the parent, and how they maintain the low mood.
- Third, with a shared understanding in place, you can support the parent to address the traumatic image(s) and practice with them in session how they can do this.

This work is therefore divided into three parts:

- Psychoeducation about the role and impact of traumatic images, as well as beliefs about the images, and pros and cons of working with these images. The parent will need to agree to the next step of exploring the images. Hence, discussing the use of "grounding techniques" is likely helpful in this part.
- Assessment of the parent's traumatic images and how they might maintain the depression. It is helpful to draw up a detailed conceptualization/formulation that will include what the parent believes about the nature and role of the traumatic image(s) and how they feel about working with them.
- Work together on modifying the images.

Psychoeducation Regarding Traumatic Images and Their Impact

It is important to take time to explain what traumatic images are and why it is important to address them. You can discuss with the parent the pros and cons of addressing them, and then, if the parent agrees to go ahead, you will need to prepare for this by discussing grounding techniques to manage the distress that may arise.

Brief Explanation of Traumatic Images (or Memories)

Many parents experience traumatic images in the context of postpartum depression. Traumatic images are extremely distressing cognitive experiences that often include not only visual images but also words or even feelings in the parent's body. These are focused on a personal experience, so people often describe them as a memory. They often relate to difficult experiences of giving birth. We have chosen to describe them as *images* rather than *memories* because, for many people, the traumatic image comprises features that parents do not remember but rather have created or used to fill in gaps in a memory. Please note that traumatic images are a separate phenomenon from intrusive images, which are addressed in Chapter 15/Session 13).

Rationale for Addressing Traumatic Images

It is important to address traumatic images because these can contribute to the maintenance of the depression. For example, the parent may be so focused on the traumatic images that they sleep very poorly and are therefore too tired during the day to engage in activities that will help them recover from the depression. Addressing the impact of these negative images can feel quite strange to some parents because often people tend to do a lot of thinking with words, rather than images. It can also be frightening because it means reliving a difficult experience.

It is important to explain clearly to the parent why it is helpful to address traumatic images.

A useful analogy is to compare describing the details of a traumatic image to opening a computer file. Although the file's icon or title might give some useful information, there is a greater wealth of detail within the file, so it is necessary to open it to understand the meaning of the content. It is the same with a traumatic image—we need to take a good look at details to understand what they mean and their effects on the parent.

The way humans store the details of a traumatic image is generally different from the way less upsetting memories are stored. With traumatic images or memories, we tend to store the information in our brains without processing it in the way we typically process information. This is because processing the information can itself be so distressing that, understandably, we may avoid processing it.

This is a bit like stuffing your clothes into a suitcase without folding them or sorting them into categories. Unfortunately, because the information is unsorted, the memory or image can "burst out" of its storage space (just like clothes can "explode" out of a suitcase in a confused mess). In reality, this can mean the traumatic memory pops up unexpectedly and in a distressing way when it is triggered by something. Hence, it is necessary to sort the information and put it away "neatly" so that it is stored in a manageable way that will no longer "burst out". Sorting the information involves exploring it in detail. Once you have done this, it is less likely that the parent's traumatic image will "burst out" in an unexpected way, and the parent will be less likely to be preoccupied with the traumatic image(s).

Weigh the Pros and Cons of Addressing Traumatic Imagery

Some parents may have developed an avoidant response to traumatic images and want to avoid engaging with the images. If this is the case, it is helpful to weigh the pros and cons of examining the material. This weighing process might provide information relevant to understanding the parent's beliefs about the images (e.g., it will be emotionally overwhelming, and they would be unable to cope). Weighing the pros and cons may involve a discussion of what the parent expects might happen to their feelings if they deliberately bring up the traumatic image (for example, being overwhelmed by negative feelings) and, alternatively, why it might be helpful to deal with the images, etc.

Preparation for Evoking Traumatic Images (Grounding and Timing)

It is good practice to plan and prepare a procedure that includes "grounding" the parent back to the day-to-day world in the session. This is because, even though you will be exploring traumatic images (but not *severely* traumatic images), the parent may still be overwhelmed by a vivid flashback when bringing up the image. Some ideas for grounding include distraction, refocusing on elements in the environment (e.g., what the parent can hear, see, smell, touch), and the use of grounding words, objects, images, or phrases.

It is also important to ensure there will be adequate time in your session after the parent has brought up their image(s) to reflect on the experience of engaging with the image and going through it in detail. You may need to plan for a longer session than usual.

Assessment of Traumatic Images

You may now explain to the parent that you will be asking questions about the specific traumatic images, encouraging them to bring these image(s) to mind so that you can both begin to understand details of their content and meaning. You will also be looking together at the role of these images in maintaining the depression.

Exploration of the Traumatic Image(s)

The task now is to sensitively help the parent to describe the image(s) (so that you have a clear sense of its content) and to express their feelings and thoughts about the image(s) (so that you have a clear sense of the parent's' emotional and behavioral responses to the image[s] and the meaning[s] of the image[s] and the parent's beliefs about them).

Useful questions for this part of the session are listed in Box 16.1.

Revisiting the meaning of the traumatic image can help to consolidate the shared understanding of the image. Ask what the image meant, if the image represents current reality, and if the parent's beliefs about the image have altered at all since starting this session.

Working Out What Keeps the Traumatic Images Going

Having explored the traumatic image(s) in detail, the next step is to develop a formulation/conceptualization of what keeps the traumatic image going. You can use Worksheet 21: What Can Keep Traumatic Images Going? As you complete this with the parent, you might become aware of other unhelpful appraisals of the image, for example, believing that engaging with it could emotionally overwhelm the parent.

Let's see how the discussion went with Sarah.

Sarah had a traumatic birth experience. She went into labor 6 weeks prematurely, and the labor was long and painful. After many hours, she was told that her baby was in distress and that she would need to have a C-section to get her baby out as quickly as possible. She was terrified that there would be something seriously wrong with her baby. After the C-section, her baby was taken away for what seemed to Sarah like hours, although in reality it was only 10 minutes. During this time, she replayed in her head

Box 16.1 Questions for exploring the traumatic image

Ask the parent to describe the content of the image as if it is happening now, from their own perspective:

Source

- *Where does the image come from?*

Content

- *What is in the image? (Ask for details from all senses that are active in the parent's perception of the image.)*
- *Do you see it in your mind's eye/hear it in your mind's ear?*
- *Does it feel as if it is happening now?*
- *What happens next? Then what happens?*

Meaning and beliefs

- *What does this image mean to you? (About yourself, others, the world, the future?)*
- *What is the significance of having the image? (Is it a premonition, is it dangerous, can it affect the future?)*
- *What message does the image carry for you?*
- *Is it as if it is a warning to you? (If so, from whom?)*
- *What might happen if you hold the image in mind?*
- *What do you feel right now?*
- *How does it affect your feelings in this moment? (Many parents report more than one important emotion.)*

Current impact

- *What is the impact of having the image in the present? (For example, does the parent feel [physically] threatened, or panicked?)*

Behavioral and cognitive responses (what is making the image persist as a problem?)

How do you respond to the occurrence of the image(s)? Do you try to:

- *distract yourself from it?*
- *suppress it?*
- *put a different image in its place?*
- *dwell on it?*
- *feel worried about it?*
- *seek reassurance about it?*
- *do something to prevent something bad happening?*

scenarios of being told that her baby was dead or brain-damaged. Eventually, they brought her baby to her, and she was able to give her a cuddle briefly before they took her to the neonatal intensive care unit (NICU). Sarah kept replaying over and over in her mind the scenario of lying there helpless after the C-section without her baby. These images would pop up unexpectedly at night and disrupt her sleep, and she would feel panicked and threatened by a risk to her baby's life. This impacted her mood and made it hard for her to feel relaxed with Chloe.

See Figure 16.1 for the diagram that was drawn up with Sarah to explain how her traumatic images had become stuck.

Based on what the parent has reported about their traumatic image(s), you can test their appraisals of the image when you begin to experiment with the image.

Transforming Traumatic Images

Having collaboratively developed a shared understanding of what keeps the image(s) going, you can now address the impact of the image(s) with the parent, by transforming the image itself, as well as changing the beliefs the parent may hold about the image. The aim in transforming the traumatic image might be to make it less threatening and/or more realistic. This can be done in a number of different ways.

Running the Image On

This refers to expanding the context by "running the image on in time." Often, images stop at the worst point of a scenario (e.g., the parent faints, they vomit, they receive very bad news). It can be helpful to add to the context of the traumatic image by running the image on in time, to see what might happen next and how the parent might cope in the situation (time projection).

Sarah and her therapist expanded Sarah's image by updating it to include what happened next.

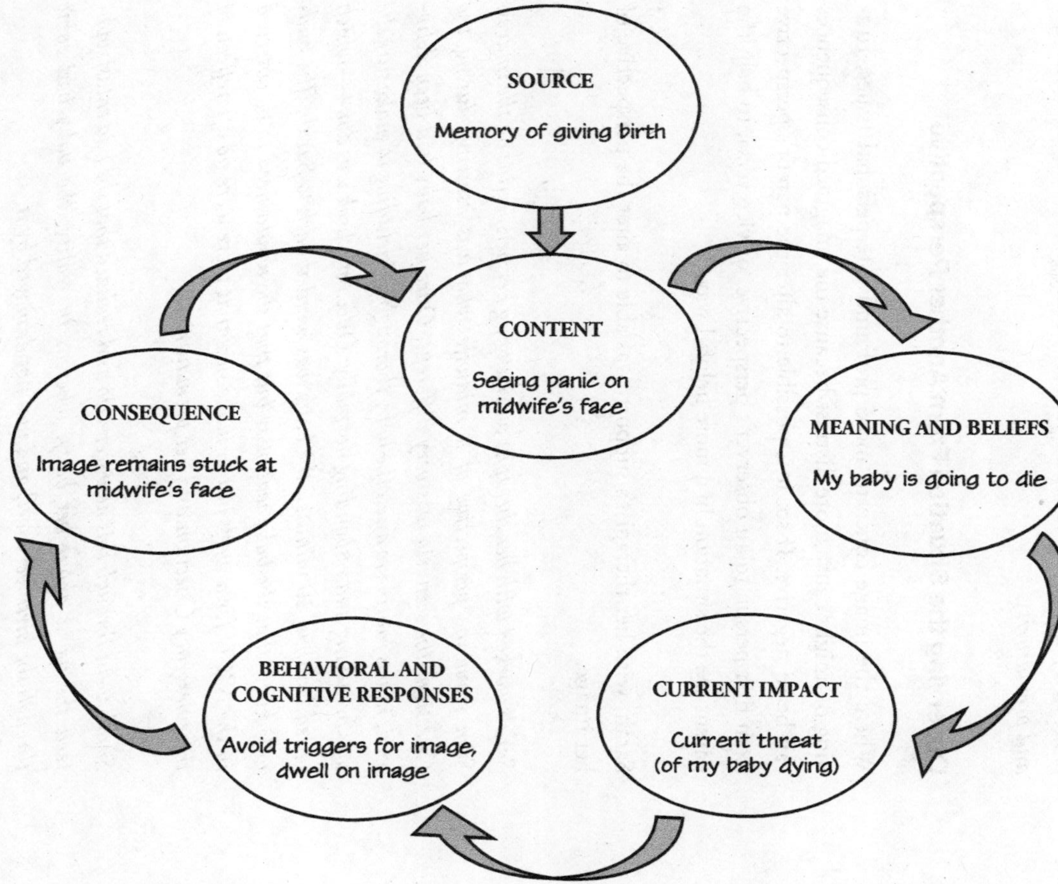

Figure 16.1
Sarah's Completed Worksheet 21: What Can Keep Traumatic Images Going?

Sarah worked with her therapist on updating the image to include what happened after her image typically stopped. In particular, Sarah added to her image two key features. First, she added in the midwife telling her that, as with all babies, her baby was being taken for routine checks. Second, she added in the process of her baby being returned to her by the midwife and being told that her baby was okay but that she would need to spend a few days in the NICU for monitoring given the traumatic birth and prematurity.

Observing the Situation From Another Perspective

Where the image concerns more profound interpersonal issues, running on might cause more distress because the imagined consequences can be so negative. If so, it is possible to alter the parent's perspective from first person to an observer's perspective, or vice versa, to help the parent see the situation in a more helpful way.

Sarah, with her therapist's support, was able to alter the perspective of her image.

Sarah worked with her therapist on changing her perspective on the images. Seen from the perspective of a midwife who was assisting during the C-section, the scenario was very different. Once her baby had been delivered, it was routine to assess the baby thoroughly, including to make sure she was breathing and responding normally. Once this check was done—which lasted less than 10 minutes, the baby was handed back to Sarah. The midwife knew that the baby was okay but that she would need to be observed in the NICU for a week just to make sure that there were no aftereffects of the emergency C-section and her prematurity.

Sarah went through this new scenario and realized that she had catastrophized the worst about her baby, whereas in reality, the baby had come through the birth very well and was not damaged by it.

Changing the Image

Changing the image might involve shrinking the image so that it takes up less space in the parent's mind's eye or turning the sound down. It can be helpful to encourage the parent to imagine seeing the image on a screen, with a remote control in their hands, so that they can turn the sound down, minimize the image, speed it up, or change the color.

Let's see what happened with Sarah.

As well as changing the perspective of the image as described earlier, Sarah found this strategy helpful, particularly when the images popped up without warning at night. When she experienced these images, she imagined that the images were on a screen and that she was able to shrink them so that they took up very little space on the screen. This left more space for other thoughts and images of a positive nature (e.g., seeing the delivery from the midwife's perspective), and these new images began to take over.

Taking Actions Not Taken at the Time

Parents can sometimes be convinced that, if they had done something different in the past, then a better outcome would have occurred. Updating the image to include taking an action that the parent did not take at the time can be helpful to reduce the negative impact of the traumatic image.

Here is how Sarah used this strategy.

Sarah and her therapist worked to alter the image (from Sarah's perspective) so that it included Sarah asking the midwife whether it is usual practice for a baby born via C-section to be taken away for a checkup. In the image, the midwife responded affirmatively and told Sarah that all babies are routinely assessed. Sarah found this to be reassuring (and this change helped to prevent the associated panic of the unaltered image from Sarah's perspective).

Transforming the Meaning of the Image

This is likely to happen naturally during the process of the work as the parent begins to see that they are able to cope and are not overwhelmed by the images. Some specific discussion with the parent about the meaning of the images is, however, often helpful.

Sarah and her therapist identified key features of the meaning of her image and examined these together.

The key meaning for Sarah was that her baby was going to die ("My baby is going to die," shown in Figure 16.1). They discussed where this came from and found that it rested on Sarah's belief that the midwife's face showed panic, which meant that something was terribly wrong with her baby and that, therefore, baby Chloe was taken away because of something really serious. When they discussed that all *babies are taken away for brief assessment, Sarah was able to see that the look on the midwife's face did not mean something was terribly wrong (and, in fact, that the midwife's face showed concentration on the task of the assessment rather than panic). Sarah was able to alter the meaning of the image to, "All babies are taken away for assessment."*

Debrief

Exploring traumatic images is an unusual and distressing experience, so it is likely to be helpful to ask the parent about their experience of the process.

Useful questions for this part of the session include:

- *What was it like talking about your image(s)?*
- *What happened to the image(s)?*
- *How do you feel now?*
- *What do you think about the impact of the image(s)?*
- *What do you need to do now to ground yourself?*

You may prompt the parent to use one or more of the grounding techniques discussed earlier in the session. Furthermore, in keeping with standard best practice, you should *ensure that the parent is in a suitable emotional and mental state to end the session safely.* For example, if the parent appears to be dissociated, then you might help ground them by asking them to give a detailed verbal description of an object in the room.

Troubleshooting

Although the parent may agree to talk about their images, they may be reluctant to start the process. It is important to make sure there is plenty of time for this session, particularly so that there can be an adequate debrief and time for grounding the parent before they get back to their normal activities.

Home Practice

Parents are unlikely to be able to re-create the altered or updated image without support. In addition to completing Worksheet 21: What Can Keep Traumatic Images Going?, the parent can make an audio recording of this session and listen to it as part of home practice to support themselves to test the strategies you have identified in the session.

Plan with the parent which strategy they will put to use between sessions. This will most likely be the one that they perceive to have been the most helpful in the session (e.g., changing perspective, transforming the meaning of the image).

Summary of This Session and Feedback

It is important now to check that the parent has understood the key issues in the session and knows what to work on before the next session. It is helpful to hear from the parent how they found the session and whether they need more discussion/grounding before the session is finished. It can be very challenging working through traumatic images, and it is important that the parent feels grounded in the present again at the end of the session.

Key Points

- Traumatic images can be very distressing and help to maintain depression in the postnatal period.
- Developing a different relationship to the images can reduce their impact.
- There are specific ways to change the nature of the images and thereby reduce their impact.
- Working with images can be distressing, and it is important to have strategies to ground oneself.

Beyond This Treatment Program

The formal therapy program has now finished. Chapter 17 (the first chapter in this final section) describes the booster sessions that may be arranged with the parent a few months following the end of therapy. Then in Chapter 18, we describe the outcome for the six parents who we have been following throughout, along with comments from one of the research participants. Finally, there is discussion of recent research in this area as well as ideas for further research.

CHAPTER 17

Booster Sessions and Moving On

Aim of This Chapter

The aim of this chapter is to consider the advantages of booster sessions and how to deliver them.

Outline

- Rationale for booster sessions 256
- How to introduce the idea of booster sessions 256
- Booster Session 1 257
- Booster Session 2 260
- Troubleshooting 260
- Summary and feedback 260
- Key points 260

When to Conduct These Sessions

The two booster sessions can be conducted approximately 4 months after the formal treatment program has ended.

Materials Needed

- Worksheet 22: Booster Session Review
- Parent's completed Worksheet 19: Staying Well Plan

Postpartum Depression. Anne Stewart et al., Oxford University Press. © Oxford University Press (2026).
DOI: 10.1093/med-psych/9780197759707.003.0017

Worksheets appear in Appendix A at the end of this therapist guide and in Appendix A at the end of the parent workbook. Worksheets can also be accessed by searching for this book's title on the Oxford Academic platform, at academic.oup.com. Note that when more than one copy of a worksheet is required, you may photocopy the worksheets for the parent, ask the parent to make their own photocopies, or direct the parent to the book website to print their own.

Rationale for Booster Sessions

In the research study that evaluated this program, the parents received two booster sessions 2 weeks apart at around 4 to 5 months following the end of treatment. These sessions were designed to consolidate the treatment that the parent had received, build on the experiences since ending therapy, and identify helpful strategies to manage low mood in the long term. Having booster sessions a few months following the end of therapy gives the parent a chance to manage on their own, before touching base with the therapist again to review how they are progressing; this is an opportunity to brainstorm options for dealing with any problems that may have arisen, using the skills acquired during the therapy.

The National Institute for Health and Care Excellence (NICE) guidance for depression (evidence-based recommendations for health and care in England and Wales) recommends the use of follow-up sessions to assess early signs of the depression returning and to prevent relapse (NICE, 2022). Some parents prefer to finish therapy completely and go it alone with support from family and friends. Others find it supportive knowing that there is a chance to check in with the therapist again and brainstorm how to deal with any challenges or setbacks that have cropped up.

How to Introduce the Idea of Booster Sessions

In Module 4: Heading to the Future: Planning How to Stay Well, having a 4- to-5-month gap is discussed as a "testing ground" for the parent to continue using the strategies learned in therapy. Meeting up after this gap can be a helpful way of reviewing how things are going, consolidating skills, and ensuring that the parent is continuing to do things that keep them well.

However, we realize that this might not always be possible, either due to the parent declining this opportunity or it not being possible for the therapist. If this is the case, you can encourage the parent to check in with their family doctor or primary care physician a few months after finishing therapy so that there is a chance to review how things are going. Alternatively, they may prefer to do their own review with a partner, family member, or friend. Worksheet 22: Booster Session Review will be helpful in providing a framework for this.

Booster Session 1

After a gap of a few months, the first booster session is designed to be an opportunity to review their experiences since finishing therapy. In this session the parent will be encouraged to talk about what has gone well, what the challenges have been, and how the parent has been able to continue some of the skills they have learned. Worksheet 22: Booster Session Review gives a framework for the booster sessions and can be introduced in Booster Session 1 as described below:

- *What Skills Does the Parent Remember From Therapy That Were Helpful to Them?* You can discuss first with the parent what they have taken from the therapy and used in a helpful way since therapy ended. For example, this may be learning the skill of being kind to themselves, ensuring that they get enough sleep, or being able to manage negative thinking.
- *What Has Gone Well Since the End of Therapy?* The next step is to discuss with the parent what has gone well since the end of therapy. Perhaps they have enjoyed watching their baby develop, they have begun to spend more time with friends, or they have coped with going back to work. Perhaps they have noticed that their mood is more consistently normal or that they are getting on better with their partner. Whatever it is, you can celebrate with the parent the positive changes that have happened, however small.
- *What Have the Challenges Been?* There will undoubtedly have been challenges since finishing therapy. Now is the chance to discuss what these challenges have been. It may be that their baby is still waking up regularly at night or that the parent's

plans for starting work have not gone well. They may have noticed times when their mood seemed to drop again. It is important to normalize these challenges. All parents will have challenges, and these booster sessions are a chance to consider how to cope with the challenges.

- *How Did the Parent Cope With the Challenges?* You can check with the parent how they have been coping with the challenges. Are there skills they have used or changes they have put in place to manage these challenges? For example, have they prioritized having a period of relaxation before bedtime to improve their sleep?
- *Are There Skills That Have Previously Been Helpful That the Parent Could Have Used to Respond to Those Challenges?* Perhaps there are skills or habits the parent used during therapy that they have forgotten about but would be useful now. It is useful to refer to the parent's Staying Well Plan (Worksheet 19), which has ideas for how to stay well. You can discuss with the parent what might be useful to try.
- *Has the Parent Been Aware of Any Unhelpful Responses?* It may be the case that the parent has slipped back into some habits that have not been helpful, for example, skipping meals or not getting out of the house. You can discuss what the impact of these responses has been on their well-being.
- *How Can the Parent Minimize These Unhelpful Responses?* This can lead to a discussion on how to minimize these unhelpful responses. Could the parent, for example, arrange to do activities with a friend out of the house or prioritize having a meal out with their partner on a regular basis?
- *What/Who Will Support the Parent to Continue Living in a Way That Gives Meaning and Value to Their Life?* It is important to discuss the things that will support the parent to continue to bring meaning and value to their life; this might be connecting more with friends and family or taking up interests that they have neglected. Watching their baby grow and develop and noticing and being curious about the small changes can enhance this period of life despite the challenges.

Figure 17.1 shows how Mila got on completing her Worksheet 22: Booster Session Review.

Question	Notes
What skills do you remember from therapy that were helpful to you?	Important things for me were learning how to be more compassionate to myself and not expecting myself to be a perfect mother. I also learned the importance of keeping in contact with my friends.
What has gone well since the end of therapy?	My partner Sophie and I have gotten a lot closer and support each other better.
What have the challenges been?	My mood started becoming low again a couple of months after finishing therapy. This was at the point of going back to work.
How did you cope with the challenges?	I reminded myself of my Staying Well Plan, and I started eating better and going out for walks regularly.s
Are there any skills that have previously been helpful that you *could* have used to respond to those challenges?	I should have thought of myself a bit more rather than running around trying to fix everything for other people. I need to keep reminding myself to look after myself!
Have you been aware of any unhelpful responses?	Skipping meals wasn't a good idea.
How can you minimize these unhelpful responses?	Get Sophie's support to make sure I eat regularly and get out for regular exercise—both of which definitely help my mood.
What/who will support you to continue living in a way that gives meaning and value to your life?	My partner and my friends will help keep me on track. It's important for me to be open with Sophie.

Figure 17.1

Mila's Completed Worksheet 22: Booster Session Review.

Booster Session 2

The second booster session (around 2 weeks later) is a final session to identify and put into place helpful strategies to enable the parent to cope with challenges or to discuss unhelpful responses and how to minimize these and to refine the plan for the future. You can check out if the parent has put into place any of the ideas discussed in the previous session and see if there are any amendments they would like to make to their Staying Well Plan. As this is the final session, it is important to ensure that the parent knows how to get additional help in the future if needed. Finally, it is important to allow any discussion about the ending of therapy and saying goodbye. Some parents will be keen to get on with their lives without therapy; others may find it hard to come to the final end of therapy.

Troubleshooting

It is not uncommon for the parent to attend the first booster session and to describe challenging experiences over the past few months, including difficulty in settling back to work and a return of some of the depressive symptoms. You can acknowledge any setbacks as an important part of the process. Everyone has setbacks from time to time; you can encourage the parent to think of ways to deal with setbacks. It can be helpful to discuss how progress is likely to be up and down and that coping with difficulties can build resilience and help to consolidate their skills.

Summary and Feedback

At the end of the two booster sessions, you can check out what the parent has gained from these sessions to take forward in their life. What are the things they have learned from these sessions? What has been helpful? You can reiterate the sources of help in the future and remind them of how far they have come to this point.

Key Points

- It is common to have setbacks after finishing therapy.
- Setbacks are a good opportunity to put skills into practice.
- Reviewing after a few months can help to consolidate skills learned.

CHAPTER 18

Growth and Change Through Treatment and Beyond

Aim of This Chapter

The aim of this chapter is to describe the outcome for the parents (case examples) who we have been following throughout this book, to hear the perspective of one of the participants in the research trial of this treatment, and to discuss further developments in the field since the original research was conducted.

Outline

- Outcome of therapy 261
- Comments from a participant in the research trial 267
- Other developments in the field 268
- Final remarks 269
- Key points 270

Throughout this book we have been following six women from diverse cultures and a range of ages, circumstances, and family situations. Now is the chance to hear how they got on with therapy and what the outcome was for each of them in their lives.

Outcome of Therapy

The outcome of all these women is also described in the parent workbook.

Postpartum Depression. Anne Stewart et al., Oxford University Press. © Oxford University Press (2026).
DOI: 10.1093/med-psych/9780197759707.003.0018

LUCY

Lucy struggled during her pregnancy and the postpartum period as a young single mother. She hadn't planned to get pregnant and found it very challenging to cope with this big change in her life while she was still a teenager. It took her a while to pluck up the courage to get help when she became depressed. However, as her symptoms continued, she sought support and ended up completing 12 therapy sessions.

One of the things that changed for Lucy was her ability to both seek and accept support from others. She began to start seeing her friends more and was surprised at how interested they were in her son, Jackson, and how keen they were to help and support her. She also developed a better relationship with her parents, who enjoyed looking after the baby while she did other things.

The additional support meant that Lucy could consider going back to her course in catering. She got in touch with the program, and they accepted her back as a part-time student. Her parents looked after Jackson for 2 days a week, and though it wasn't easy, Lucy managed to find a daycare that was within her budget for the other day. She was excited about all of this and enjoyed getting back to the catering program and spending time with like-minded people.

There were, understandably, times when Lucy felt tired and worn out, but when this happened, she knew she had to prioritize herself, making sure she got sufficient rest and did not skip meals. She reviewed how things were going with her therapist after 4 months and felt confident that she was managing to look after herself and her baby, with support from family and friends. Jackson grew into a happy toddler, giving a lot of pleasure to those around him, and Lucy felt proud of what they were accomplishing as a family.

ZAINAB

Zainab felt she had "failed everyone" when she became depressed after giving birth to her son, Amir. She had been depressed 4 years previously after giving birth to Layla, her first child, and was hoping that things would be different this time. She felt she was a bad mother and was embarrassed that she needed help "yet again". However, she found it a relief to see a therapist who empathized with how overwhelmed she was feeling and helped Zainab to tackle her problems systematically one by one.

She gradually got out of the house more and learned to deal with her negative thinking, be kinder to herself, and not expect herself to be the perfect mother. She accepted help from her mother-in-law, who offered to babysit so she and her husband Tauseef could go out for a meal.

Zainab began to take an interest in gardening and was pleased when Layla joined her too—this special time together had a positive effect on Layla's mood and behavior. Zainab's relationship with Tauseef also improved as they prioritized time together.

As her depression lifted, she became more confident as a mother and a person. Zainab knew that she had a history of depression and realized the importance of being aware of the warning signs of her depression returning and the need to address these signs early before depression gets a hold again. She continued to have check-ins with her family doctor and her psychiatrist, who monitored her progress and medication over a period of 6 months. Her therapist also let her know that she could have further therapy sessions if needed.

KENISE

Kenise had a tough time coping with her twins Serena and Jayden as well as her 6-year-old, Maya. Her husband, Demar, was frequently away for work, and her mother lived in another city, 4 hours away, so she lacked the close support of immediate family. She began to feel she was a bad mother and got stuck in cycles of negative thinking that kept her awake at night. It was hard to find time for therapy, but Kenise persisted and with her therapist's support, completed 10 sessions. Her aunties and cousins who live nearby visited regularly and encouraged her to get out.

Over time, Kenise learned the importance of having regular contact with her friends and family and being more compassionate and forgiving of herself. As she began to feel more able to leave the house and take on new things, she joined a local twins group through social media and started meeting up with other twin-moms. She found this really helpful in terms of making sense of her experience and feeling like she had a community of parents who understood what she was dealing with. She began to take more interest in Jayden and Serena's development. When Demar was home, they found ways to share some of the household tasks, and this created some opportunities for them to have moments together relaxing—and their relationship improved.

Kenise found that raising three children under age 6 is not an easy task, but she became more relaxed in her expectations for herself, learned how to ask more directly for support, and began to have moments of fun with her children.

SARAH

Sarah had given birth at the age of 38 and struggled with exhaustion and low mood, alongside experiencing recurrent images about the traumatic birth of her daughter, Chloe, which she couldn't get out of her head.

Her therapy initially focused on becoming more active, which helped a little in lifting her mood. In addition, she learned to trust other people, including her husband, Richard, to look after Chloe, which meant that she became less exhausted. She found the work on problem solving helpful as it gave her a tool to address the many demands in her life. Halfway through the module on 'Thinking', Sarah required some additional therapeutic work focused specifically on the traumatic images about the birth.

Sarah had previously really enjoyed her work as a senior manager in retail. As her depression gradually lifted, she began to consider going back to work; she contacted her employer and was pleased that they were happy for her to return to work in a flexible capacity. They agreed that she could do remote work managing the inventory/supply chain side of the job 2 days a week, which meant that she only needed to be in the office 3 days a week. For the 2 days working from home, Sarah found a great opportunity to share with a neighbor a local babysitter, who could be based at home. Sarah and her husband Richard agreed to share the management of this. He would do the morning handover to the sitter, and she would do the evening handover. This meant that each of them had a bit of flexibility in their work schedule at one part of the day. This provided Sarah with a lot of relief. For 2 of the days Sarah worked in the office, she managed to get Chloe into a nursery close to her work, and on the other day her parents (who had retired) came to look after Chloe in their home.

There were times when certain situations, such as driving past the hospital where she had given birth, triggered a memory of the birth. However, she now had strategies to deal with this. Sarah found it wasn't easy coping with a high-level job and looking after Chloe, but she was aware of the importance of looking after herself, which meant having regular meals, taking time for exercise, and engaging in enjoyable activities that she valued. Her cousin (who lived nearby and had been very supportive when she was depressed) offered to look after Chloe from time to time and this enabled her to go out for a meal with Richard every few weeks, which had a positive impact on their relationship. At the 4-month booster review, Sarah refreshed her strategies to manage negative thinking and was encouraged to keep going with looking after herself.

MILA

Mila was diagnosed with depression 2 months after giving birth to Marta and struggled to look after herself. She began to skip meals, and her energy levels dropped. When Mila first saw her therapist, the main problems she identified were feeling exhausted and not getting any enjoyment from life. She also acknowledged having thoughts about harming her baby, which just popped into her head and worried her.

Her therapist helped her to set goals, keep herself safe, and tackle her problems one by one. Mila was encouraged to meet up with other mothers with babies the same age, which she found helpful because this gave her a chance to talk over difficulties that they were all experiencing and exchange tips on how to manage. She also learned to be more compassionate to herself and not expect herself to be a perfect mother. Mila engaged in additional work with her therapist to manage the intrusive thoughts that she was having regarding harming her baby. She realized that these thoughts were normal, and they ceased to bother her.

Mila found the therapy helpful and was anxious about being discharged. Her therapist encouraged her to prioritize regular time with her friends and continue with her mother and baby group. She practiced different ways of asking for support from her partner, Sophie, and they became a lot closer. At the end of therapy, Mila brought Sophie along to one of the final sessions so that they could discuss the warning signs of depression together and how to manage them as a couple.

A few months later, Mila started to become depressed again. It was Sophie who noticed that Mila was skipping meals, losing energy, and complaining of feeling tired. She had also stopped going to her mother and baby group. They reminded themselves of the Staying Well Plan, and Sophie supported Mila to start eating regularly again and get out for walks each day. She rejoined her mother and baby group, even though she didn't feel like it. Her mood gradually improved, and she realized the importance of support from her partner and her friends. She had arranged to have booster sessions with her therapist after 4 months, and at the first booster session she was able to discuss the blip with her therapist and how she got back on track with support from family and friends. Mila had a final session a couple of weeks later and felt confident to finish therapy, knowing that she had strategies to keep herself well and could get help if needed.

ISABELLA

Isabella found it hard coping with having a baby, particularly as Isabella is autistic, and she found the change involved in having a baby very unsettling. She was previously in a familiar routine with her job in IT and a structured life with her partner, Jack, and the arrival of Margarita changed everything. Part of her resented how Margarita had changed her life.

Isabella struggled with the therapy to start with and didn't feel understood. However, the therapist encouraged her to give feedback and adapted the therapy to make it more concrete and predictable.

Isabella spent some time going through her values as a parent with her therapist and identified that her values were around daily structure and an orderly home and feeling loved and valued. With her therapist's help, she managed to develop a routine at home that she felt comfortable with. This included asking for and accepting help from her mother at times that Isabella had control over. Isabella has learned to be clear with her mother about how she wants to parent Margarita, in a way that doesn't cause conflict and resentment. She also developed a pattern of inviting her wider family over for short periods of time on the weekends. Isabella found that it worked for her and Margarita to have a schedule for feeding times and sleep. She began to resent the demands associated with parenting less and took more interest in Margarita's development.

Over time, Isabella's mood started to lift, and she got used to her new life with the baby. She and Jack felt more comfortable traveling with Margarita, and following the ending of the therapy, they were able to take a vacation in Argentina where they have family. When Margarita reached 10 months old, Isabella considered returning to her IT job and, in preparation for this, made arrangements for daycare for Margarita as well as a day a week spent with Isabella's mother. Prior to starting back to work, Isabella had a review with her family doctor and felt reassured that she could get further help in the future if she needed it.

Comments From a Participant in the Research Trial

Here are some comments from Olivia, who introduced herself in Chapter 2 and who completed the program during the research evaluation. She describes what she thought of the program and how things turned out for her.

OLIVIA

When I enrolled as a participant in the OPP [Oxford Postnatal Programme] study, I was suicidal: by the time I completed the program outlined in this book, I was well on the road to recovery. I didn't get better overnight, and at times it was hard going. However, the program gave me the tools to understand why I became so unwell, and it also gave me the knowledge I needed to keep myself safe.

When my first child was 4, I had a second baby, and I stayed well. There is no way I would have been able to go on to have another baby had it not been for the treatment I received via the OPP study. The birth of my second child really showed me how life-saving my participation in the OPP had been. It brought with it an element of grief as I mourned the experiences I missed with my first baby, but it also allowed me to see that my relationship with that baby, forged as it was in such difficulty, was unharmed: that in fact our bond was strong precisely because of the experiences we weathered together. Both my children have brought me so much joy over the years, and I have learned so much as a result of being their mom. I know though that I am a better, more compassionate mother as a result of having had, and recovered from, postpartum depression. That might seem an odd thing to write, but through my illness and recovery I had to learn the true meaning of self-compassion and the importance of treating both my and my children's mental health with the same seriousness that as parents we're primed to bring to our care of our children's physical health.

Several years have passed since I had postpartum depression, and in the intervening period I've continued to learn from my participation in the program. I know now that recovery from depression is not always straightforward, and I have seen that my own recovery has been a journey on which there have been stumbling blocks as well as milestones. I have learned that staying well is an active process and that relapse prevention plans that are manageable and meaningful are really important. I have continued to understand more of the story of my first child's babyhood as I have learned that change does not mean getting back to where you were before but rather involves finding new ways to be, new ways to look after both yourself and those around you. I am enormously grateful to have been a participant in the original OPP study, and I am so glad this book makes it possible for other people to benefit from the therapy program too.

Other Developments in the Field

Since the research was carried out to evaluate this treatment program, there have been further studies on cognitive behavioral therapy (CBT; including behavioral activation [BA] approaches) for postpartum depression in the field across high-, middle-, and low-income countries, demonstrating further evidence of the effectiveness of CBT for maternal postpartum depression, anxiety, and stress when compared to either treatment-as-usual or waitlist (Fatori et al., 2023; Pettman et al., 2023) and whether delivered in home settings, online, or in groups (Branquinho et al. 2021; Cuijpers et al., 2023; X. Li et al., 2022; Pettman et al., 2023). Recognizing the increased support needs in the postpartum period, a number of CBT programs have included components focusing on building support with close others. For example, a meta-analysis found that interventions that included the partner in the treatment were effective at reducing maternal perinatal depression (X. Li et al. 2022). In a process analysis of a peer-delivered CBT treatment for perinatal depression called the "Thinking Healthy Programme" conducted in India, Singla et al. (2021) found that both activation and support mediated outcomes, suggesting CBT for postpartum depression should include components that focus on both elements. Several studies have also now demonstrated that CBT effectively reduces perinatal depression relative to the control condition in women with low incomes, in both high-income (Ammerman et al., 2015; Jesse et al., 2015; H. O'Mahen et al., 2013) and low- and middle-income (Arisoyin et al., 2023; Rahman et al., 2008; Sarfraz et al., 2024) countries, with results sustained over longer-term follow-up.

Several postpartum depression CBT interventions have included components focused on developing parenting confidence and skills (Amani et al., 2023; Merza et al., 2023; Pettman et al., 2023), though few have included video-feedback parent–infant work as was done in the Stein et al. (2018) study. The current Insika-Yomama trial in South Africa is testing BA alongside a parent–infant intervention across pregnancy and the transition to parenthood compared to treatment as usual (Rochat et al., 2021). Some studies, such as a CBT intervention for young mothers in Nigeria, have embedded CBT content into broader public health parenting education elements (Gureje et al., 2022).

Recent studies have focused on improving the reach of CBT, focusing on delivery by a range of mental health, health, and non-specialist providers. The results thus far have been mixed, with a recent meta-analysis (Pettman et al. 2023) finding better outcomes in trials where CBT was delivered by mental health professionals or co-delivered by a mental health professional and a health or non-specialist provider, compared to interventions delivered solely by health or non-specialist providers. These findings highlight the need for robust training and supervision of therapy providers.

Further research needs to identify which components of CBT are the most effective, clarify what works for whom, and evaluate parent/baby interventions within CBT.

Final Remarks

Olivia, who went through the program, emphasized the importance of sticking with the program even if you don't feel like it. Change doesn't happen immediately but can occur if there are small, persistent changes that can contribute to gradually feeling better in oneself and more able to deal with life. A key role for the therapist is encouraging small steps, acknowledging the efforts the parent is making, and helping the parent build their own support network. Understanding the challenges of parenthood is a crucial element to this.

Key Points

- Postpartum depression is a serious condition that can disrupt the lives of parents and babies.
- It is possible for parents from a range of diverse cultures and countries to benefit from this program.
- Therapy can be tough at times, but with support, parents can get through the challenging times.
- It is possible for parents to recover from depression and get on with their lives.

Appendix A

Worksheets

Worksheet 1: Preparation for Assessment

Worksheet 2: Motivational Balance

Worksheet 3: Coping Strategies

Worksheet 4: How Changes in Life Can Lead to Low Mood

Worksheet 5: Safety Plan

Worksheet 6: Mood Monitoring Record

Worksheet 7: Working Out Your Values

Worksheet 8: Setting Goals for Therapy

Worksheet 9: Weekly Goal Planner

Worksheet 10: Weekly Goal Record

Worksheet 11: Weekly Routine

Worksheet 12: Daily Routine

Worksheet 13: Nourishing and Depleting Activities

Worksheet 14: Problem Solving

Worksheet 15: Understanding How We Get Stuck in Our Thoughts

Worksheet 16: Getting Stuck in Your Thoughts Record

Worksheet 17: Alternative Strategies to Getting Stuck in Our Thoughts

Worksheet 18: Using an Image to Practice Self-Compassion

Worksheet 19: Staying Well Plan

Worksheet 20: What Can Keep Intrusive Thoughts Going?

Worksheet 21: What Can Keep Traumatic Images Going?

Worksheet 22: Booster Session Review

Worksheet 1: Preparation for Assessment

Question	Notes
What are your current concerns?	
What would you like to be different?	
What would you like to achieve in therapy?	
What are your strengths?	
Who can support you to make changes?	

This worksheet can also be accessed online at academic.oup.com

Worksheet 2: Motivational Balance

Pros of doing this therapy	Cons of doing this therapy

This worksheet can also be accessed online at academic.oup.com

Worksheet 3: Coping Strategies

Sometimes we experience emotions or situations that can feel overwhelmingly distressing and difficult to manage. This worksheet has some ideas for strategies that you can use to try and cope with feelings of anger, stress, sadness, or worry in the short term.

Coping strategy	Examples
Distraction	Go for a walk, get out of the house, read a book, watch a film, listen to music.
Strong sensations	Squeeze ice cubes, punch a pillow, bite into a lemon or lime, snap an elastic band against your wrist.
Nurture yourself	Apply hand cream, take a 20-minute nap, run a warm bath, make a soothing hot drink, light a scented candle.
Talk	Call a family member or friend, talk about your feelings or just about everyday things, remember positive times, or have a laugh and a joke together.
Find nature	Go for a walk, sit in your car or on a bench, or take a picnic to a beautiful place outside in nature: a forest, a beach, a park, near the sea.
Creative expression	Write down your feelings, keep a journal or make a scrapbook, draw, paint, put on some music and dance.
Physical exercise	Go for a jog or walk, join an exercise class, or try out an online yoga, fitness, or dance routine.
Slow breathing	Take five deep, slow breaths: breathe in for a count of 4 through your nose, and feel your rib cage expand and your stomach rise, then slowly exhale through your mouth for a count of 6. Repeat four more times, each time remembering to make the out breath (exhale) longer than the in breath (inhale).
Muscle relaxation	Squeeze each of your muscle groups in turn for 10 seconds and then let go of the tension: start with your shoulders and neck, then arms and hands, then your stomach, move down to your thighs and lower legs, and finally curl up your toes and release.

Coping strategies you already use and find helpful

____

____

____

New coping strategies to try

____

____

____

This worksheet can also be accessed online at academic.oup.com

Worksheet 4: How Changes in Life Can Lead to Low Mood

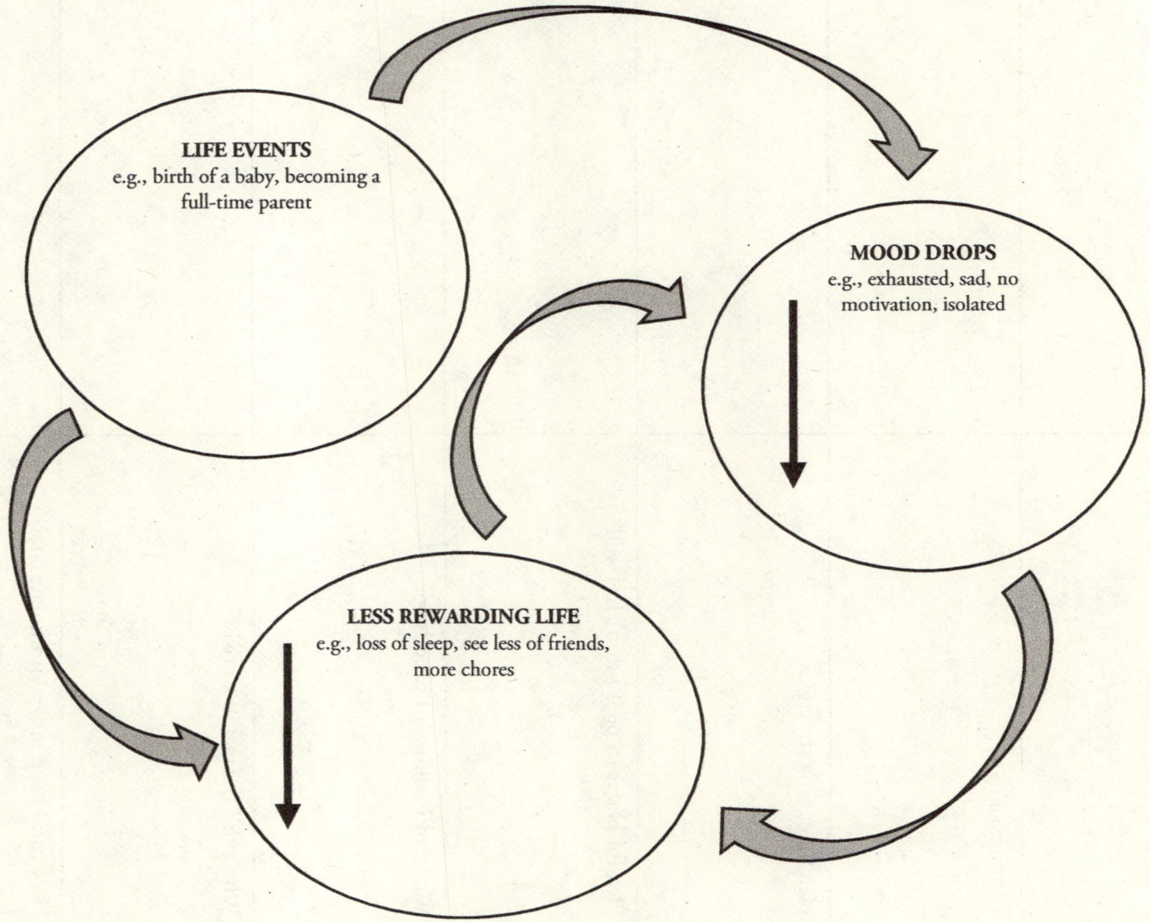

This worksheet can also be accessed online at academic.oup.com

Worksheet 5: Safety Plan

Think about	Actions
Triggers	
Warning signs	
Helpful coping strategies	
Helpful places to be if I don't feel well	
Who can I talk to if I need help?	
Who can I contact in a crisis?	
How can I keep my environment safe?	

This worksheet can also be accessed online at academic.oup.com

Worksheet 6: Mood Monitoring Record

Completely overwhelmed	Low much of the time Frequent symptoms	Low sometimes. Generally coping. Occasional symptoms		Content much of the time Managing most challenges	Enjoying life to the full

1_____2_____3_____4_____5_____6_____7_____8_____9_____10

Day	Time	Rating	Note anything that has happened to change your mood
Monday	AM		
	PM		
	EVE		
Tuesday	AM		
	PM		
	EVE		
Wednesday	AM		
	PM		
	EVE		
Thursday	AM		
	PM		
	EVE		
Friday	AM		
	PM		
	EVE		
Saturday	AM		
	PM		
	EVE		
Sunday	AM		
	PM		
	EVE		

This worksheet can also be accessed online at academic.oup.com

Worksheet 7: Working Out Your Values

Working out your values	Three words to describe these values	What does this look like? What would you be doing? When do you do that now in your daily life? What helps you to do that?
Values as a parent		
Values as a family		
Values as an individual		

This worksheet can also be accessed online at academic.oup.com

Worksheet 8: Setting Goals for Therapy

Goals for therapy	My goal is . . .	What does this goal look like? Remember, think SMART (specific, measurable, achievable, relevant, time-based)
Therapy goal 1		
Therapy goal 2		
Therapy goal 3		

This worksheet can also be accessed online at academic.oup.com

Worksheet 9: Weekly Goal Planner

Question	Notes
What is your goal for this week?	
What do you need to carry it out?	
When will you carry it out?	
What might get in the way of carrying it out?	
How will you overcome any obstacles?	

This worksheet can also be accessed online at academic.oup.com

Worksheet 10: Weekly Goal Record

Goal(s) for this week: ____________________

Day	When did you try the goal(s) today?	What went well?	What went not so well?
Monday			
Tuesday			
Wednesday			
Thursday			
Friday			
Saturday			
Sunday			

This worksheet can also be accessed online at academic.oup.com

Worksheet 11: Weekly Routine

Day	Morning	Afternoon	Evening
Monday			
Tuesday			
Wednesday			
Thursday			
Friday			
Saturday			
Sunday			

This worksheet can also be accessed online at academic.oup.com

Worksheet 12: Daily Routine

Time of day	Baby	Parent	Family
Morning			
Afternoon			
Evening			

This worksheet can also be accessed online at academic.oup.com

Worksheet 13: Nourishing and Depleting Activities[1]

Time/Day	Activity	Nourishing or depleting

[1] Developed from *Mindfulness: a practical guide to finding peace in a frantic world* (Williams & Penman, 2011).

This worksheet can also be accessed online at academic.oup.com

Worksheet 14: Problem Solving

Problem	Possible solutions	Advantages	Disadvantages	Best solution
When?				
What was happening?				
Who was involved?				
What were you doing?				

This worksheet can also be accessed online at academic.oup.com

Worksheet 15: Understanding How We Get Stuck in Our Thoughts[2]

Brief description of situation where I can get stuck in my thoughts	
Context Where, when, who with, what, and how does it happen?	
Usefulness How did it help? How did I feel? What did it avoid? What are the consequences?	
Development When did it start? Where did I learn this from? Who did I learn this from?	
Options Are there times when I don't get stuck in my thoughts? What is different when my thoughts feel helpful?	

[2] Developed from *Rumination-focused cognitive behavioural therapy for depression* by Ed Watkins (2016).

This worksheet can also be accessed online at academic.oup.com

Worksheet 16: Getting Stuck in Your Thoughts Record[3]

When *e.g., Tuesday, after lunch*	**Where** *e.g., in my kitchen*	**Focus** *e.g., I've failed as a parent*	**Feelings** *e.g., worried, angry*	**What stopped it** *e.g., baby waking up*

[3] Developed from *Rumination-focused cognitive behavioural therapy for depression* by Ed Watkins (2016).

This worksheet can also be accessed online at academic.oup.com

Worksheet 17: Alternative Strategies to Getting Stuck in Our Thoughts

Brief description of situation where I can get stuck in my thoughts	
Right Now: Move toward a focus on the "here and now." What is the next thing you need to do *right now*?	
Action: Move toward action. What could you do to *act* on what you are thinking about?	
Distraction: What activities really engage your attention that you could use to distract? Or those that give you a sense of satisfaction?	
Absorption: Practice absorbing yourself in your immediate experience to change your focus of attention. What could help remind you to do this?	

This worksheet can also be accessed online at academic.oup.com

Worksheet 18: Using an Image to Practice Self-Compassion[4]

	Describe in detail (hold in mind the qualities of strength, wisdom, warmth, and acceptance)
My compassionate image is:	
Where are you?	
What can you see in your image? *(e.g., color, shape, movement)*	
What can you hear in your image? *(e.g., voice, other sounds)*	
What does your image want you to feel?	
What does your image want to say to you?	
What does your image want you to know?	
What else is important to you about this image?	

[4] Developed from compassion-focused imagery work by Paul Gilbert (2010).

This worksheet can also be accessed online at academic.oup.com

Worksheet 19: Staying Well Plan

Question	Notes
How did your low mood come about?	
What kept your low mood going?	
What have you learned that has been helpful to you in dealing with this?	
How can you build on what you now know to continue to make changes?	
Who or what can support you to continue living in a way that lifts your mood?	
What challenges lie ahead, and what would the signs be that you are becoming increasingly stressed or low?	
How can you cope with these challenges and look after yourself well?	

This worksheet can also be accessed online at academic.oup.com

Worksheet 20: What Can Keep Intrusive Thoughts Going?

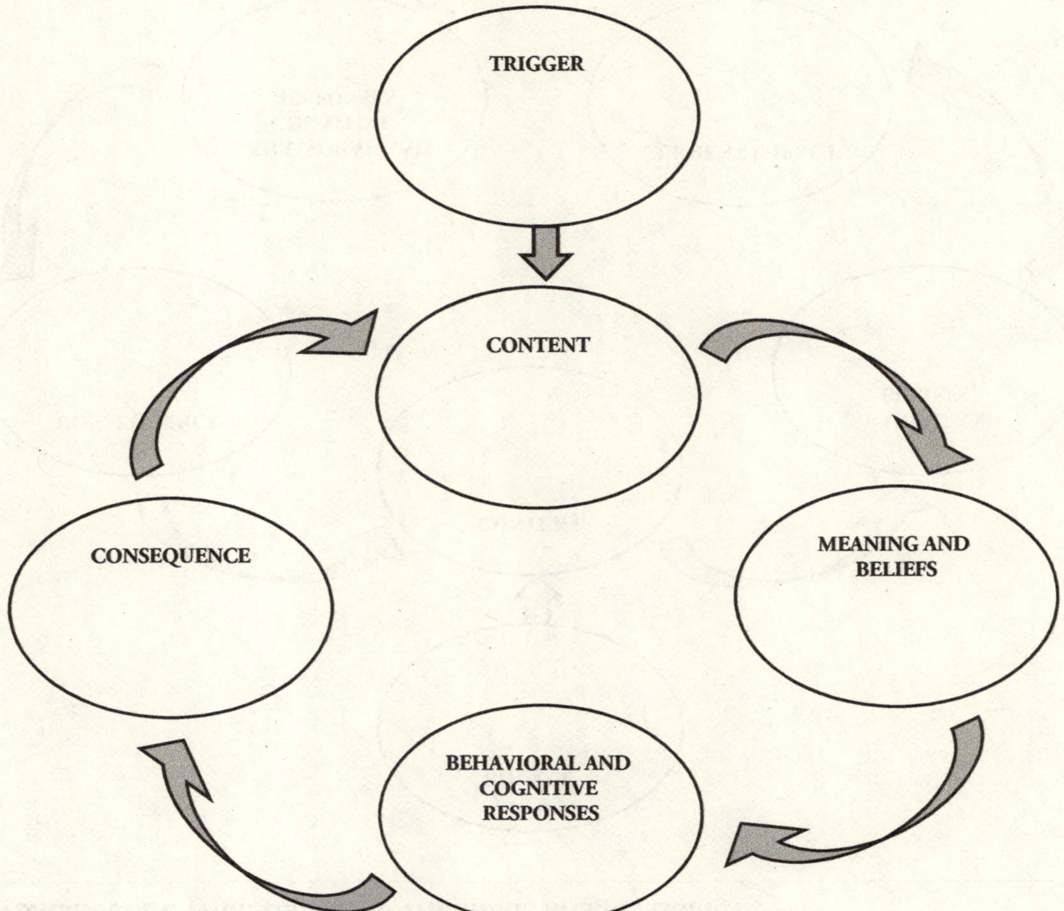

This worksheet can also be accessed online at academic.oup.com

Worksheet 21: What Can Keep Traumatic Images Going?

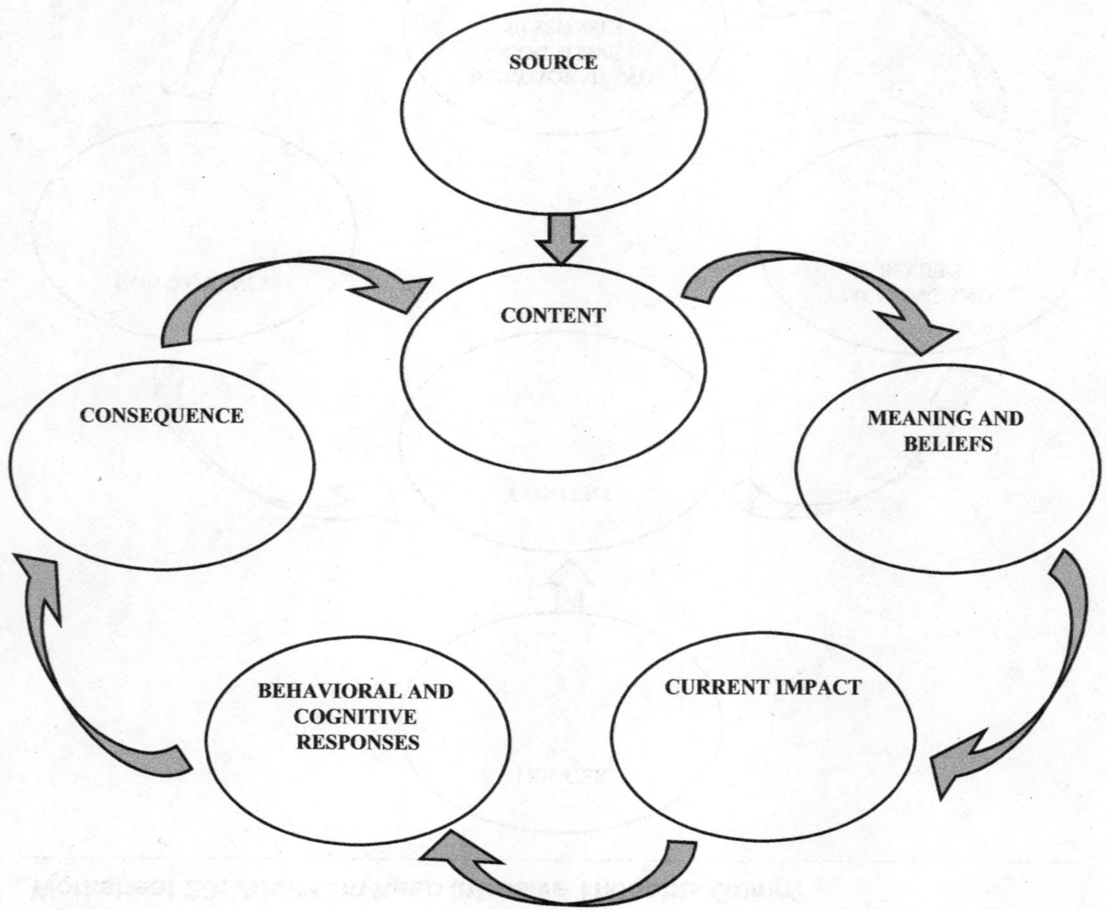

This worksheet can also be accessed online at academic.oup.com

Worksheet 22: Booster Session Review

Question	Notes
What skills do you remember from therapy that were helpful to you?	
What has gone well since the end of therapy?	
What have the challenges been?	
How did you cope with the challenges?	
Are there any skills that have previously been helpful that you *could* have used to respond to those challenges?	
Have you been aware of any unhelpful responses?	
How can you minimize these unhelpful responses?	
What/who will support you to continue living in a way that gives meaning and value to your life?	

This worksheet can also be accessed online at academic.oup.com

Appendix B

Assessment Questionnaire

Name:
Any adverse childhood experiences and/or previous mental health difficulties
Previous experience of therapy and expectations of therapy
Motivation: Level of motivation, pros and cons of therapy

Current context, concerns, recent events, mood, anxiety, triggers

Self-care: sleeping, eating, exercise and energy, time for self

Pregnancy, delivery and early months, other sources of help, use of medication

Typical day and week

Managing strong feelings: overthinking, overactivity, and avoidance

Coping: current and past strategies, what's working, substance use

Social support: practical and emotional issues, local network, crisis support

Risk: present/past suicidal ideation/intent, self-harm, harm to others (including the baby), domestic violence, protective factors

Formulation/case conceptualization

Future life and goals for therapy: sense of how parent would like life to be, what aiming for

References

Adams, A. M., Nababan, H. Y., Hanifi, S. M. M. A. (2015). Building social networks for maternal and newborn health in poor urban settlements: A cross-sectional study in Bangladesh. *PLoS ONE, 10*(4), e0123817. https://doi.org/10.1371/journal.pone.0123817

Amani, B., Krzeczkowski, J. E., Savoy, C., Schmidt, L. A., & Van Lieshout, R. J. (2023). The impact of peer-delivered cognitive behavioral therapy for postpartum depression on infant emotion regulation. *Journal of Affective Disorders, 338*, 380–383.

American Psychiatric Association. (2013). *Diagnostic and statistical manual of mental disorders* (5th ed.). https://doi.org/10.1176/appi.books.9780890425596

Ammerman, R. T., Altaye, M., Putnam, F. W., Teeters, A. R., Zou, Y., & Van Ginkel, J. B. (2015). Depression improvement and parenting in low-income mothers in home visiting. *Archives of Women's Mental Health, 18*, 555–563.

Arisoyin, A. E., Salawu, M. A., Folorunsho, I. L., Olaleye, K. T., Afolayan, A. Y., Adeyemo, D. A., Mbaezue, R. N., Ibeneme, C. N., Ballagan, J. S., Rai, S., Fagbenle, O. E., Oraekwute, I. M., Lopez Pantoja, S. C., Okunromade, O., & Haddad, M. M. (2023). Effectiveness of cognitive behavioral therapy for post-partum depression in low and middle-income countries: A systematic review. *Journal of Advances in Medicine and Medical Research, 35*(18), 33–40.

Beck, A. T., Rush, A. J., Shaw, B. F. & Emery, G. (1979). *Cognitive Therapy of Depression*. Guilford.

Beck, A. T., Steer, R. A., & Brown, G. K. (1996). *Manual for the Beck Depression Inventory–II*. Psychological Corporation.

Belloch, A., Morillo, C., Lucero, M., Cabedo, E., & Carrio, C. (2004). Intrusive thoughts in non-clinical subjects: The role of frequency and unpleasantness on appraisal ratings and control strategies. *Clinical Psychology and Psychotherapy, 11*, 100–110.

Boath, E. H., & Henshaw, C. (2001). The treatment of postnatal depression: A comprehensive literature review. *Journal of Reproductive and Infant Psychology, 19*(3), 215–248.

Boath, E. H., Pryce, A. J., & Cox, J. L. (1998). Postnatal depression: The impact on the family. *Journal of Reproductive and Infant Psychology, 16*(2–3), 199–203.

Bradshaw, H., Riddle, J. N., Salimgaraev, R., Zhaunova, L., & Payne, J. L. (2022). Risk factors associated with postpartum depressive symptoms: A multinational study. *Journal of Affective Disorders, 301*, 345–351.

Branquinho, M., de la Fe Rodriguez-Munoz, M., Maia, B.R., Marques, M., Matos, M., Osma, J., Moreno-Peral, P., Conejo-Ceron, S., Fonseca, A., & Vousoura, E. (2021). Effectiveness of psychological interventions in the treatment of perinatal depression: A systematic review of systematic reviews and meta-analyses. *Journal of Affective Disorders, 291*, 294–306.

Brown, J. V. A. Wilson, C. A., Ayre, K., Robertson, L., South, E., Molyneaux, E., Trevillion, K., Howard, L. M., & Khalifeh, H. (2021). Antidepressant treatment for postnatal depression. *Cochrane Database of Systematic Reviews, 2*, Article CD013560. https://doi.org/10.1002/14651858.CD013560.pub2

Cooper, P., & Murray, L. (1998). Postnatal depression. *British Medical Journal, 316*, 1884–1886.

Cornish, A. M., McMahon, C. A., Ungerer, J. A., Barnet, B., Kowalenko, N., & Tennant, C. (2005). Postnatal depression and infant cognitive and motor development in the second postnatal year: The impact of depression chronicity and infant gender. *Infant Behaviour and Development, 28*, 407–417.

Cox, J. L., Holden, J. M., & Sagovsky, R. (1987). Detection of postnatal depression. Development of the 10-item Edinburgh Postnatal Depression Scale. *British Journal of Psychiatry, 150*, 782–786.

Cuijpers, P., Franco, P., Ciharova, M., Miguel, C., Segre, L., Quero, S., & Karyotaki, E. (2023). Psychological treatment of perinatal depression: A meta-analysis, *Psychological Medicine, 53*(6), 2596–2608.

Ekers, D., Webster, L., Van Straten, A., Cuijpers, P., Richards, D., & Gilbody, S. (2014). Behavioural activation for depression: an update of meta-analysis of effectiveness and subgroup analysis. *PLOS ONE*, *9*(6), Article e100100. https://doi.org/10.1371/journal.pone.0100100

Elwood, J., Murray, E., Bell, A., Sinclair, M., Kernohan, W. G., & Stockdale, J. (2019). A systematic review investigating if genetic or epigenetic markers are associated with postnatal depression. *Journal of Affective Disorders, 253*, 51–62.

Erdur-Baker, O., & Bugay, A. (2010). The short version of ruminative response scale: Reliability, validity and its relation to psychological symptoms. *Procedia Social and Behavioural Sciences, 5*, 2178–2181.

Fairbrother, N., & Woody, S. R. (2008). New mothers' thoughts of harm related to the newborn. *Archives of Women's Mental Health, 11*, 221–229. https://doi.org/10.1007/s00737-008-0016-7.

Fatori, D., Zuccolo, P., Xavier, M. O., Matijasevich, A., & Polanczyk, G. V. (2023). Smartphone-assisted online brief cognitive behavioral therapy to treat maternal depression: Findings of a randomized controlled trial. *Brazilian Journal of Psychiatry, 45*(1), 50–53. https://doi.org/10.47626/1516-4446-2022-2679

Felitti, V. J., Anda, R. F., Edwards, V., Nordenberg, D., Williamson, D. F., Spitz, A. M., Koss, M. P., & Marks, J. S. (1998). Relationship of childhood abuse and household dysfunction to many of the leading causes of death in adults. *American Journal of Preventive Medicine, 14*(4), 245–258.

Ghaedrahmati, M., Kazemi, A., Khierabadi, G., Ebrahimi, A., & Bahrami, M. (2017). Postpartum depression risk factors: A narrative review. *Journal of Education and Health Promotion, 6*(1), 60–66. https://doi.org/10.4103/jehp.jehp_9_16

Gilbert, P. (2010). *Training our minds in, with and for compassion: An introduction to concepts and compassion focused exercises.* Compassionate Mind Foundation.

Gilbert, P. (2014). The origins and nature of compassion-focussed therapy. *British Journal of Clinical Psychology, 53*(1), 6–41.

Gureje, O., Oladeji, B. D., Kola, L., Bello, T., Ayinde, O., Faregh, N., Bennett, I., & Zelkowitz, P. (2022). Effect of intervention delivered by frontline maternal care providers to improve outcome and parenting skills among adolescents with perinatal depression in Nigeria (the RAPiD study): A cluster randomized controlled trial. *Journal of Affective Disorders, 312*, 169–176. https://doi.org/10.1016/j.jad.2022.06.032

Howard, L. M., Piot, P., & Stein, A. (2014). No health without perinatal health. *Lancet, 384*, 1723–1724.

Huang, L. H., Zhao, Y., Qiang, C., & Bozhen, F. (2018). Is cognitive behavioural therapy a better choice for women with postnatal depression? A systematic review and meta-analysis. *PLOS ONE, 13*(10), Article e205243.

Hutchens, B. F., & Kearney, J. (2020). Risk factors for postpartum depression: An umbrella review. *Journal of Midwifery and Women's Health, 60*, 96–108.

Jankovic, J., Parsons, J., Jovanovic, N., Berrisford, G., Copello, A., Fazil, Q., & Priebe, S. (2020). Differences in access and utilisation of mental health services in the perinatal period for women from ethnic minorities—A population-based study. *BMC Medicine, 18*, 1–12.

Jesse, D. E., Gaynes, B. N., Feldhousen, E. B., Newton, E. R., Bunch, S., & Hollon, S. D. (2015). Performance of a culturally tailored cognitive-behavioural intervention integrated in a public health setting to reduce risk of antepartum depression: a randomized controlled trial. *Journal of Midwifery & Women's Health, 60*, 578–592.

Jones, I., & Smith, S. (2009). Puerperal psychosis: Identifying and caring for women at risk. *Advances in Psychiatric Treatment, 15*, 411–418.

Kroenke, K., & Spitzer, R. L. (2002). A new depression and diagnostic severity measure. *Psychiatric Annals, 32*, 509–521.

Lawrence, P. J., Craske, M. G., Kempton, C., Stewart, A., & Stein, A. (2017). Intrusive thoughts and images of intentional harm to infants in the context of maternal postnatal depression, anxiety, and OCD. *British Journal of General Practice, 67*(661), 376–377. https://doi.org/10.3399/bjgp17X692105

Lee, D., & James, S. (2012). *The compassionate mind approach to recovering from trauma: Using compassion focused therapy*. Hachette.

Li, S., Zimri, S. Y., Kim, H.-J., Briggs, J., Duffy, M., Frechette-Hagan, A., Cohen, L. J., & Galynker, I. I. (2018). Entrapment as a mediator of suicide crises. *BMC Psychiatry, 18*, Article 4. https://doi.org/10.1186/s12888-018-1587-0

Li, X., Laplante, D. P., Paquin, V., Lafortune, S., Elgbeili, G., & King, S. (2022). Effectiveness of cognitive behavioural therapy for perinatal maternal depression, anxiety and stress: A systematic review and meta-analysis of randomised controlled trials. *Clinical Psychology Review, 92*, 102–129.

Lindahl, V., Pearson, J. L., & Colpe, L. (2005). Prevalence of suicidality during pregnancy and the postpartum. *Archives of Women's Mental Health*, *8*, 77–87.

Liu, C., Ystrom, E., & McAdams, T. (2023). Long-term maternal and child outcomes following postnatal SSRI treatment. *JAMA NetworkOpen*, *6*(8), Article e2331270. https://doi.org/10.1001/jamanetworkopen.2023.31270

Lovibond, S. H., & Lovibond, P. F. (1995). *Manual for the depression anxiety stress scales* (2nd ed.). Psychological Foundation.

McMahon, C. A., Barnet, B., Kowalenko, N. M., & Tennant, C. (2006). Maternal attachment state of mind moderates the impact of postnatal depression on infant attachment. *Journal of Child Psychology and Psychiatry*, *47*(7), 660–669.

Martell, C. R., Dimidjian, S. & Herman-Dunn, R. (2010). *Behavioral Activation for Depression: A Cliician's Guide*. Guilford Press.

Merza, D., Amani, B., Savoy, C., Babiy, Z., Bieling, P. J., Streiner, D. L., Ferro, M. A., & Van Lieshout, R. J. (2024). Online peer-delivered group cognitive-behavioral therapy for postpartum depression: A randomized controlled trial. *Acta Psychiatrica Scandinavica*, *150*(5), 422–432. https://doi.org/10.1111/acps.13611

Milgrom, J., Westley, D. T., & Gemmil, A. W. (2004). The mediating role of maternal responsiveness in some longer-term effects of postnatal depression on infant development. *Infant Behaviour and Development*, *27*(4), 443–454.

Mitchell, A. R., Gordon, H., Lindquist, A., Walker, S. P., Homer, C. S. E., Middleton, A., Cluver, C. A., Tong, S., & Hastie, R. (2023). Prevalence of peri-natal depression in low- and middle-income countries: A systematic review and meta-analysis. *JAMA Psychiatry*, *80*(5), 425–431.

Nath, S., Psychogiou, L., Kuyken, W., Ford, T., Ryan, E., & Russell, G. (2016). The prevalence of depressive symptoms among fathers and associated risk factors during the first seven years of their child's life: Findings from the Millennium Cohort Study. *BMC Public Health*, *16*, Article 509. https://doi.org/10.1186/s12889-016-3168-9

Netsi, E., Pearson, R., Murray, L., Cooper, P., Craske, M., & Stein, A. (2018). Association of persistent and severe postnatal depression with child outcomes. *Journal of the American Medical Association of Psychiatry, 75*(3), 247–253.

National Institue for Health and Care Excellence (NICE) (2022). Depression in adults: treatment and management. https://www.nice.org.uk/Guidance/ng222

Neff, K. D. (2011). Self-compassion, self-esteem, and well-being. *Social and Personality Psychology Compass, 5*(1), 1–12.

Nolem-Hoeksema, S. (1998). 'Ruminative Coping with Depression', in Heckhausen, J., Dweck, C.S. (eds.). *Motivation and Self-Regulation across the Life Span*. Cambridge: Cambridge University Press, pp 237–256.

O'Connor, R., & Portzky, G. (2018). The relationship between entrapment and suicidal behaviour through the lens of the integrated motivational–volitional model of suicidal behaviour. *Current Opinion in Psychology, 22*, 12–17.

O'Mahen, H., Himle, J. A., Fedock, G., Henshaw, E., & Flynn, H. (2013). A pilot randomized controlled trial of cognitive behavioural therapy for perinatal depression adapted for women with low incomes. *Depression and Anxiety, 30*(7), 679–687.

O'Mahen, H. A., Woodford, J., McGinley, J., Warren, F. C., Richards, D. A., Lynch, T. R., & Taylor, R. S. (2013). Internet-based behavioural activation treatment for postnatal depression (Netmums): A randomised controlled trial. *Journal of Affective Disorders, 150*(3), 814–822.

O'Mahen, H. A., Richards, D. A., Woodford, J., Wilkinson, E., McGinley, J., Taylor, R. S., & Warren, F. C. (2014). Netmums: A phase II randomised controlled trial of a guided Internet behavioural activation treatment for postpartum depression. *Psychological Medicine, 44*, 1675–1689.

O'Mahen, H. A., Grieve, H., Jones, J., McGinley, J., Woodford, J., & Wilkinson, E. (2015). Women's experience of factors affecting treatment engagement and adherence in internet delivered behavioural activation for postnatal depression. *Internet Interventions, 2*(1), 84–90.

Orsolini, L., Valchera, A., Vechiotti, R., Tomasetti, C., Lasevoli, F., Fornaro, M., De Berardis, D., Perna, G., Pompili, M., & Bellantuono, C. (2016). Suicide during the perinatal period: Epidemiology, risk factors and clinical correlates. *Frontiers in Psychiatry, 7*, Article 138. https://doi.org/10.3389/fpsyt.2016.00138

Pawlby, S., Fernyhough, C., Meins, E., Pariante, C., Senevirante, G., & Bentall, R. P. (2010). Mind-mindedness and maternal responsiveness in infant–mother interaction in mothers with severe mental illness. *Psychological Medicine*, *40*, 1861–1869.

Pettman, D., O'Mahen, H., Blomberg, O., Svanberg, A. S., von Essen, L., & Woodford, J. (2023). Effectiveness of cognitive behavioural therapy–based interventions for maternal perinatal depression: A systematic review and meta-analysis. *BMC Psychiatry*, *23*(1), 1–25.

Preschl, B., Maercker, A., & Wagner, B. (2011). The working alliance in a randomized controlled trial comparing online with face-to-face cognitive-behavioural therapy for depression. *BMC Psychiatry*, *11*, Article 189. http://www.biomedcentral.com/1471-244X/11/189

Rahman, A., Malik, A., Sikander, S., Roberts, C., & Creed, F. (2008). Cognitive behaviour therapy–based intervention by community health workers for mothers with depression and their infants in rural Pakistan: A cluster-randomised controlled trial. *The Lancet*, *372*(9642), 902–909.

Reid, H. E., Pratt, D., Edge, D., & Wittkoski, A. (2022). Maternal suicide ideation and behaviour during pregnancy and the first postpartum year: A systematic review of psychological and psychosocial risk factors. *Frontiers in Psychiatry*, *13*, Article 765118. https://doi.org/10.3389/fpsyt.2022.765118

Richards, D. A., Ekers, D., McMillan, D., Taylor, R. S., Byford, S., Warren, F. C., Barrett, B., Farrand, P. A., Gilbody, S., Kuyken, W., O'Mahen, H., Watkins, E. R., Wright, K. A., Hollon, S. D., Reen, N., Rhodes, S., Fletcher, E., & Finning, K. (2016). Cost and outcome of behavioural activation versus cognitive behavioural therapy for depression (COBRA): A randomised, controlled non-inferiority trial. *The Lancet*, 388(10047), 871–880.

Rochat, T. J., Dube, S., Herbst, K., Hoegfeldt, C. A., Redinger, S., Khoza, T., Bland, R. M., Richter, L., Linsell, L., Desmond, C., Yousafzai, A. K., Craske, M., Juszczak, E., Abas, M., Edwards, T., Ekers, D., & Stein, A. (2021). An evaluation of a combined psychological and parenting intervention for HIV-positive women depressed in the perinatal period, to enhance child development and reduce maternal depression: Study protocol for the Insika Yomama cluster randomised controlled trial. *Trials*, *22*(1), Article 914. https://doi.org/10.1186/s13063-021-05672-0

Rokicki, S., Patel, M., Suplee, P. D., & D'Oria, R. (2024). Racial and ethnic disparities in access to community-based perinatal mental health programs: Results from a cross-sectional survey. *BMC Public Health*, *24*(1), Article 1094. https://doi.org/10.1186/s12889-024-18517-7

Sarfraz, Z., Sarfraz, A., & Amin, S. Z. (2024). Evaluating cognitive behavioral therapy as a solution for postnatal depression in economically disadvantaged regions. *Archives of Women's Mental Health*, *27*(3), 459–475.

Schneider, L. (2025). FDA panel casts SSRIs during pregnancy as risky–many experts disagree. *The Journal of the American Medical Association*, *334*, 937–939. doi:10.1001/jama.2025.14105

Segre, L. S., O'Hara, M. W., Arndt, S., & Stuart, S. (2007). The prevalence of postpartum depression: The relative significance of three social status indices. *Social Psychiatry and Psychiatric Epidemiology*, *42*, 316–321. https://doi.org/10.1007/s00127-007-0168-1

Silverman, M. E., Reichenberg, A., Savitz, D. A., Cnattingius, S., Lichtenstein, P., Hultman, C. M., Larsson, H., & Sandin, S. (2017). The risk factors for postnatal depression: A population-based study. *Depression and Anxiety*, *34*(2), 178–187.

Singla, D. R., MacKinnon, D. P., Fuhr, D. C., Sikander, S., Rahman, A., & Patel, V. (2021). Multiple mediation analysis of the peer-delivered Thinking Healthy Programme for perinatal depression: Findings from two parallel, randomised controlled trials. *The British Journal of Psychiatry*, *218*(3), 143–150. https://doi.org/10.1192/bjp.2019.184

Slomian, J., Honvo, H., Emonts, P., Reginster, J.-Y., & Bruyere, O. (2019). Consequences of maternal depression: A systematic review of maternal and infant outcomes. *Women's Health*, *15*, 1–55.

Stein, A., Netsi, E., Lawrence, P. J., Granger, C., Kempton, C., Craske, M., Nickless, A., Mollison, J., Stewart, D. A., Rapa, E., West, V., Scerif, G., Cooper, P. J., & Murray, L. (2018). Mitigating the effects of persistent postnatal depression on child outcomes through an intervention to treat depression and improve parenting: A randomised controlled trial. *The Lancet Psychiatry*, *5*(2), 134–144.

Stein, A., Pearson, R. M., Goodman, S. H., Rapa, E., Rahman, A., McCallum, M., Howard, L. M., & Pariante, C. M. (2014). Effects of perinatal mental disorders on the fetus and child. *The Lancet*, *384*, 1800–1819.

Stephens, S., Ford, E., Paudyal, P., & Smith, H. (2016). Effectiveness of psychological interventions for postnatal depression in primary care: A meta-analysis. *The Annals of Family Medicine*, *14*(5), 463–472. https://doi.org/10.1370/afm.1967

VanderKruik, R., Barreix, M., Chou, D., Allen, T., Say, L., Cohen, L. S. and on behalf of the Maternity Mor bidity Working Group (2017), *BMC Psychiatry*, *17*: 272. https://doi.org/10.1186/s12888-017-1427-7

Watkins, E. R. (2016). *Rumination-focused cognitive behavioural therapy for depression*. Guilford Press.

Webb, R., Uddin, N., Constantinou, G., Ford, E., Easter, A., Shakespeare, J., Hann, A., Roberts, N., Alderdice, F., Sinesi, A., Coates, R., Hogg, S., & Ayers, S. (2023). Meta-review of the barriers and facilitators to women accessing perinatal mental healthcare. *BMJ Open*, *13*(7), Article e066703.

Williams, M., & Penman, D. (2011). *Mindfulness: A practical guide to finding peace in a frantic world*. Piatkus.

Wisner, K. L., Parry, B. L., & Piontek, C. M. (2002). Postpartum depression. *New England Journal of Medicine*, *347*, 194–199.

Zaidi, F., Nigam, A., Anjum, R., & Agarwalla, R. (2017). Postpartum depression in women: A risk factor analysis. *Journal of Clinical and Diagnostic Research*, *11*(8), QC13–QC16.